NOT AS I DO:

A Father's Report

by Ed Lowe

Newsday

ANDREWS and McMEEL
A Universal Press Syndicate Company
Kansas City

Additional copies of this book may be ordered by calling (800) 642–6480.

Library of Congress Cataloging-in-Publication Data
Lowe, Ed, 1946–
    Not as I do : a father's report / by Ed Lowe.
        p. cm.
    ISBN 0-8362-7045-2
    1. Fatherhood. 2. Fathers—Psychology. 3. Father and child.
I. Title.
HQ756.L73 1995
306.874'2—dc20   94–44752
                                                                        CIP

CONTENTS

ACKNOWLEDGMENTS

The material in this book began as a column called "Fathering," which appeared on the cover of a Saturday section of *Newsday* and *New York Newsday* every other week, alternating with a very fine column called "Mothering," by Pulitzer Prize–winning feature writer Madeline Blais. The whole section was invented by Phyllis Singer, assistant managing editor of *Newsday* and *New York Newsday*, who was my wife at the time and also was (and to this very day remains) the mother of two of the children mentioned frequently in the following pages, Jed and Danny Lowe, without whose existence and daily contributions to my life I would not have had much to say on the subject of Fathering. Phyllis Singer also was and is the capable and extremely influential stepmother to my daughters, T.C. and Colleen, and my gratitude for that generosity never will diminish.

Bob Heisler of *Newsday* pitched the idea to Jake Morrissey of Andrews and McMeel about publishing this material in book form and distributing it beyond the boundaries of New York and Long Island, where Heisler suspected other parents and children might also exist. I read a copy of his proposal and although its effusiveness embarrassed me, I'm glad he wrote it. I'm glad Morrissey agreed with him, too.

Every time I sat down to write an episode of this series, my stomach knotted, and I wished I had not agreed to the project. If initially I had intended to write and deliver it as a book, I would not have been able to summon or sustain the courage to keep going. But readers encouraged me relentlessly, through hundreds of letters, notes, cards and calls. Addressing me almost as if I were a brother, a cousin or an uncle, they shared their own experiences and often referred to my children with hauntingly deep and genuine concern and affection. In a profound and mysterious way, they became part of my family, and I theirs, and I am incalculably richer for the connection.

Ed Lowe
January 1995

For Edward J. Lowe, Sr.
1915–1985

INTRODUCTION

September 1989

Not since I wished for a red wagon had I actively longed for a specific present for myself, but, in anticipation of my forty-second birthday, which I hoped would arrive without fanfare in late March of 1988, I wished aloud, fervently and often that my younger son would urinate in the toilet. He had developed a habit of soaking his Pampers all night and then sitting on my head in the morning.

By late spring, he acquired the requisite knowledge and self-control to relieve himself (and, thus, me), whereupon we began the process of convincing him to behave similarly regarding the other, less delicate exercise.

That accomplished, the year I thought would never end went the way of other years I thought would never end, and the last of my four children—I hope he is the last—now uses the toilet regularly. I would indulge myself some wistfulness regarding the passage of those stages if I weren't so perilously close to starting all over again with grandchildren, a condition that would place me once again in the leading wave of yet another generational trend.

As much as I loathe trends, fashion, the shackles of popular custom and tradition, I have managed to stumble headlong into nearly every major demographic turn and twist common to my age and my gender. I am a reluctantly modern man; Quitter of Smoking, Eater of Roughage, Examiner of Self, Husband of an Executive, Blender of Religions and a father of both young adults and old toddlers.

I am a baby boomer by three months. I am fashionably twice married, gaudily and liturgically the first time to a baptized Irish-German-American; more serenely and secularly the second time, to a Bat-Mitzva'd, Eastern Euro-American.

I started out with no credentials in the fatherhood trade and now have four, born in 1968, '69, '81 and '85. My first two—pre-Lamaze daughters—were born while I paced appropriately at home, chain-smoking my then-acceptable Lucky Strikes. The girls were raised imperfectly in the turmoil of divorce, which had by then become fashionable, at least statistically, though nobody in my experience seemed particularly proud of it.

Later, I watched in trendy anticipation as the newspaper-executive-biological-clock-ticking-maturing-feminist-mother of my third and fourth children—boys, this time—huffed, puffed, counted and pushed them into the modern world. How modern? Danny, 3, already a second semester Montessori student, can name both Super Mario brothers. Jed, 7, boots up the compatible to play Math Blaster.

I like to think that my sons will benefit from fathering lessons I learned before they were born. I ache, though, to ponder that my daughters might suffer for what I bungled during my on-the-job training. The girls seem beyond my influence. One is planning to marry earlier than I would have recommended (next month, in fact); the other is away at college, fortifying my credit rating.

I have been asked to chronicle some of the adventures of fatherhood. I said I would take a swing at it, in two-week intervals. The material is plentiful enough. In July, I will have been fumbling at the job for 21 years without a text and will be facing almost the same amount of hard time ahead. Also, I know men who are very good at being fathers. I talk to them often and steal what I can from their superior patience and wisdom.

We commiserate—good fathers and not-so-good—and laugh at the sometimes inescapable suspicion that we may have no idea what we're doing.

YEAR ONE

Yecch, the Love Part Again

My wife casually informed me last week that our older son knew what gay meant. The boy is scheduled to turn 8 in April. "Wonderful," I said, hiding behind sarcasm. "He elaborated, did he?"

"We were watching something on television," she said. "Somebody mentioned being gay, or gay rights, and he turned to me and said, 'I know what "gay" means.' I said, 'You do?' He said, 'Yeah, I do,' and then he shrugged, as if to say, 'Doesn't everybody?'"

"What did he say it meant?"

"He said, 'It means when guys like to make out with guys.'"

"Terrific," I muttered again, wondering why I suddenly felt so chagrined. "I'm so pleased."

"I understand how you feel, but don't take it so hard."

"Shouldn't 'gay' mean happy and giddy for longer than second grade?" I asked. I mean, am I wrong to think that my son should understand fractions and know how to spell breakfast before I have to warn him about sexually transmitted diseases? God. At 7 we're dealing with sexuality?

Without my conscious assistance, and indeed beyond my control, all my intellectual energies immediately boarded a high-speed time machine, shot back to 1953, and scoured the territory for any memory that might help me comprehend this new fact. When I was 7, did I have any information, however inaccurate, or any suspicions, however remote, about sex, let alone about homosexuality?

Blank. A vast, sexual desert.

I tried 1954, a more fertile year. I was in the fourth grade. My teacher was Pat Sanford, Mrs. Sanford. Blond hair, blue eyes, crimson lipstick. She wore straight skirts, high heels and pull-over sweaters, and she reminded me of Doris Day. When she smiled, my chest tightened and my knees loosened.

All right, so I did have some sexual feelings when I was 8. I worked that corner of my memory's attic for more discoveries. I found one or two suspicions and curiosities, but still about heterosexuality. I smiled idiotically as I unearthed a clear recollection of a purloined deck of cards; photographs of a woman printed on the back of each card. The women wore cowboy hats, cowboy boots, strategically fringed gun belts and broad smiles.

Still, I located no facts, no knowledge, not even a reference about alternative lovestyles; nothing even within range of the phrase . . . "when guys make out with guys."

I felt unarmed. Every day that I am the father of James Edward Lowe—Jed—is another first day, in a way, because I have not been the father of boys before. In the absence of a fatherhood manual, or a college major in fathering, I am forced to rely on my reasoning powers and my own experiences for materials with which I can build rules, expectations and assistance programs that would permit the boy to grow happily into a good man. If I cannot find references to his experiences from my own, I feel uninformed. I feel ignorant, like a trail guide on a new trail.

"When I was 7," I said, not even knowing whether my wife was listening, "and my father took me to the movies, mostly to see cowboy pictures or cop pictures; and the hero beat up the bad guys and saved the girl; and the hero and the girl started staring at each other as if they were going to lean forward and kiss, which they were, I almost always said the equivalent of, 'Yecch, the love part!' and closed my eyes. Has time changed our species so much since then, or am I a dinosaur? Is there no place any more for innocence?"

She smiled and shrugged.

The following night, I attended a Safety Kids program at Jed's school. Pupils from kindergarten through third grade assembled on stage, each class clad in a brightly colored Safety Kids T-shirt. The assemblage belted out their safety songs with surprising verve and energy, far more than they mustered for Christmas carols. One song, about memorizing your home telephone number, fractured me, because in the refrain, each individual sang his own telephone number. The last four syllables of the song consisted of an unintelligible mess, as each kid shouted digits different from the others. The next song was about screaming if somebody touched your body in the wrong place, and kids loved the part of the song where they got to scream. I was impressed with the program's cleverness and amused at the

2

kids' enthusiasm; also dismayed by the necessity to prepare children so young for dangers so disturbingly creepy.

We drove home and later watched a stupid movie Jed wanted to see on Home Box Office: *The Boy Who Could Fly*. My wife, returning home from a particularly long day at work, landed just in time to have to endure the last quarter of the film, during which the patient, angelic and pretty girl-next-door character breaks through the seemingly impenetrable emotional barriers of the troubled, orphaned neighbor boy, who appears to believe he can fly, and then does. Toward the end, the boy's eyes meet the girl's eyes, and the boy's hand moves slowly and dramatically toward the girl's hand, clearly with the ultimate goal of holding hands, possibly even kissing, as well.

"Yeccch!" Jed suddenly interrupted as he sat on the couch. "Not the love part!"

My wife and I looked at each other. "Wonderful," I said, without a trace of sarcasm.

Daddy's Little Girl

Fathers of brides-to-be sit next to each other in diners and restaurants with a coincidental frequency as uncanny as that with which gout sufferers stumble across each other at bars. The fathers seem to recite from the same text, too, which is how they learn of each other's presence.

Twice in the last week, I unwittingly have rested my worried elbows on a countertop next to the luncheon plates of men who already had ordered the tuxedos from the specific stores and in the specific colors their betrothed daughters had selected for them. In one instance of mutually eavesdropped conversations, I sat next to two retired New York City detectives. One faced a wedding that his daughter and son-in-law would perpetrate the following Saturday; the other had just begun preparing for May nuptials by transferring his certificates of deposit into his checking account. I identified myself to them as a fellow fretter, with a wedding chronologically in between theirs.

In each instance, the paternal lamentations were nearly identical, differing, if they did, only in dollar amounts. Both retired detectives, for instance, bemused by the notion of a young couple spilling a small fortune into the punchbowl of a four-hour party instead of, say, the foundation of a house, had offered their children thousands-plus in what basically would amount to a dowry, if only they would not squander it in a catering hall.

"I told my daughter I would give her $10,000 toward a down payment on a house—more, if I could raise it—and a wedding party under a tent at the house," said one ex-cop. "I figured we could have a terrific wingding for less than $1,500. What did she say? No good. She wants a wedding, a big wedding."

"They want what they want," said the other man. "I'm staring down the same barrel. Prices of houses being as high as they are now, you would think that they would think that . . ."

"They don't think; that's the problem," said the first man, echoing every father I've heard. "You can't talk to them, either. Besides, their mothers agree with them. I now have both my wife and my daughter yelling at me: 'After all,' they tell me, 'you only get married once! Blah blah blah.' I hope they're right. I know I'm not paying for any second wedding."

"I'm more worried about my daughter's youth," I said. "I made two lifelong commitments at 20 and didn't stick to either one. I didn't stay in teaching and I didn't stay married. I never know if I'm handling this one right. I tell my daughter I support her decisions, and then I privately worry myself into gastrointestinal trouble about her future."

"Only makes you the same as everybody else," one said.

I stared at my own plate.

When they were much younger, little girls, really, I frequently would tell my daughters that I looked forward to knowing them as adults. It was the truth, too.

Now, two weeks before T.C.'s wedding, I find myself looking backward, hoping to seize and hold what images and textures I can of my little girls, who seem to be at once long-gone, yet so recently escaped.

I had successfully avoided indulging in such reverie until this moment, no doubt frightened by what I would find. I always eschewed sentimentality. Now, unable to avoid it, I felt like a common cliché, a sentimentalist, a personified, sophomoric lyric in a simplistic ditty by a mediocre composer.

Strangely, my most vivid memory of the bride, the image that continues to snap back like a recurring television commercial and interrupt all others, is far from a happy, lyrical, daddy-daughter reminiscence. It is one of the more horrible replays I can conjure. For some reason, though, I cannot subdue its persistent, involuntary resurrection, perhaps because it represents the last time I faced losing her.

Her tiny body—I think we still measured her age in weeks—burned with a fever of 104 degrees, at least. I cannot recall the name of whatever cruel virus had taken up residence in her, but, according to instructions from our doctor, we were to periodically apply rubbing alcohol to her entire body, dabbing her with soaked cotton balls, until the fever subsided.

Mine was the late watch. I remember no other details of the episode, but with a terrifying vividness, my mind easily reconstructs my standing over her flimsy, plastic-covered dressing table at 3 or 4 A.M., a skinny, 22-year-old schoolteacher staring down at an astonishingly beautiful little baby.

I unsnapped her pale yellow terrycloth stretchie and felt the heat rising inches high from her skin. My left hand supported her right shoulder in its palm, her left shoulder in its fingertips. My right hand dunked cotton balls into a breakfast bowl of pungent, clear liquid and then dabbed them—gingerly, hesitantly—on her chest, belly, legs and back. She wailed a high-pitched, dry and breathy rasp, and I continued dabbing, clenching my teeth, praying that I could cool her, straining to hold back tears.

As joyous and festive as it is designed to be, this wedding could be a little rough on me.

When Cuddly Things Go Bump in the Night

As a young child . . . and an only child, at that . . . I frequently would awaken an hour or so sooner than I had reason to awaken, and then shuffle sleepily from my room into my parents' room. I would climb up, and forward, from the foot of their bed to the pillows, plotting to wedge myself between my mother and my father.

Often without waking either entitled occupant, I then would press my backside against a pillow, slide feet-first beneath their covers, squirm into sufficient comfort, and thus cap off my night's repose in the kind of communal warmth that puppies and kittens must feel during their first few weeks of life, when they sleep draped over one another, like cards from a discarded deck.

My father was big in those days, outweighing my mother by 100 pounds, so that when I did intrude, I had to sleep on an incline that favored his side of the bed. Whenever he coughed, (he smoked heavily and coughed mightily), I cringed at the noise, but I enjoyed the bouncing.

His favored sleeping position was the oddest I ever had seen or imagined. He reclined on his left side, as he did on the living room floor Sunday evenings when he watched the "Ed Sullivan Show," and planted his left cheek in the palm of his left hand, the weight of his head and chest supported by a propped elbow. If ever he sneezed and rolled over backwards, he smothered me, first, then inaugurated a snore whose timbre and volume loosened the planks in the oak flooring. (My mother snored too, and handsomely, though my uncorroborated testimony has not convinced her.)

My parents never objected to my pre-dawn presumptuousness and always allowed me to believe that they even enjoyed my company. So I, in turn, felt similarly about like intrusions from my own children, lately my sons, who still are young enough to require nocturnal proximity and cuddly enough to make it palatable. Whenever I am tempted to expel them from my bed (Danny especially, because he sleeps like a helicopter blade during business hours), I remind myself that in a fleeting decade, they will be gawky and hairy; they will have acne, deep voices and smelly feet; and if I touch them with more affection than implied by a handshake, they will recoil with embarrassment, breaking my heart, just as I broke Pop's.

Softened by those trepidations, I have given my sons more slack—too much—and they have taken it; taken it and demanded more still.

Other parents warned me for years about this trait they said was common to all children. In the seventies, when my daughters were little, a friend cautioned me as kindly as she could: "Unless you pay attention to yourself once in a while, she said, you will find that your children will crave your attention—all of it, all of the time, all of their lives, until you have no self left for yourself."

Another acquaintance, a retired city fireman, issued his warning with more melodramatic emphasis. "Eddie," he said, "they are assassins. You know this. Ed, you're a father. You know they're cannibals. They live to devour you. Listen to me. My father, a Brooklyn Russian, had a saying. In Russian, it would sound like: 'Muhzsh-nah zshidt. Nah dai-yen.' Ed, memorize this. Keep it in your heart. To a Russian, you don't even have to say the whole thing. You could say: 'Muhzsh-nah . . .' and then you could shrug. Just shrug. He'll know. Eddie, he will know. And he'll love you for it. Loosely translated, it means, 'You could live; but they won't let you.' Ed, you could live, but will they let you? No. Why? Because they're assassins."

I seem to have abdicated all rights to my bed. The boys used to shuffle in at 5 A.M., sleepy and snuggly and welcomed, having slept most of the night in their own beds. Now, they will not exit consciousness outside the marital bed. And they must have food and drink immediately before slumber, so that later, when I do seize a sliver of my own bed, I sleep on crumbs and spill spots. I dream that I am reclining on a beach of clamshells, sometimes on a rising tide.

My remedies for these indignities are two; one more cowardly than the other. I let them have their way, initially, then lug them to their respective bunks after they have lapsed into somnolence. Or, I let them have their way, initially, then let them keep it. I go to sleep elsewhere, hoping that, someday, before we all grow senile and die, they will go to bed on their own, to beds of their own.

Hefting their limp bodies is more work than I have done since the 1960s. A sleeping Danny, at 40 pounds and 40 inches long, carries like three bowling balls. Jed is heavier, and has grown lanky, as well. I have to turn sideways to get him through a doorway without bruising one end or the other. In portage, his center of gravity changes from step to step. Relocating him into the bottom half of a bunk bed is like placing a corpse into the vegetable drawer of a refrigerator. I either fall onto him while trying to avoid banging my head on the top bunk, in which case I awaken him; or I bang my head on the top bunk, in which case I curse, and awaken him. He requires that I scratch his back until he falls asleep again.

He sleeps oddly, my boy, reclining on his left side, his cheek resting in the open palm of his hand, his upper body weight supported by a propped left elbow.

He Survives

I could kick myself for my skepticism. I don't know where it originates or if I control it, but I know that it often causes fretting that turns out to be foolish; it nearly ruins such good times as I ought to feel entitled to; and it almost always leaves me wondering why I don't listen to people who freely offer the lessons of their experience.

I doubted I would have a good time at my daughter's wedding. I doubted that the catering complex she chose would deliver much more than a mediocre affair, plus cold, chewy food. I doubted the reassurances of all the people who repeatedly insisted that my bleak fears were unfounded—maybe because most of them were mothers. My truly infuriating mistakes always have stemmed from doubting the advice of my mother. Regarding a wedding, the people said, "Everything will come together perfectly. You'll see. You shouldn't worry."

I worried, anyway.

T.C. had designated her brother, Daniel, as her ring-bearer, to accompany a young lady, Danielle, whose name and age were purely coincidental. Like Danny, she is 3 years old, but far more trustworthy, I suspected, to carry out her ceremonial, flower-bearing task than my Dan would be to walk a church-length straight line without running away or whining insufferably.

T.C. also had ordered that Jed, not yet 8, act as a similarly tuxedoed, full-fledged usher. I saw potential disaster in the selection—this is a boy, for heaven's sake, who hates to don any garment save sweats and sneakers; a boy who cringes, even weeps, at the very notion of appearing before more than two adults, let alone the terminally embarrassing lens of a camera; a boy who would rather take three showers than escort a girl, let alone a bridesmaid, down an aisle, in front of people, in any form of pageantry, anywhere, ever. Two nights before the wedding, Jed actually cried himself to sleep in terror of serving this sentence, while his mother tore her soul into shards of guilt, comforting him with half her tortured self, while not relenting with the sterner half, because she so ached to see him in a tuxedo.

Finally, T.C.'s co-maid of honor would be her sister, Colleen. Wonderful, I mused.

Chronologically, they are separated by 13 months. Over the

years, their relationship has fluctuated between hot and cold: the heat of all-out nuclear war and the cold of mutual ostracism. In temperament, T.C. is a child of the 1950s; relatively conservative, fiercely traditional. Colleen was born in 1969 and still lives there. A college sophomore hopelessly in love with the North Country, personal freedom and The Grateful Dead, she listens to Bob Dylan tapes and clothes herself in layers of flannel and denim. For weeks, in telephone calls from Plattsburgh, she groused about having to wear a dress (of all the ridiculous . . . blah, blah); about having to interrupt her semester and return to the awful, crowded and tacky Island; about having to even attend the ceremony, much less participate in it.

So what happens?

T.C. personally orchestrates every detail like a symphony conductor. She emerges so beautiful and radiant a bride that her joy dominates St. Patrick's Day, the wedding day.

Danny steals the show at church by abandoning Danielle during the wedding march and delivering the white satin ring pillow to his 3-year-old girlfriend, Katie Kretz, who is tucked demurely into a mid-church pew. Hysterical congregants quickly shove Danny back on track, while the throng guffaws at the cuteness. On the altar, Colleen, also looking radiant, reaches behind her cousin's back, grasps T.C.'s hand, in full view of everyone. They hold onto each other for much of the ceremony, Colleen sobbing so that an altar boy is compelled to retreat to gather tissues. People who have known the Lowe sisters nearly collapse at the sight, their father, mother and stepmother included.

Jed, though clearly pained by the attention, performs flawlessly as a parental support. He endures the entire nighttime reception without the company of one chronological peer. He then, at 1 A.M., in the backseat of a limousine, falls asleep, finally, resting against the delicate arm of his still-beaming sister, the bride.

The catered affair at the gaudy catering complex turns out to be perfect. I start my evening by planting a giant smooch on the left cheek of my ex-mother-in-law, and then dance with as many women as I can from 8:30 P.M. until after midnight, including my wife, her friends, my mother, her friends, my mother-in-law, my daughters, their friends, my cousins, their friends, and T.C.'s pal, Patty Muir, one of the kids who used to call me Dad.

Next day, as we nurse our aching muscles, my wife reminds

me that we are taking the boys to Disney World in a week. "It'll be good," she says. "We need the rest."

"It'll be awful," I mutter.

"No, it'll be fine," she says.

"Are you kidding? First, we're busted. Danny's not old enough, anyway. It'll be stinking hot. It'll be crowded. We'll have to hear Whine-on-Line . . ."

For Whom the Alarm Bell Tolls

My brain long ago developed a father's alarm system. It dings, when triggered. It responds to stimuli that appear innocent and non-threatening but actually are foreboding and even terrifying. Certain Sunday morning telephone calls can set it off, for instance, or civil questions posed too sweetly.

"I have a collect call for anyone from Colleen, in Plattsburgh, New York. Will you pay for the call?"

. . . ding . . .

"Yes, of course. Hi, Colleen."

"Hi, Dad! How are you . . . ?"

. . . ding ding . . .

". . . and how was your trip to Disney World?"

The mind races. Colleen is asking how I am. When did she last ask that? 1979. Also, this is Sunday morning. Sundays, Colleen rises at the crack of dusk. Also, her voice is sweet and melodious, as if she were rehearsing a television commercial for a breakfast cereal. This is another man's Colleen. How am I, her father? And how was Disney World? What could these questions mean? What is she leading up to? I keep hearing my friend Bill's warnings: Eddie, They're assassins. We are surrounded by assassins. They operate without anesthesia, these kids.

In an attempt to give her the benefit of the doubt, I talk to her over the dinging and the ruminating in my brain. I try not to sound suspicious, skeptical; not to sound fatherly. After all, she will be 20 years old this year. Maybe she has completely passed through the stage she entered when she became a teenager, when she developed a sarcasm gland. She was wonderful at her sister's wedding— happy, ebullient, involved. Perhaps I should reprogram my alarm system, at least until the boys hit their teens.

"Disney World was okay," I tell her. "I mean, you know me. I love to stand on line for 45 minutes with 50 thousand other people, sweating. I love to watch 1,200 dolls singing, 'It's a Small World After All,' over and over and over and over, until I can escape to another long, hot line.

"But, the boys had a great time, and I survived. I made friends with the bus driver from the hotel. He called The Magic Kingdom 'Rat World,' so we got along with each other right away. I must tell you, now that I think of it, I had one sort of nice, nostalgic moment that involved you, directly."

"Really?"

"Yeah. We were sitting at one of the luncheon places, eating our deep-fried plastic, when I looked across the way and saw the exit ramp from the Swiss Family Robinson tree house . . ."

"Oooh!" Colleen squeaked a high-pitched, little-girlish whine of reminiscence. Twelve years ago (which suddenly felt like 12 days ago), I took the girls to Disney World. Puffy-faced with a homicidal sunburn we all had acquired the day before, our first ever in the Florida sun, Colleen fell forward while exiting the Swiss Family Robinson exhibit and belly-flopped on the pavement. We drew a small crowd as we wiped away tears from her burning cheeks and blood from her scraped knees, and hugged her and stroked her hair.

"Oh, I remember that!" she said. Then she abruptly changed the subject. "Dad, want to hear what I did?"

. . . ding ding . . .

"What do you mean, what you did? What did you do?"

"Well, Wednesday, Kate and I and another girl, Michelle, decided to go to a Grateful Dead concert . . ."

. . . ding ding ding . . .

The mind resumes its racing. How many concerts is enough, especially Dead concerts, with thousands of 20-year-old Volkswagen vans and 40-year-old bearded guys in tie-dyed shirts?

". . . in Greensboro, North Carolina."

DING DONG DING DONG

"So, we got in the car . . ."

"YOUR car?" She drives my late father's 1976 Chevy Nova. Faded-maroon, garnished with dents, it seems to be slouching toward automotive senility, sinking into the pavement. People applaud when she returns to the house from 7-Eleven.

". . . and drove to North Carolina."

"Colleen! I don't believe this."

We got there in the middle of the concert, so we were bummed; but we knew there was another concert the next night. So, we stayed overnight in a Quality Inn . . ."

"Well, at least . . ."

". . . parking space. We slept in the car, behind the motel. The next morning, we made signs, like, 'Need 3 Dead Tickets!' We walked around town, holding them up."

Billy's right. She's trying to assassinate me.

"Finally, this guy sold us three tickets for forty dollars each, so we were dancing around all day, like, 'Yay! We got tickets! We got tickets!' Then we went to the concert. We gave the guy our tickets, and he says, 'These are counterfeits.'"

"Oh, Coll!"

"Yeah. We were so bummed, we got right in the car and drove all the way back. But it was fun. We got back last night. For the last two hours, we were cheering the car for making it."

"Colleen."

"Yeah?"

"You're broke, right?"

"Yeah. Well, not completely, but, yeah, close. I got a few more days' worth left."

"It's nice to know you're alive. I love you."

"Love you, too, Dad."

Son's Debut

I approached consciousness early on a recent Thursday, stirred by familiar stimuli assaulting two senses: I heard the high whine of the hair dryer, and I felt Danny's 3-year-old heel pressing against my right eye.

I opened my remaining eye. The darkness streaming through the bedroom window warned me that the hour was earlier than I might normally have expected to awaken.

The hair dryer ceased its screaming, and the bathroom door clicked open. I tried to articulate an inquiry regarding the predawn festivities. My mind instructed my mouth to ask, "Why are you up so early? What's going on?" but I am slow to motor-coordinate upon emerging from slumber. My mouth growled,

"Dorlf rildem." Uncannily, my wife answered, as if she had heard the thought instead of the question.

"I told you . . ." she began. (Answers to all questions posed early in the morning seem to require this introductory clause) ". . . Jed had to be at school an hour and a half early, because a television crew from "Good Day, New York" is doing something there, live. I've already driven him to school. The show comes on at seven. Channel Five. We have to watch."

I scanned the room for the source of the eerie blue light. "It follows 'Popeye,' then?" I managed to ask.

"Evidently."

Danny woke up, whining, but removing the heel from my eye. He had a cold, and so had begun each day making ridiculous demands of his mother, who acquiesced to every one of them before she left for work. On this morning, he ordered her to take him to 7-Eleven to buy Twinkies. "Do you think I can go?" she asked, as the show's blue logo appeared on screen. "If I miss Jed, I'll shoot myself."

"Yeah, go," I said. "They're bound to do the news about the battleship *Iowa* before they tell the world about life at the Grace Day School." As I spoke, the logo began shrinking to reveal behind it a gymnasium filled with youngsters in uniform—blue blazers, gray slacks, plaid ties and skirts.

"Oops," I said. "There's Kip. Do you see Jed anywhere?" The shot dissolved, and the show's attention shifted to the South Street Seaport, then the news of the *Iowa* explosion. My wife whisked a grouchy Danny off to buy the Twinkies.

I meditated. This is dopey. I am a reasonably smart man. I've managed to summon and sustain a certain degree of pride and dignity. Why should I allow myself to get excited over seeing my kid on television? I see him every day, in the flesh. I know exactly what he looks like. I could pick him out of a crowded stadium. I'm simply not going to fall for this. I am going to remain cool.

The power of television has always impressed me (the nature of the impressions range from awe to disgust and back), but never so much as on the two, purely fortuitous occasions when a child of mine appeared on the screen. While I lazily awaited Jed's appearance, I recalled Colleen's.

Five years ago, someone in the office alerted me that somebody knew somebody who knew someone at "CBS Morning

News" who was looking for a teenager who lived in a stepfamily situation, preferably with stepsiblings, but mainly with a stepmother or stepfather. The producers had lined up two such youngsters and felt they needed one more. Ever the trendoid, I telephoned my Colleen, who lived with me and her stepmother. Then approaching 15, Colleen agreed to appear on the show, once she learned that we would ride in a limousine from our hotel room to the studio. Why did I volunteer her? Why did we board a train to New York, stay overnight in a hotel, rise early, skip work and follow instructions to serve the whims of a network news show producer?

I don't know.

Worse, the interview was mildly humiliating for her, although she didn't care nearly as much as I did. Before the segment, a woman prepared Colleen for two questions about the relationship between her and her stepmother, but during the interview, a poorly prepared Bill Kurtis asked her to list the problems she had living with stepsiblings. Colleen had no stepsiblings. Jed, her half brother, was 3, and they were crazy about each other. Colleen could not answer, so Kurtis dismissed her with a gratuitous wisecrack. I would have thrown a folding chair at him were it not for the kindness of his co-host, Diane Sawyer, who stood next to me. Sawyer had somehow spotted me, a total stranger, straining to see the set from the darkened rear of the studio, no doubt looking almost as out-of-place and as stupid as I felt. She appeared from out of nowhere and asked, "Can I help you?" I told her why I was there, and she escorted me through a slalom course of technicians and cameras until she found a spot close to the set, where I could watch the segment.

"DID I MISS ANYTHING?" my wife suddenly screamed from downstairs. I yelled back, "No, but turn on the TV down there." She stayed downstairs. I lay in bed, thinking, this is ridiculous. I thus blanketed myself in sophisticated boredom, as segment after segment appeared—news, weather, sports, Grace Day School; commercials, South Street, news, weather, sports . . . JED!

I jumped up, staring bug-eyed at the set.

"WOW! HIS WHOLE FACE, RIGHT THERE ON TELEVISION! MY BOY! HOLY SMOKE! LOOK AT THAT! HEY, JED! WAY TO GO!"

Emotion Gets Its Chance

I must remind myself often that I am divided. I am the reasoning me and the feeling me: the intellectual Ed Lowe, whose controlled responses to stimuli follow after careful deliberation, and the emotional Ed Lowe, whose gut reactions are honest, but not always convenient.

The two selves frequently struggle against each other, until they achieve a balance satisfactory to both. Usually, the emotional self responds first, and then is tempered by its counterpart. For example: The emotional self, angered by the 50th whine from a boy whose brother is torturing him mercilessly in the backseat of the car during an interminable traffic jam on a rainy morning, might burst, uncontrolled, into shouting and ranting. Later, the intellectual self, concluding that the initial response was exaggerated and counter-productive, might request a calming, perhaps an apology.

I discovered recently that sometimes the process is reversed.

Since my father died in March 1985, both my wife and my ex-wife have asked me several times if I miss him, because they do, sometimes overwhelmingly, and because it must appear to them that I do not. I have answered that I do not miss him, for that matter, and have explained why, in these terms:

My father may well have been the best human I ever met, certainly the best man. Had I only met him—encountered him briefly, exchanged pleasantries, shaken hands—I suspect I still would be bragging about the moment to younger men in my town who had not enjoyed such privilege. I might even lengthen the encounter in my reminiscences; I've seen other men do it. Had I been his acquaintance or, better, his friend, I might feel the presence of that relationship lifelong, as if I were wearing an invisible badge or ribbon of honor. I wouldn't need to boast. It would be known, and part of me.

So. I was his son. His only son. His only child. And during the 39 years I enjoyed that exalted station, he and I covered nearly perfectly the classic cycle of a father-son relationship. When I was a small boy, he was a big cop. He visited my first-grade classroom in uniformed splendor and spoke to the whole class about the virtues and benefits of being good, honest, careful, safe and respectful of other people. When I grew to awkward

15

rebelliousness and then, later, to reasoned, philosophical opposition to his firmly held beliefs, we scowled and argued and stormed away from the dinner table, each disgusted by the other's intransigence. When I divorced, he asked no questions; just showed up one night with a six-pack and let me weep. When he grew infirm, we reversed roles, and I became his adviser. When he died, in the wee hours during heart surgery in North Shore University Hospital, I sat in his chair and wondered how I might miss him. I determined that it would be sacrilegiously greedy to allow myself do so. To expend any time or energy longing for another moment in the man's company after 39 years of exclusivity seemed unconscionable. So, I would not.

For Jed's eighth birthday, besides the customary hoopla and the requisite skateboard, I took him to a Mets game. He was very excited about it, though less, I learned, about seeing the Mets than about the idea of our going together—me and my Dad, without Danny, without Mommy, without a group of fathers and sons. He mentioned it in the car on the way to Shea, and I was touched. Thus began the erosion of my resolve about my own father.

Walter O'Malley lived in Amityville when I was a boy. He owned the Brooklyn Dodgers, and he often bestowed upon a friend in the Amityville Police Department tickets for box seats at the rail behind the Dodger dugout. The friend shared the tickets with his friends, so that, when my father and I took those seats at Ebbets Field, I could see whether Duke Snider had shaved that morning. I still have a clear, tactile memory of the sand paint atop the Dodger dugout, which was green. The Dodgers always lost when we attended.

Jed played in the backseat of the car while I struggled with these cherished memories. I maneuvered the car into the clogged, right lane of Grand Central Parkway in Flushing. I flipped on the radio for distraction, and it assaulted me with the sweet strains of a song whose lyrics I suspect I had been consciously avoiding hearing. The song, "The Living Years," was written by Mike Rutherford and B.A. Robertson, of Mike and the Mechanics.

"I wasn't there that morning when my father passed away ..."

I put my hand to my mouth; I quickly spied Jed in the rearview mirror. The song continued. I don't know why I didn't switch the radio off.

"... I think I caught his spirit later that same year/I'm sure I heard his echo in my baby's newborn tears ..."

Danny was born in November 1985. The scene now felt rigged, as if I had been set up. Evidently, the emotional Ed Lowe had been waiting patiently for the balance denied him by the reasoning Ed Lowe. Waited four years. I bit into the knuckle of my forefinger. The reasoning self thought: What an inconvenient time to fall apart. Ebbets Field rose up, followed soon after by tears. I quit trying to control. I just whispered into my fist, over and over: "I miss my Dad. I miss my Dad ..."

The Mets won.

Creeping Nintendonism

It is 11:30 P.M. on a Friday. I arrive home from dropping off the babysitter, Jennifer. As I enter the kitchen from the garage, I imagine that I hear my wife telling my older son to kill himself. It almost sounds like, ... "the last time I'm going to tell you to kill yourself. It's late, and you were supposed to be in bed more than an hour ago!"

I smile, amused at the optical-illusion-like tricks my auditory equipment can play on my brains. I shake my head and wonder what she actually could have said. . . . spilled something on yourself . . . probably.

"JED!" I hear her shouting from upstairs, breaking my concentration. "IF YOU DON'T DIE THIS MINUTE, I SWEAR I'LL THROW ZELDA IN THE GARBAGE, AND THAT'LL BE THE END OF IT!"

I bound upstairs.

"Mom," Jed's voice pleads, "this is not Zelda! This is Link!"

Good Lord! I think, dashing to rescue my boy from his poor, overworked, stressed-out, suddenly insane mother. I knew her birthday was approaching, but I never suspected for a second that it might trigger this profound a reaction.

She meets me at the top of the stairs. She is growling. "This Nintendo business is going to drive me out of my mind!" she howls.

"Sounds to me like you're using the wrong tense," I say, before giving myself a proper chance to think about her state of mind and refrain from any potentially insulting wisecracks.

"Oh yeah? Well, you deal with this, then. Your son has been at that damned game since dinnertime."

"Hey, I didn't buy Zelda! You did!" (Another bad move. She storms away, furious.)

"This is not Zelda, Dad! This is Link!" He sounds insulted. They're both mad at me. I just walked in!

"Jed, you die, now, or I'll pull the plug on you in one second!" Menacingly, I enter the blue light of his room. I know, now, what's happening. I made the mistake once before of turning off the Nintendofied TV set while he was playing Zelda. I thus erased three hours worth of (however dubious) accomplishments, forcing him to start over, next time.

"Okay, okay. I'm dying, I'm dying. Hold on, hold on. I have to die four more times."

"Listen to us, though. Have I slipped into another dimension? Do we really talk like this, now?"

"Dad, please, don't turn it off. Please, please! It's not mine. It's not my Link game. It's Mark's. If you turn it off, you'll be erasing everything Mark did. Look, look. I just died, again. Three more, Dad. That's all."

Mark. He is Jennifer's 13-year-old brother. One day, when Jennifer was booked already, Mark watched Jed and Danny for us. Mark apparently is as Nintendotic as Jed, so Jed now prefers Mark to Jennifer. When Jennifer does watch the boys, Jed calls Mark, anyway. Mark sometimes gets one of his parents to drive him to our house, where Jennifer already is babysitting. Mark and Jennifer's parents must think this is as nutty as we do.

"Okay. See, Dad. There's all my life. Dad, want to know what I got? I got Shield. I got Jump. I got Life-With-Magic. I got Fairy—makes you turn into a fairy, which means you can fly over everything. I got Fire, Reflect, Spell. Spell means you can turn the enemies into ghosts, so you only have to shoot him once instead of three times . . ."

He has no notion that I'm angry. I have no idea what he's talking about.

"I got Thunder. That kills everything on the whole board. I got Candle, Glove, Raft, Boot, Whistle, which destroys the monster and lets you get to the Sixth Palace. I got Cross, which lets you see invisible enemies. Then I got Hammer and Magical Key, and that's the end. I won the game."

"Great, Jed." I am absolutely dumbfounded. "I'm so proud." I know he doesn't believe me, and, frankly, I'm not telling the truth. I'm afraid I've sired an alien. "Please, now, brush your teeth. You have to go to bed before tomorrow."

Days later, I am at lunch, meditating over tuna salad on toast. The Nintendo argument has preoccupied parents in my neighborhood for two years. On the positive side, Nintendo requires participation and is thus better than staring impassively at the same cartoons for hours. The more sophisticated games also require an understanding of rules, exceptions, complex shortcuts; practice, failure, triumph and, lately, some reading. On the negative side, it gets expensive and appears to be addictive. One neighborhood father is tempted to cut his child off entirely for her apparently acute Nintendonism; a mother swears that Nintendiscipline is saving her sanity. She can stop her son in midair by threatening deprivation.

Me, I just want to play catch now and then, or shoot some hoops, or just understand what's going on.

Richie and Jerry sit down near me. Richie is 42. Jerry looks older and smokes cigars. Suddenly, I am distracted from my reverie by the word, candle. Jerry is saying, "I finally got the Candle." I eavesdrop more aggressively. Richie says he's up to Raft. He says he's been at it for weeks. He says his wife thinks he's lost all the aces in his deck. I decide to jump in the conversation.

"You guys are only up to Raft? Heck, I got an 8-year-old who got the Magical Key. He's practically bored with Link, already."

Tipoff to Adventure: "Hey, Dad"

My Danny has developed a profound interest in women. He has a girlfriend in the neighborhood—Katie—and one at school—Gina. He frequently awakens with either name first to escape his lips.

His romances are public knowledge. During a parental visit to his Maria Montessori school class, I noticed other tots approaching him with these words of comfort: "Don't worry, Danny, Gina is coming. She's just late, today. That's all. Don't worry." Gina, a doe-eyed brunette, finally arrived and stared at me and my wife, as if measuring us for in-law status. Later, at home, I eavesdropped as the sultry 3-year-old Katie Kretz asked coquettishly, "Danny, is Gina pretty?"

"Yes," my rogue son answered.

"Does she have blonde hair, like me?" Katie pressed. Danny said that, yes, Gina had blonde hair, just like Katie. A boldfaced, lover's lie. My son!

I hope that someday Danny will nurture a similarly abiding affection for tact, because while sometimes his observations about the opposite sex are endearing and amusing, sometimes they are downright dangerous. To me, not him.

For instance, I like to take Danny for boat rides across Great South Bay to Gilgo Beach. It is an act that fills many otherwise conflicting needs in our house. Danny loves to go; his mother loves to see him go, because his absence permits her to rest, read, garden or perform necessary household tasks without worrying about him roaring out into the street on his Hot Wheels. Danny's older brother almost never wants to go, but prefers instead to play with his friends. So, I get to take a boat ride with a person who is unaccompanied by a co-conspirator to hit, tease, whine with or be tortured by; who is delighted beyond measure to accompany me; who rarely disagrees with me, and who comes along on a moment's notice, unencumbered by the toting of folding chairs and canvas bags containing towels, sun block, visors, hats and sweatshirts. We just go. Danny and Dad. Free.

Last week, when we arrived, we followed our standard routine upon hitting the beach. Danny threw a couple of stones into the water. We proceeded to the Gilgo Beach Inn. I bought Danny a hot dog with ketchup, and something for myself, and we walked together through the underpass and toward the ocean. Danny immediately noticed women who were not wearing very much clothing. He thus stared at them, shielded by a 3-year-old's guileless curiosity.

The first two women we encountered in the shadows of the underpass appeared to be wearing no clothing at all. They were walking from the ocean side back toward the inn. When they strolled past us, we looked back and saw that they had donned, or applied, a few flesh-colored strings, though to what end I had no notion.

For purely educational reasons, I continued to watch the progress of their strolling, while I tried to imagine what it might feel like to wear a piece of string in the manner of their dress.

After several moments of meditation, I concluded that it would be uncomfortable and made a personal vow never to do it.

"Hey Dad!" yelped Dan, rousing me from contemplation. That already would have been sufficiently embarrassing, but I knew that Danny's "Hey Dad's" generally served an introductory function. In this particular case, I had every right to expect him to follow with an exhortation like, "Hey Dad! Look at that lady's butt!"

"Butt" seems to have emerged as a compromise curse word for children of our era and place. I object less vociferously to Danny's calling his brother Jed a butt-head or butt-breath, so that my angry howls have more impact in my endless and probably futile attempt to erase "You [anatomically correct noun for an exclusively male appendage]!" and "[Gas-expulsion]-face!" from their vocabulary.

Anyway, "Hey Dad! Look at that lady's butt!" was the (unnecessary) directive I expected, and, before I could reach down to gag the boy, I got it. We still were in the concrete echo chamber of the underpass, which amplified his comment to a public bellow: "HEY DAD! LOOK AT THAT LADY'S BUTT!"

Heads turned. I quickly scooped up his 45 pounds of public humiliation and hastened with him toward the beach, while he tried to twist my head back in the direction of the . . . Strings, saying, "Dad! Dad! Those ladies don't have any clothes on their butts! Look, Dad!"

"I know, Dan," I whispered. "I know. Look! There's the ocean! Look! Don't you want to see the ocean!"

I longed to stay on the beach until nightfall, to avoid any chance of meeting the Strings on their way back from the inn. Danny finally turned his attentions toward the Atlantic, but his eyes evidently tripped over another scantily clad woman, this one of considerable girth. His jaw dropped open, and I somehow managed to spot simultaneously both her massive, sunbathing form and Danny's awed expression. Still carrying him, I raced back toward the underpass before he could "Hey Dad!" me.

I knew what he was scheming. He had nearly killed his mother by observing aloud that the neighborhood ice-cream vendor was fat. "Mom, look! Isn't the ice-cream lady FAT?"

"Danny, just tell me what you want," his mother begged.

"BUT, MOM, LOOK AT HER. SHE'S SO FAT! WHY ARE YOU SO FAT, ICE-CREAM LADY?"

Assembly—Plus
Sweat and Blood—Required

The final score of the final game of the 1989 NBA Championship flashed onto the television screen at around midnight. I rose from the chair to walk home from my neighbor's house, and he said, "Want to help me put together a trampoline?"

I cannot recall ever wanting to help anybody put together a trampoline, let alone at midnight, but the question swooped down so fast from nowhere, it caught me with my powers dimmed. I must have somehow indicated in response that I did want to help assemble a trampoline—however insane a notion it now seems—or at least that I would not kill to avoid it, because he next said, and with maddening exuberance: "Great! Let's go."

Trudging behind him to the garage, I marveled at the speed and ease with which he had sprung and closed this trap. I knew that his son, Eamonn, had turned 5 years old at midnight. I then correctly deduced that the day's birthday celebration was to include presenting to the celebrant an assembled trampoline, whose assembly my neighbor had procrastinated until this, the very last, possible moment.

My neighbor must have suspected that I would sympathize with him, because of my reputation in town. For more than 20 years, I had procrastinated about the assemblage of every similarly devious contraption known to Sears and its corporate co-conspirators in the endless campaign to drive up the blood pressure of America's fathers and dispatch them, blithering, to the asylums. I commenced each assembly immediately before, or on, or at, or during, or after whichever deadline required the work. It is my legacy.

I began with cribs and proceeded quite typically to the smaller, ride-on toys, to Hot Wheels, to hideously complicated and burdensome swing-and-slide sets, and beyond. I can't count the Christmas Eves and birthday midnights I have spent on my knees in a basement or garage, cursing. Adding to the misery, my daughters' birthdays fell on the same days, every damned year—July 7 and Aug. 8, in heat and humidity invented specifically for death-by-perspiration.

One of my more unforgettable tortures involved screwing

together a multicolored semi-polyhedron, which an anonymous, evil sorcerer marketed as a climbing-toy for the offspring of his intended victims. Once completed, it looked from a distance like a hemisphere made of red and blue straws; cute, clever. However, when you dumped it, pre-assemblage, out of the box, it more closely resembled a pile of red and blue pipes, their ends squeezed by giant pliers and drilled through, once.

Following the clanging pipes, a bag of nuts and stove bolts tumbled out of the box with an ominously weighty thud. The instructions recommended laying out about six pipe sections in a circle, on the freshly mowed and thus itchy, buggy, humid, summer lawn. At ground level, you had to hold three ends together at a time, in an inverted T, then pierce them with a stovebolt of appropriate length and secure the mating with a nut. At the next level up, four flattened ends of pipe had to meet and marry, requiring two strong hands to squeeze the ends together, plus two, separate sets of fingers to run the bolt through the holes in the pipes and spin on each nut. Possessed of only a couple of hands, I waited until the birthday party guests arrived to ensnare another innocent father, then another. We growled through the entire party.

At the apex of the hemisphere, all the remaining ends of pipe—five or six—were to gather in a bunch and be secured by a long bolt. A series of grueling, grunting trials revealed that the length of the bolt exactly matched the thickness of the bunched-up pipe-ends. No matter how hard we squeezed or how many other hands assisted ours, we could not make the bolt stick out far enough to meet the nut.

Enraged, and convinced that the semi-polyhedron's manufacturer was rolling on his floor somewhere, cackling, then guffawing, then retching with hysteria at his own evil wit, I abandoned the party and stomped to a local hardware store, brandishing the murderous stove-bolt. I bought a bolt of matching thickness, but eight times the length. I asked for the longest such bolt manufactured in the Northern Hemisphere, and I got it. I could have used this bolt as a clothesline, or a fishing pole.

I also bought a hacksaw.

I returned just as the party guests were leaving. Ignoring them, I reclined for the next hour on my back—my legs serving as ankle-McNuggets for the fast-food, gnat crowd—and twirled the tiny nut up the entire length of the oversized bolt. I sawed off the excess bolt, then announced the polyhedron's completed construction to the gathering crowd of fireflies.

The girls played on the climbing toy for 10 minutes or so. After dusk, they draped a blanket over it and made a tent. I glared at them from a distant lawn chair, muttering repeatedly: "A tent. A tent. I could've gotten a tent."

The trampoline seemed uncomplicated. String the bungee cord over the bar, through the hook and under the bar. Then, stretch the cord. Over, through, under; stretch. Over, through, under; stretch. Maybe 75 times. We were three-quarters done when I noticed an under-through-under in the middle, and we had to start over. I got home at 1:30 A.M. The kids loved the trampoline. For a whole day.

Pacifism's Limits

We were at opposite ends of the kitchen. My wife was telling her friend, Ellie, of her wrenching, maternal, pacifist agony over a two-day-old incident involving our son, Jed, that I was now learning about for the first time. The story seemed to be headed in the direction of some sort of violence.

I leaned backward against the stove, listening intently and with mixed emotions, deeply interested in the narrative's details but mildly resentful of my ignorance of them. Moreover, my wife seemed to be addressing Ellie directly and more or less including me, rather than the other way around. I tried not to be distracted by ripples of paranoia that repeatedly asked annoying little questions, like, "Why am I hearing about this for the first time? Why do I, the father of this boy, feel like the third party here? Why isn't she even looking at me during the reweaving of this tale?"

My wife described a scene two days earlier wherein she had tried in vain to comfort her anguished son as he tearfully lamented about the extent to which he endured physical guff from his compadres. He told her that he was thoroughly fed up with trying to act as if he was neither hurt nor bothered by the punching, pushing, shoving, jumping-on; by the too-obviously overenthusiastic backslaps and by the fake-but-nonetheless-painful choking that he said his friends customarily indulged in, often with him serving as the punching bag.

"I'm too nice," he had told his mother. Crying with an intensity so heart-rending that its misery remained vivid and moving two days later, even via hearsay evidence, when he swore to his mom that he would no longer permit his own exploitation. Borrowing from sentiments expressed in the movie *Network*, he was mad as hell and was not going to take it any more. The next time anybody shoved, choked, punched or pushed him gratuitously, he would punch the offender right in the face.

"Oh, no!" his mother had responded. She told him not to punch anybody in the face but instead to tell her about such incidents, or, in her absence, to tell another adult. Hearing this, I looked down at the floor. But Jed insisted, she continued. He was adamant. "He said, 'No, Mom, you're wrong. I'm gonna do it.'"

Now I knew why I was hearing this tale two days late, and why my wife was not addressing me directly. On the immediate horizon loomed a fundamental, philosophical difference in parental approach. I did not interrupt, however, but I began formulating my argument. I also tried to read Ellie's expression. She had raised two sons and a daughter to adulthood. She, too, was listening intently.

I ruminated. I have punched somebody in the face twice in my whole life. (This does not count one swing that missed and one feeble punch into a stomach. In that case, my antagonist looked down at his ample and unharmed belly and asked, "Is that it?" I answered, "Yeah. That's pretty much my show." He said, "Good," and we both laughed.)

I don't condone fighting, would not recommend it for any of my children and still have a sickening memory of my 7- or 8-year-old fist hitting into the flesh of another boy's cheekbone. When I was about Jed's age, a slightly older, significantly bigger neighborhood boy developed a habit of punching me and my best friend in the stomach, on short notice. It almost always made us cry. After the fourth or fifth time, my father called me over to his seat at the kitchen table and said, "Listen to me. I don't want you fighting, and I never want to hear from anyone that you started a fight or caused a fight in any way. But, if he punches you in the stomach like that ever again, and if you, then, punch him in the nose, I will give you a quarter."

Two days later, the bigger boy punched me in the stomach again. I doubled over, started crying, straightened up and flung a hard right into his left cheekbone. I then stood dumbfounded, arms at my sides, stunned that I had hit him (and offering, in my defenseless stupefaction, a wide-open opportunity for him to hit me back). He raised his hand to his face. He looked just as shocked as I was. He began to cry, a phenomenon I never had seen nor imagined. He said he was going tell his mother. I couldn't believe it. Until that moment, I had thought of him as a grown man, not a boy who would cry or tell his mother. I ran home, collected my quarter and never again got punched in the stomach.

"I didn't know what to tell Jed," my wife was saying. But the very next day, one of the boys mashed a ball into Jed's face, hard, and Jed hauled off and socked him, right in the face, so that he ran home, crying.

Perfect, I thought, trying not to reveal my satisfaction. I looked for Ellie's reaction.

"Perfect," Ellie said. "That'll be the end of it. Once they know that this very nice boy also refuses to be pushed around, they'll stop pushing him around."

"Really?" my wife asked. "You think so?"

"Hey, I went all through this with all three of my kids," Ellie said. "If we lived in a perfect world, it would be different. But we don't. Some kids will always take advantage of other kids, until they find out that they'd better stop, or they'll get hurt. Period."

I nodded. I didn't even have to enter the discussion.

Lessons in Siblinghood

In most of my private deliberations regarding what a good father ought to do in certain situations, I rely heavily on my experiences as a son. In the main, I know how and where I benefited from the decisions my parents made and the courses of action they took. I also harbor some reasoned suspicions about how and where they might have damaged me, by offering too much or too little discipline, for instance, or encouragement, trust, denial, assistance or independence. As any good student might, I try to do what I most admired in my parents and fight off the temptations to duplicate their shortcomings.

One example: My father performed a great many chores about the house, and a great variety. He fixed broken items, ranging from the brakes on the car to the dials on the clock; and he manufactured other items—lamps, bookcases, a patio, a finished attic room. Qualitatively, his handiwork ranged from mediocre to high-mediocre, but he loved to tinker, and the creativity gave him tremendous satisfaction. Whenever I sought his company during these periods, however, and asked with a son's rapt admiration if I could help him, he answered, too truthfully, that I could best help him by leaving, by going outside or into another room. I was devastated on those occasions.

So, as much as I hate the very idea of handing a spray can of Rustoleum paint to a 3-year-old boy while I am trying to whiten the wrought-iron patio furniture, I try to remember how I felt in my banishment and then shrug off the sticky consequences. It is not easy, but I trust the lessons of experience.

I have no experience as a sibling, though, and frequently am confounded by the range of possibilities represented by the relationship, exacerbated as they are in the case of my children by chronological distance and half-sibling relationships. My daughters are beginning their third decade; my sons are at opposite ends of their first. T.C. is married and not around much, but the boys miss her and talk about her and love her visits. T.C.'s relationship with Colleen, 13 months her junior, has been stormy for many years, though since T.C.'s wedding, the girls have begun to develop at least a curiosity about each other's lives, if not an actual concern, however embryonic.

I marvel at the evidence of genetic bonds, how much my older son, Jed, looks and acts like T.C., who owes her dazzling smile to her mother, who is not related to Jed; and how my younger son, Danny, looks exactly the way my younger daughter, Colleen, looked, and displays precisely her temperament, though Colleen and Danny also have in common only my genetic code.

My one sibling was stillborn. I wear his absence like a birthmark, wondering now and then about its effect on my close friendships, which sometimes seem actually fraternal. Perhaps because I know I missed some profound characteristic of life, I want my four children to feel connected to one another and to cherish and nurture the ties. I have no idea how to successfully encourage them, except with words, and my words would come from reality imagined, not experienced. Danny already knows more than I ever will about being someone's brother.

Armed with no knowledge, I have chosen so far to do nothing. But I watch. And in recent weeks, I have seen and heard indications that, I confess, strike me as quietly but deeply thrilling.

We had promised Jed we would take him to see the Beach Boys at the Jones Beach Marine Theater. We got four tickets and told Jed that he could invite a friend. He immediately telephoned Colleen, at work in a local ice-cream parlor. She later reported the conversation gleefully: "Don't you want to take your best friend?" she had asked him.

"You are my best friend," he said.

Days later, at about the time of evening the younger residents of the house should have been asleep, I climbed the stairs expecting to find my 8-year-old boy in his room playing Nintendo and my 3-year-old boy watching over his shoulder. As always, the door to Colleen's room was closed, but I could hear an extended conversation was in process. Colleen and Jed? I turned away, so as not to eavesdrop or interrupt, but I did hear Jed's voice: "So college is like a huge slumber party?" he asked.

"That's right, Jed," Colleen answered. "In fact, that's a pretty smart comparison!" They talked on, my son and my daughter.

Last Monday evening, unnerved by the peace downstairs in the house, I asked my wife where the boys were. They were upstairs in Colleen's room, again, listening to Grateful Dead tapes, learning to braid multicolored string bracelets and discussing such subjects as chronologically-distant, opposite-gender, half-siblings must discuss when their father is out of earshot.

I returned to the kitchen in time to answer a telephone call from T.C. She asked distractingly mundane questions about my health. I was busy envying the richness of the growing bond between the kids upstairs.

"How do you feel about the name Pop?" T.C. asked.

Pop, I thought. The girls called my father Pop, their grandfather. Grandfather!

"Teace! What are you saying?"

"What does it sound like I'm saying, Pop?"

Diving into Competition

My ambivalence about competitiveness has cost me weeks of sleep during my years in the parenthood trade.

Year in, year out, I hear hundreds of what seem to be sound arguments about the value of competition in so competitive a society; how organized contests prepare children for life in the real world; how being a good loser first means being a loser. Moreover, whenever someone whom I care about triumphs in a contest, I feel all the appropriate surges of adrenaline and who-knows-what other biochemicals that inspire bursts of joyous applause and exclamation. I also wrestle with feelings of disappointment when they do not triumph, when they lose or fail.

Still, I am forever doubtful that the achievement of individual excellence really requires another individual's defeat or failure. I do not accept that finishing last in a race is less an achievement for that contestant than first place was for the winner.

I once met and wrote about a man who had started and coached a high school rifle team in a tiny school in the Northwest. He asked each team member, each day, to strive to match their last performance, and he congratulated them profusely when they did. When they bettered their previous performance, he absolutely rejoiced and invited other team members to rejoice, as well. His fledgling rifle team won matches all over the United States and in England, and were noted particularly for their sportsmanship. Losing a match to someone else was a concept alien to their training. They encouraged their competing colleagues; they competed with their own yesterdays.

Sixteen years ago, my oldest child broke my heart during a kindergarten race. She entered it with unbridled enthusiasm and made triple-certain that I was watching. Clearly, she wanted to please me, make me proud of her. The race began. I loved watching her run. I loved watching her do anything. Early in the race, I saw her become aware that another child was passing her, then another, then another and another. Suddenly, my daughter fell. She appeared to slip and fall, but to this day I suspect that she reached a point where, consciously or subconsciously, she actually determined to stumble and fall rather than finish last. I guessed that, somehow, she had concluded that I would not be proud or happy to watch her run if she ran slower than other children. I ached to think that I might have conveyed that message, for it was untrue.

Ten years later she joined a swim team—for one session. She insisted that I accompany her and watch her swim in a practice heat, and I did. When the other swimmers began to pass her, she choked and gagged; she stopped swimming and appeared so distressed that her coach dove to rescue her.

I hate thinking I might share some responsibility for those two moments, hate it desperately.

Jed has joined a swim team. Jed takes his time becoming confident at an endeavor, then learns it suddenly and progresses at an accelerated rate. He insisted on keeping the training wheels on his bicycle for a long time, despite my offers to help him learn to ride without them. One day, he asked me to remove the training wheels before I left for work. That evening, he repeatedly rode around the block with his friend, as if he had been riding a two-wheeler for months. He knows himself, and I am beginning to trust, and be very proud of him for that.

From the earliest, he was almost neurotically timid about swimming, clinging to pool ladders and splashing in knee-deep beach water until, one week, he plunged into a pool and moved through the water like an amphibian.

With him, however, I feared that the jump from swimming to competitive swimming was going to resemble the difference between ladder-clinging and board-diving. Frankly, I didn't want to witness the painful part of the process and ran out of excuses to miss swim meets only this week.

A swim meet turns out to be as long and as hot as a dancing school recital was 15 years ago, but less torturous because of the excitement of competition, inevitably between us and them. I found myself cheering loudest for one of them. A 4-year-old named Marybeth was entered a year shy of eligibility into a backstroke contest, apparently because a real team member failed to show. Marybeth's backstroke bore a striking resemblance to drowning, but she would not quit and was still flapping her spindly arms in her lane long after the other backstrokers had wrapped themselves in towels. I started yelling "Come on Marybeth!" along with a woman I took to be her mother. My eyes filled as Marybeth's wild flailing drew her inches closer to the end of the pool, by which time everyone was cheering madly for Marybeth, the triumphant loser of the race.

Jed, who shares his father's disdain for keeping eyes open in a pool, lost his goggles in one heat and fell back from a possible victory; then swam wonderfully in two relays, his team taking second place in one. Later, I heard his mother asking, "Where's your ribbon? You didn't forget to pick up your ribbon, did you?"

"Mom," he said, "the ribbon means nothing in the world to me."

My boy.

What Did I Just Say?

The envelopes from the State University of New York at Plattsburgh have collected on the kitchen counter, increased in number during the summer and now display the kitchen wounds and circular blemishes more common to the brown envelopes from the telephone company. An envelope from the State Department of Motor Vehicles appeared atop the pile one day, and, following it, one from an automobile insurance company. All the envelopes are addressed to Colleen Lowe.

Colleen Lowe procrastinates. I long to scold her for that, or even criticize her, or simply remind her to prudently accomplish what she ought to accomplish, but I cannot. I am gagged by the knowledge that her tendency to ignore, put off, avoid, neglect and/or forget comes directly from my DNA. My grandmother would say: "It ain't off the grass she gets it." Still, I become angrier as, day by day, the salad-dressing stains increase in number on the unopened envelopes. I know that the deadlines are approaching. I know, too, that they are more my deadlines than Colleen's, because I have the credit rating and because I have not attended eight Grateful Dead concerts this summer, at God-knows-what-cost. The proximity of the deadlines, coupled with my stupid reluctance to pick up the envelopes and put into motion the payment of the tuition bill and the renewal of the car insurance policy, makes me short-tempered and anxious.

It is Saturday morning, hot and humid. Her car insurance expires Wednesday. The tuition payment must be postmarked Monday, or Colleen will have to re-register, no doubt missing some courses that she dearly wanted. She then will blame her difficulties on me, and she will be right.

I pace the kitchen. My daughter T.C. is visiting, and she and her sister and my wife are in the kitchen, too, talking as if I am not there. Danny and Jed are in the den, giggling. I catch sight of Jed just as he pushes Danny's head into the couch. I tell him not to do that; it will lead to trouble. Danny laughs and hits Jed with a throw pillow. I say, "Danny, stop!" I then say, "Jed, you know where this is going: You tickle him; he hits you; you kick him; he cries, and I get mad at you for kicking him. Why don't you just cut it out, now! Stop it before it starts!" I am very edgy.

Jed laughs and hits Danny back. Danny throws his stubby, 3-year-old fist into the air and plants it in Jed's left eye. Danny turns to run; Jed howls and thrusts out his long, lean, 8-year-old leg, driving the heel of his sneaker into Danny's back. Jed is now holding his eye and screaming with more anguish than his pain deserves, because he knows I'm already storming angrily into the den, about to bellow and then repeat the obnoxiously, parental question: "WHAT DID I JUST SAY? HAH? WHAT DID I JUST SAY?" He is right, too. I do exactly that. Danny, shuffling forward, leaning backward, his contorted face aimed at the ceiling, is wailing with almost supernatural grief. He knows that the louder he wails, the angrier I will be at Jed, and not at him. He is right, too. Am I so predictable? Ugh, yes.

I am gripping the envelopes from Plattsburgh and yelling at Jed for kicking Danny in the back. I am fiercely angry. I'm angry with the boys. I'm angry with Colleen. I'm angry with me. I'm angry with the damned weather. I yell both boys into genuine grief and then storm back into the kitchen, angrier at myself for having lost control. My mind races. I would have been better at being a bachelor. I would have made a terrific uncle. I wish I were a hermit. I should have gone to sea.

I feel I have to talk to Jed. I'm sorry I yelled so. I take him aside in the den. I try to explain several profound truths at the same time, truths that I believe dearly and that I desperately want to convey to this boy. "It's bad enough that when somebody punches you in the eye, you wanted to punch him in his eye," I say. "But you go beyond that. You feel you have to escalate. If Danny takes a bite out of your cookie, you want to deprive him of meals for the next three days. If Danny hits you with his hand, intentionally or accidentally, you think it's all right to retaliate by crushing his skull with a bat. I'm exaggerating, I know, but I'm trying to make a point here. How many times have

I told you not to kick him? Jesus, Jed, he's your brother. Not only that, he's 3, and you're 8. How fair a fight is that? If you were being slammed around the room by a 13-year-old brother, wouldn't you want me to talk to him about it? I'm sorry I got so mad. I just can't stand it when you go so far. I can't take it. I love you both, but, man, what's the sense of bringing Cain and Abel into the world if one is going to cause the worst grief a parent could ever imagine, and the other invents murder! Please try to think the next time! Please!"

I kiss him and return to the kitchen. My wife is smirking. Colleen is smirking. T.C. is giggling. My wife says, "They were telling me about your lectures, how long and boring they always were."

"They said that?"

"They were feeling sorry for Jed. I told them, 'Don't worry about Jed. He's on another planet. He zoned out in the first 10 seconds after Daddy started.'"

"You said that?"

"Don't feel bad," she laughs.

I smile, but weakly. Really weakly.

Real Education

For me, taking Colleen back to college represents work: Three hours of hard labor sandwiched between two days of driving. I therefore prefer to do the job by myself—just me and my daughter, traipsing off to Plattsburgh together.

I envision us on the road for six hours (or more, depending on the transportation-bond-issue activity), listening to selections from among her tens of thousands of cassette tapes, and casually chatting during each change of the tape or at the toll booths, when I turn down the volume in sympathy for the collector.

Perhaps we stop at a way-off-the-Thruway restaurant an hour north of Albany. Later, we pop more or less randomly into a motel near Ausable Chasm in Keeseville. We rise early on Sunday and finish the journey by taking Route 9 along the shoreline of Lake Champlain. Colleen registers at her dorm, and we begin hauling a truckload of life's necessities to her new quarters.

That done, she begins the process of wiring her speakers, arranging her CDs, stacking her tapes and then unpacking her clothes, while I dash off to buy the three-prong-to-two-prong electric plug adapters that we forgot again.

Next, I take her out to lunch, give her some cash, kiss her good-bye and say that I'll see her in two weeks when she comes home again for the all-important Jerry Garcia concert. I leave Plattsburgh and drive south in meditative silence. I stop after 5½ hours to dine alone in meditative silence. I arrive home, kiss my wife, hug my sons and take a boat ride to a spot on the bay where I can sit in meditative silence. In my view, it is a perfect way to dispense with a time-consuming, annual trek.

Mine is not the only view, nor is it the prevailing one. My wife sees returning Colleen and her equipment to college as a mini-vacation for the family. Colleen seems to consider the trip a way to show her brothers dormitory life and how delightful life can be if parents appear only when summoned, and then briefly. My boys see it as an adventure and an opportunity to drink and eat junk food in the back of my Suburban, which I normally do not allow because they spill the drinks, sprinkle the chips, crush the Twinkies and sit in the mixture until they stick to it.

Colleen wanted the boys to accompany us. The boys wanted to accompany us. My wife wanted everyone to accompany us. Thus accompanied, I left home last Saturday, hours later than I wanted to leave, but this time equipped with a borrowed hand truck. Last year, I learned that it is not prudent enough to own just a vehicle that will hold most of a college student's belongings; you must also bring along the wherewithal to get the belongings from the vehicle to the room. My neighbor in the dormitory parking lot last August drove a small Toyota station wagon, but extracted from it a hand truck and blithely wheeled his daughter's trunk into the dormitory elevator. I had smugly pulled up in a vehicle that could have accommodated his station wagon, but I nearly collapsed when I realized how far I would have to lug the luggage. This year, I would be smarter.

The boys behaved decently during the ride north last weekend, though I wished they had synchronized bladders before our departure. Danny simply could not go when we stopped; we had to stop again for him to go.

My fantasy about popping into a roadside motel at random proved to be monstrously stupid. I had not made reservations at any motels, because I did not know that half the vacationing population of Canada commandeers motel rooms from Plattsburgh down to Saratoga each August and that half the population of upstate New York occupies rooms from Lake George up to Plattsburgh at the same time. We stopped at motel after motel, begging for accommodations that did not exist. One kind innkeeper, whom we roused at about 10:30 P.M., telephoned a friend who kept a camper in his driveway; but we were too large a family for the camper. The friend feared that at least one of five people wedged into his two-person camper was bound to rub up against the heater during the night and catch fire, damaging the camper and spoiling his next vacation.

At 11 P.M., faced with the bleak possibility of spending the night in the Suburban, I did what any red-blooded American father would do. I called my mother. I knew she had the address of Linda Delbel, a family friend who lived in Plattsburgh, but whom I had not seen in 22 years. I also knew that my mother would have the courage to call the woman and plead our case. She did, and the saintly Miss Delbel rose from slumber, prepared our beds and chilled a bottle of Labatt's for me. The boys played until after midnight with Thomaso, Linda's ominously cute daschund-cocker spaniel mix, and we all slept as if deceased.

I awoke to Danny and Jed's arguing over Thomaso's affections. Of course, when the little doggie wanted to go out, he invited me to accompany him.

Colleen's dorm, MacDonough Hall, a short walk away, has no elevators. Her room is on the third floor. A hand truck would hinder more than help. I stubbornly insisted on using it anyway and thereafter felt as if someone had fastened vise grips to the base of my spine.

Worse, the boys now want a dog for Christmas.

Reveille

Of the four Lowe children, only Danny ever got out of bed in the morning without the inspirational assistance of a marching band, a crowbar or an inverted bucket of ice water.

They may be fundamentally meaningless in the long run, but such minor personality traits and characteristic distinctions always have helped me appreciate the children individually, so I look for these little differences and try to alter my parental approach accordingly.

Regarding sleep, T.C., the oldest, as a child and even as a teen, is singular among my daughters and sons in her childhood understanding of the concept of bedtime. The other three required (or require) aggressive lulling, ranging from bedtime literature to food, rock music, repeated visits to the bathroom, ice water, threats of deprivation, peeks at late-night television news programs with absolutely no discernible bearing on their lives, mounting indications of fatherly impatience escalating inexorably toward frustration and rage, and—specifically in Jed's case— accompaniment in bed by a thoroughly exasperated parent willing to scratch the boy's back until he leaves consciousness.

In the mornings, particularly school mornings, T.C. and Jed shared this characteristic: You had to pull them bodily out of bed, prop them up and tell them who they were. My mother swears they got that from me.

Colleen required ingenuity. When she was about 11 years old and had begun to respond preferentially to one stimulus at the expense of almost all others, I ordered her a separate telephone line and placed a telephone on her night table. On school mornings, I called her from the kitchen. It worked mainly because of the statistically remote—but nonetheless existent—possibility that the caller each morning was not me, but somebody important.

But Danny, the youngest, always rose willingly from slumber, as if he had emerged from a different gene pool. So, on Monday, when he was to start his sophomore year in Maria Montessori preschool, on a day that his mother's job required her to be off to work earlier than usual, I calmly and willingly accepted sole responsibility for waking Danny and getting him and his brother up, washed, dressed and out of the house.

Leery of my ability, my wife roused me at 6:20 A.M. to tell me that she had reset the alarm for 7:15 A.M.; that she would be leaving the house at 6:30 A.M. and probably would remind me again just before she left; that she had draped Jed's clothes, including socks, over the end of his bunk bed; that she had draped Danny's clothes similarly over the end of his bunk bed; that she had packed Jed's lunchbox with food and his backpack with books and gym paraphernalia; that I should remember to remind him to take both the backpack and the lunchbox or he would surely leave one at home; that she felt guilty about missing Danny's first day; that if she could find a way, she would call me at 7:15 A.M., just in case the alarm clock had no effect on me or suffered a dead battery in the next 45 minutes; that she loved me, and that I should now close my eyes, relax and get some sleep. Ten minutes later, she whispered the entire litany to me again, including the exhortation to relax, now, and sleep.

Danny woke up at 6:31 A.M. and waddled into the bedroom, whining, "Where's my Mommy?" I told him, but I must not have aimed the information carefully enough. It shot past him without any appreciable effect, and he proceeded down the stairs, still whining the same question.

I rose and followed him. By the time I arrived in the kitchen, he was rock-climbing the third shelf of the pantry, whining to himself that he wanted a cookie. I would have offered my opinion of cookies-for-breakfast, but I knew I still had a 44-minute window-of-opportunity to return to bed and was willing to let Danny eat any confection if he would permit me that luxury. I offered to get a cookie for him, but he flailed at me, whining strangely that he did not want my help. In retrospect, I think he was functioning on diminished power, his engine started, but not yet idling properly. He spied a box of small doughnuts, collected four of them and marched past me, again, to the stairs, which he mounted quite deliberately, thumping his way up to the bedroom.

I returned to bed and managed to doze. The alarm beeped at 7:15. The telephone warbled two minutes later, while I was in the bathroom. I began my chores, aiming my efforts first at resurrecting James Edward Lowe and tutoring him in the complexities of placing one foot in front of another. That battle won, I turned my attentions to the easier task: Tell Danny boy to rise and watch him go.

"Dan, let's go."

No rise; no go.

Danny was on his back, his head ringed with doughnut crumbs, a white powder garnish above his lips. I shook him. No response. "Dan! Come on! All you've been talking about for days is going back to school. Don't you want to get up and go to school?"

No response.

I tickled his lip. I raised and dropped his limp limbs. I hefted him and stood him up. He was out. Gone. Comatose. Waiting for parts.

I held him up, brushed his teeth, hovered him over the toilet, dressed him and aimed him toward the kitchen, tired, but satisfied that he was one of us, at last.

Death Is Part of Life

One of my more awkward tasks as a father involves explaining to a small child why he or anybody else would want to mingle and chat in a crowded room whose occupants included a dead person; a dressed-up, made-up, laid-out, bejeweled corpse, sometimes even wearing eyeglasses.

In my household, currently, this explanation is the father's responsibility, because the mother's ethnocentric traditions do not include the viewing or waking of the dearly departed. My wife accepts the ritual wake as part of the baggage I bring to our union, and she participates for the same reason I wear one of those slippery little yarmulkes when we attend the ceremonial farewell to a fellow from her traditions. (Funny attribute of those hats: I feel like it has fallen off when it has not; I feel as if it is still in place when it has fallen off.)

But, she cannot be expected to explain what must appear to her to be a little crazy, which is unfortunate, because children seem to seek the answers to such mysteries from their mothers more than they do from their fathers. And why not? It's perfectly natural to me for a child to cling to the place of his origin while inquiring about his eventual departure.

My older son, Jed, has been particularly curious about death and its attendant liturgies since just before his fourth birthday, when his doting and often-present grandfather died, giving him the experience of permanent loss at precisely the age it was apt to become memorable. Two incidents in the next couple of years heightened my sensitivity to his sensitivity, and I must say that I marveled at the extent to which he pondered.

When Jed was 5 or 6, we spent a weekend in a small condominium in Quechee, Vermont. Jed and I took a walk one sunny morning and eventually found ourselves following a path through a meadow surrounded by purple heather and unfamiliar, tall weeds whose sprouts oozed white liquid when we broke them open. We rounded a bend and discovered a freshly mowed avenue leading off the path, down a hill to a circular patch of moist, green grass. In the center was a headstone, flanked by two young, newly planted trees, and a stone bench. For reasons I will never comprehend but always cherish, Jed and I both, to this day, remember the identity of the interred as Michael Stephen Yaroschuk. The stone's information indicated that he had died fairly recently, and at the age of 48. The inscription read, "He saw things as they were and tried to make them better. He saw people as they wished to be and tried to help."

Jed and I sat and talked about him for nearly an hour; and about death; about what might happen or not happen afterwards; about how much Michael Stephen Yaroschuk must have loved the meadow; and about how generous he was to provide a place for us to share it with him. We chose to believe that Michael Stephen Yaroschuk was a nice guy and to like him, maybe visit him again, someday. I learned later that the land was part of the property of the Quechee Inn at Marshland Farms, and that Yaroschuk and his widow, Barbara, owned it at the time, although she has since sold it. Cleverly, Jed and I agree, Michael stayed on.

That same year, as we too-frequently do, we attended a wake at D'Andrea Brothers Funeral Parlor, and Jed insisted on accompanying his mother there. "I think he was really curious about the idea of seeing a dead body," she said, "in the way kids kind of like gross things. But he also told me he was mad that we didn't let him go to Pop's funeral, and he wanted me to know that he wanted to go to the next one. I told him not to worry, there'd be one on deck soon enough."

We went into the viewing room for a minute and he looked, but then Richie D'Andrea took him into another room where an old, retarded man was laid out and completely alone. The man's brother had arranged things and was likely to be the only viewer the next day. Richie explained the embalming process. I hung back and almost didn't let him go in, but then I figured that if Jed was going to participate in an Irish Catholic life to any degree, wakes and dead bodies would be part of it. Since he was looking at someone he didn't know, I felt this was as good a time as any. He just accepted it with a kid's normal curiosity and didn't say too much about it.

My Aunt Genie died this week, and when Jed heard the news, he said immediately that he would attend the wake. He was not asking permission, and I was mildly startled by his developing self-assurance.

While there, he observed relatives kneeling in prayer at the casket and asked his mother to go kneel with him. She declined, citing our ethnic-religious differences as her reason, and so Jed was stuck with me.

We approached my aunt's body, clad in a pink dress and looking quite peaceful, given her protracted battle with the effects of multiple strokes, and Jed studied her. He winced slightly as a child might and wondered aloud why they had covered her legs. "Come on Jed," I chided, "Nobody wants to be remembered by their feet!" He smiled. I had passed on another tradition from my family. We take death very seriously for about 25 minutes, then find some reason to laugh.

Absence Makes the Call Seem Longer

Despite the customary vagaries of my chosen trade, writing for a newspaper, I never have spent much time away from my family on business, or envied people whose work assignments required frequent and sometimes extended solo journeys. I'm not crazy about traveling with the kiddies, but I'm not at all comfortable when I am out of touch.

My wife grew up in New Jersey, then Illinois, then Georgia and then Manhattan, the daughter of a successful corporate executive whose career required both periodic relocation and extended business trips with his wife, though without their son and daughter. The daughter, therefore, still remembers both characteristics of her childhood—moving away permanently and being left behind temporarily—with vivid dismay. She complains now and then that she felt rootless for years and had no locale she could consider home. Also, she sometimes yields to a burst of sadness from feeling abandoned, even now, when her parents talk of flying to Europe or the Orient. Her memories and the emotions they inspire figure heavily in our travel plans, as do mine.

As a child on an opposite end of the spectrum, I enjoyed the almost Disney World security of a household wherein my mother stayed home all day, and my father, who worked in town, took most of his meals in his own kitchen. My parents did not vacation without me until I was grown and gone, myself, and would not ever have considered it. I might add, though, that my parents vacationed in upstate New York via used car; Europe and the Orient were inaccessible to them, so the question never arose. But even when my father attended police seminars at St. Lawrence University or in Washington, my mother and I accompanied him.

Those days are long gone, I know, and doting on the memory of them is manifestly unrealistic, given our current place, time and condition. I co-preside over a family whose entire administrative staff—Mom and me—works full-time outside the home, thus requiring gymnastic management of parental time and responsibilities, not to mention the careful nurturing of the fragile feelings of the younger children, particularly.

My wife is an executive whose responsibilities include one or two extended business trips annually, and we agonize on those occasions over whether the children would be best served by my staying home with them, or the marriage best nourished by our escaping from them. In recent years, my wife simply found ways to decline some of the travel opportunities, and so rendered the dilemma moot. I, meanwhile, sought no out-of-town assignments. Nobody went anywhere without everybody.

This summer, however, saw me faced with the excruciating pain of a decision. The travel editor asked if I would accept the following, overseas assignment: Go to Ireland. Have fun. Find your grandfather's birthplace, if you can. Take notes. Then return home and write about it. My dedication to journalism thus tested to its limits, I, too, agonized for . . . oh, moments . . . over the sacrifice and the emotional damage my absence might represent, especially to my boys. (The girls might suffer, too, I thought, but from envy, not abandonment.) A slave to my craft, I let my higher instincts prevail. I would serve Truth rather than self. I flew to Ireland, promising my wife that I would telephone home, every day.

Great move. E.T. had it easier phoning home from Earth than I did from Ennis. I stood stupidly before the pay phone in the lobby of the Old Ground Hotel, unsure of the coinage and hoping to charge the call to my credit card. That required reaching an operator, and his or her reaching another operator, then calling me back.

While I waited a half-hour for the first operator to call me back with news of the second operator, I had to shoo hotel guests away from the pay phone, on the flimsy grounds that I was awaiting a telephone call. I felt discourteous, presumptuous and anxious, and was therefore in an unfriendly mood when my family answered the telephone. Jed picked up one extension, his mother another, and then Danny, when he realized who was calling, scampered upstairs and grabbed a third. My wife asked how I was (I had left home eight or nine hours before).

I started to answer, when Jed interrupted. "Dad! he began, you know what an ollie is, don't you? When I jump in the air with the skateboard? Well, I learned a new trick, a better one! Wanna hear about it?"

"How do I respond to this?" I asked my wife. She tried to comment, but Danny started to mock-belch into the telephone, presumably because he wanted to be a part of the conversation but couldn't summon any information.

"Danny, shut up!" said Jed.

"Urrrrgh! Urrrrch!" barked Danny.

"We miss you," said their mother.

"I can tell," I snapped. "Danny's burps are fraught with emotion."

". . . I flip the skateboard over . . ."

"Urrrrgh! Urrrrgh!"

"Suppose I call you at the office, next time?" I said. "And, Jed, congratulations on the skateboard move, whatever it is."

But, days after my return, Danny suddenly wrapped his little arms around my neck and said, "I missed you at Ireland!"

Hollow Feelings

Nearly 30 years ago, the Button-Down Mind of comedian Bob Newhart turned my mind's dial two clicks off-center and permanently altered the way I viewed my own, individual behavior and, moreover, the collective behavior of my species.

Newhart's weapon was sense, uncommon sense; and when he aimed and fired it at an activity, the activity crumbled into a laughable heap. He would devise a way to approach ordinary behavior as one who never had seen it before and thus sought a simple explanation. His trick reduced a description of cigarette smoking, for instance, to ". . . you roll up the leaves; you put them in your mouth; and you set them on fire!" Or, by posing as a mildly confused, Milton Bradley Co. board game executive, listening to a young Abner Doubleday eager to market his new game, Newhart reduced baseball to silly nonsense: "Eighteen players are going to require an awfully big table . . . and why three strikes, and four balls? By the way, what's a ball?"

Over the years, I found myself applying Newhart's skewed perspective to, among other events, the organized insurrections we call holidays. Under Newhart's lights, we appear to be one strange group, humans. For example, could I explain to my children, if they asked, why we mourned our slaughtered sons on Memorial Days throughout the world by parading instruments of fiery death along the boulevards of our remaining cities? Or why, on Christmas, we celebrated the birth of a baby by murdering a sapling, then dragging the carcass out of the woods, propping up the corpse in the living room and draping it in trinkets?

On Labor Day, we stayed home from work. Perfect.

For Thanksgiving, I imagined a first-generation, American-born Pilgrim explaining the tradition to his children on the holiday's 30th anniversary: "The natives had shared their food and blankets with my grandparents and basically kept them alive, when they surely would have starved to death. So, after harvest that year, they all had a big feast together and thanked the natives for their life-giving help. Then, of course, we massacred the natives and stole their property."

Typically, and I suppose because tradition is tradition and therefore not required to make much sense, I still participated in these celebrations; I still do. I take my kids to parades; I buy a Christmas tree every year, sometimes two. I take off from work on Labor Day, and I enjoy an annual Thanksgiving dinner.

But now I am looking down the barrel at Halloween. I have been a father for 21 Halloweens and never once felt comfortable participating in its liturgies. It is the holiday that crumbles most completely under Newhartian scrutiny and therefore most seriously tests my willingness to cooperate.

If ever a cultural alien asked me to explain our purpose and practices on Halloween, I would have to describe it as a celebration of the range of possibilities of what could happen to us after we were dead. What a delightful thought.

By depicting ghosts, for example, we celebrated our option to cling to physical reality without rejoining it. By depicting ghouls, we rejoiced in the idea that we might exist as playful, living beings while simultaneously decomposing. In that case, we would frolic by scaring the children of our survivors.

I also would have to explain how we taught extortion to our children. Even though extortion and the grave might seem unrelated, we annually dispatched our kids to wander the streets of their community, in small bands, and disguised. The kiddies would offer their neighbors the option of giving them free booty or suffering swift and serious property damage. The threat, masterfully elliptical in its simplicity, would be articulated thus: Trick? [Do I spoil your front door with rotten eggs?] Or treat? [Do you give me candy?] You decide, bucko.

I have participated, nonetheless, but I have hated it, too.

Last year, when Jed was 7, he wanted to dress as Freddy Krueger. I never had seen a Freddy Krueger movie, but I had spied the posters and viewed the previews on television, so I knew that my gentle, generous boy wanted to prowl about the neighborhood as a prune-faced, homicidal dead man with long razor blades instead of fingernails, with which he caressed the silken cheeks of innocent victims, causing them to bleed to death while screaming during their disfigurement. Just the kind of boy I longed to leave behind, as a legacy.

My wife, who as a child was once (no, twice!) Camper of the Year, pooh-poohed my pooh-poohing and bought the costume, anyway. My younger son, Danny, dressed as a black cat. Then pushing 3, Danny cried every time he looked at his brother, which made pure joy out of escorting them from house to house. My wife informed me only this year that she paid $90 for the wretched Krueger costume. I flipped. Ninety dollars to make this child look like a homicidal maniac!

This year, Jed wanted to dress as a skateboarder, for which he would require knee and elbow pads, and a helmet. I have not been able to hide my glee. First, he is a skateboarder, so he is basically going as himself. Second, I have begged him to let me provide him with pads and a helmet.

Danny wanted a Batman costume. I can live with that.

Children, Meet Dinner

Jed approached me on the sidelines at the start of his Sunday soccer game and asked, "Dad, if I score a goal, will you take me to that restaurant that has octopus?"

The woman standing next to me groaned an involuntary noise whose depth and timbre revealed all anybody could wish to know about her opinion of humans who ate octopus. To punctuate it, though, she shot me a look that could have meant a variety of reactions—all pretty disdainful—from accusations of elitism to mere expressions of disgust. I toyed with the notion of telling her that my son also had eaten jellyfish at the Japanese restaurant in question, but I decided against it. Jed considered the jellyfish too spicy for him, anyway.

In general, my kids' attitude toward food is vastly different from what I remember as my own, and even more so from those of members of generations before them. At 73, the boys' maternal grandfather swears he will not stay in the same building with an onion, for example. His top-10 favorite delicacies all fall into the same food category: cake.

My parents' eating habits ran a gamut that extended from bland up to basic: meat, potatoes and frozen vegetables. I was over 30 when my second wife introduced me to the following new foods: the artichoke, chopped liver, fresh vegetables and pork chops that were not cooked for so many hours you could hammer nails with them.

As a child, I ate Cheerios for breakfast; cream cheese and jelly sandwiches for lunch; pot roast (or, hash, now that I recollect) and frozen peas and carrots for dinner. My mother made the hash from the heels of old pieces of meat languishing in the refrigerator. I helped turn the grinder, but I couldn't bear to eat the results. In both taste and texture, the hash resembled gravel. I smothered it in ketchup or slipped it under the table to Bootsie, our cocker spaniel.

My father wanted me to vary my vegetable intake by eating frozen spinach, as well as the frozen peas, but I resisted that, too. Frozen spinach tasted to me like soggy aluminum foil, and nauseated me. My father did not press the issue with much enthusiasm, because he could not eat day-old lamb, and I could. The aroma of day-old lamb reminded him of the government-issue mutton he had been served during the war, and nauseated him.

Evidently because of our proximity to the bay, I ate clams on the halfshell as a child, and without prodding. Three of my children did the same, although my second-oldest has since cured herself of the habit.

When my daughters were 3 and 4 respectively, we attended a backyard barbecue whose host had bought a bushel of hard-shell, little-neck clams, which he did not know how to open. I thus presided over the task, standing at the end of a picnic table, placing the opened clams onto large paper plates. I had intended to fill several plates and then distribute them about the backyard, but I could not seem to get a plate filled, even though most guests had not yet arrived. I discovered that the girls were underneath the picnic table, sneaking clams and sauce and conducting their own private party. I pretended to be angry, but I was amused, even proud. While I think I understand before-the-fact revulsion, which is essentially fear of the unknown, I admire such courage as it takes to be curious about food.

Years later, I accompanied Colleen's sixth-grade class to the Museum of Natural History, where she encountered a huge model of a mollusk, with each organ labeled: stomach, brain, kidney, foot. She made a noise not unlike the woman at the soccer game, though higher in pitch and more extended in dramatic delivery. *"Eeewwww!"* she yelped.

A museum guide approached her and asked if she was familiar with hardshell clams. Colleen said that she was. He asked her if she ate clams raw, on the halfshell. Colleen said that she did. He then asked, "Did you know that, when you eat a raw clam, it's still alive?"

I almost had to catch her. Heads turned at her howling. Museum guests must have thought we were torturing someone.

So now, T.C., my older girl, and Jed, my older boy, are the hardshell clam-on-the-halfshell consumers in our family. Colleen won't even think about them, and Danny, days away from his fourth birthday, simply has not exhibited much culinary adventurism. Nor am I pushing it.

Danny accompanied Jed and me to the Japanese restaurant Wednesday evening. We were alone—the Lowe boys—because my wife had obtained tickets to see Sting star in "3 Penny Opera." Fortunately for me (I had no desire to watch a rock star bomb in a Broadway show), we couldn't find anybody to watch the kids.

Jed ate octopus, mackerel, raw tuna and a piece of cooked eel. Danny, following in his grandfather's footsteps, declined every opportunity to taste a new food and ordered vanilla ice cream for dinner. He said he had eaten meat balls and spaghetti earlier in the day.

I could see from his shirt that he was telling the truth.

Ties That Bind

I was on my back, on the couch, meditating about the next 24 hours, which were to be dominated by acknowledgments of Daniel Philip Lowe's attaining the age of 4, uninjured.

I fixed my eyes on the ceiling and closed them, as I tried to recreate the scene wherein my neighbor and I assembled the trampoline he bought for his son Eamonn's fifth birthday, back in June. Despite an astute observation by another father in the neighborhood ("If there's one kid in the world who doesn't need a trampoline," he said, "it's Danny Lowe"), my wife bought a sister trampoline of Eamonn's for Danny.

We hoped secretly that Danny would exhaust his calves and thighs bounding on and soaring over the trampoline, and then use the beds in our house for purposes closer to their intended design. My job, later in the evening, after the boys drifted off to sleep, once again would be to kneel in the basement until after midnight, putting the thing together.

Also, while employing the couch for its intended purpose, I pondered my having agreed (he said, as if he had a choice to disagree) to leave work early the next day, so I could attend the celebration of Danny's milestone anniversary. Staring meditatively at the ceiling (through closed lids, so as to avoid reality's distractions), I conjured the birthday party, too. The scene consisted of me surrounded by a horde of Danny's chronological peers, plus a yet-to-be-determined number of their mothers, Danny's included. I knew I would be the only man present at the birthday party. I knew from prior experience that I would feel awkward and out-of-place in my own house and environs. I knew I would hate the confusion, real or apparent; I would clench my teeth and fists at the cacophony; I would sicken at the unbridled consumption of sweets. I would worry too much when the children began running the cyclical course from the den to the kitchen to the dining room to the living room, where they would have to pass a glass-topped, metal coffee table whose corners could seriously damage any young forehead that fell on it with minimal velocity. I would sit on it.

Also, I would have to record the frivolity on 35 mm film, despite my antipathy toward fathers with cameras. My wife and the concentric circles of worried family members collectively fret about the possibility that second children grow up dismayed that more photographs exist of their older siblings than do of them. More do exist, I am sure, but for the same reason that a new camera's owner consumes more film during the first three months following the purchase than in the next six. The infatuation is with the newness, not the camera, nor the child.

The doorbell interrupted my ruminating, and my married daughter, T.C., entered the den. She kissed my forehead and proceeded to the kitchen to talk with her stepmother about pregnancy. The boys meanwhile played with a puzzle that would have been a birthday present had Danny not discovered it, unwrapped, in the closet. I continued meditating.

T.C. had proceeded in stages from pregnant-by-declaration to pregnant-by-silhouette, and, as the visible manifestations of her condition grew, so did her passion for talking about every change and nuance. Her enthusiasm is boundless. I consider it one of the more bizarre trappings of modern life that we already have magneted to our refrigerator door a picture of my unborn grandchild, a photocopy of a sonogram printout. From what I can see, the child will be born with a head and some ancillary parts that could prove useful.

Otherwise I have no personal experiences with any of the changes and nuances associated with pregnancy, and, though I have shared life with a pregnant person four times, my sympathies are purely intellectual, and mainly boring. I decided to leave the conversing to them, and so continued meditating.

While I could barely hear the murmur of the women's conversation, it distracted me into thinking about their relationship, as well as other, mildly complicated relationships created by my life-choices.

My wife has loved and cared deeply about my daughters for

13 years. She considers herself a pending grandmother, regarding T.C.'s pregnancy, and a real one; not a step-grandmother. My sons have older sisters—half sisters, technically—with whom they have magically developed real, sibling relationships, despite the distances of miles and years and the complexities of mixed ancestry.

Frequently, Colleen will telephone from school, exchange news and pleasantries with us for a few minutes and then stay on the phone for a half hour talking with her 8-year-old brother. When Danny and Jed visit T.C. and Bill, their brother-in-law, they often sit for dinner (to the extent that Danny sits) with my ex-wife, whom they know and like. I marvel.

I must have dozed, for suddenly I was aware of T.C.'s voice mixed in with those of the boys, instead of my wife. They were talking about someone kicking. I am forever admonishing my sons for kicking one another; I am furious at the idea of it. I opened my eyes and turned my head to look, and saw T.C. lying flat on her back, guiding her brothers' hands around the ball containing their future niece or nephew. My wife watched, tears glistening in her eyes.

Doctor's Office

In my first adulthood, and for as many excuses as reasons, I rarely took my children to the doctor.

One excuse, and the most convenient, was work. For a while, I worked two jobs—three, for a short time—until I switched trades; but even then I devoted long days and nights to my labors in the paragraph factory and so steadfastly maintained that I could not be expected to accompany the kids for medical examinations or periodic healings.

Another excuse involved gender. My children were female, and I was not. In debate, I suggested that the female parent of daughters would better understand and sympathize with their physiological discomforts than the male parent. It sounded so perfectly logical, not only did my first wife buy the argument, I did, too.

Actually, I simply didn't want the assignment. I didn't want to see the doctor, myself, for that matter. I never liked the aroma of his office. The sight of the equipment made me perspire nervously (though not as much as dental paraphernalia; and I still plead shamelessly to be spared that awful chore).

But because I was in a traditional marriage, I got away with evading office visits. Mothers took the kids to doctors. Fathers took kids to emergency rooms, sporting events and hardware stores.

Another decade and another marriage forced me to change my act. My second wife, an executive who works longer hours than I, rendered moot my work-related excuse. How can you effectively debate the comparative importance of your job with a spouse who earns a higher salary at hers? Moreover, the two children she bore are males, and so am I. That destroyed my different-gender excuse. My wife, with generous pity, eventually agreed to accompany the boys to the dentist, thus vaulting me into a parental indebtedness payable only in doctor visits.

From the beginning, marked by Jed's birth in April 1981, I visited the pediatrician's office every time he did, sometimes accompanied by his mother, as well, but just as often alone. Now that I recall, she was so scared she might drop the baby and break him, I bathed Jed every night for the first year of his life. He was her first child, but my third, giving me the dubious distinction of veteran.

Jed spoiled me for doctor visits and haircuts. He was absolutely serene at all times. Haircutters marveled when he allowed them to place his 13-month-old head in a specific attitude convenient to their task, and keep it there until the work was done. He never wept. He never resisted. At the doctor's office, he cried in response to two specific stimuli: the aftershock of a stab from a needle, and the aftergag from the pediatrician's stabbing the wall of his throat with an extended Q-tip designed to mine for traces of strep throat. Otherwise, though he appeared to be terrified, he made no sounds; he inhaled on request, and he said "Aaaah" without rancor. He objected only to stripping while the door was unlocked. He is fiercely modest, my boy.

In 1985, and by cesarean section, Danny Lowe entered the physical world, railing from the instant of entry against the entire medical establishment. Before long he, too, developed a response to the notion of visiting the doctor's office. The stimulus he required was the sound of the syllables *doc* and *tor*, uttered in succession. If you said "doctor," Danny's body would freeze on the spot, all four limbs suddenly extended and stiff. His mouth would open into a huge circle. His eyes would shut tight and commence leaking; he would inhale a gymnasium of air and then bellow a howl that would summon two county police departments and the Air National Guard.

"I DON'T WANT TO GO TO THE DOCTOR!" he would bellow, in case one of us had missed his initial point. He then cried in the car until the ride calmed him some; he resumed crying upon sighting any landmark heralding our approach to the doctor's neighborhood. He took an intermission in the waiting room, all the while watching the other victims and, presumably, wondering what tortures they were in for; and then he resumed crying again upon entering the examination room. He cried and bellowed steadily until I rebuttoned his coat. Once, for a strep culture, two adults had to hold down his arms and legs, while the doctor leaned on his torso and waited for him to unclench his teeth and yell his rage, permitting the Q-tip's entry.

Those days are gone, thank everything. He is cuter, now. In his new maturity, Danny tries to deal his way out of the doctor's office, or at least to evade the discomforts he most loathes. Wednesday morning, he awoke with a canine cough and a slight fever. He eavesdropped on my conversation with his mother and proposed that I visit the doctor and get him some pink medicine. She said, "It doesn't work that way. Daddy is going to take you to the doctor." He approached me and, in what honestly can best be described as a manly fashion, he said (and obviously as a condition of his cooperation): "No laying down on my back, and no stick in the mouth."

"I can't promise you anything, Dan," I said, "but I'll try to talk the doctor out of the stick." Later, when he had to lie on his back and have his intestines kneaded, I felt as if I had betrayed him, but he didn't fight; he didn't cry. Despite his fever and his bark, he skipped happily back to the car, free at last.

A Lavish Gift, Lavishly Intended

I once bought a car for less money than I spent this year on one Christmas present for my 8-year-old son.

Mitigating circumstances will soften the implication of that statistic (I bought the car 24 years ago, for instance; it was a five-year-old Chevrolet Corvair; and this year's gift is very special, not my usual, more reasonable generosity), but the bare fact of the comparison gnaws at me, anyway, in that it raises the specter of potential child spoilage.

One of my most constant fears since I entered the paternity business has been that I would spoil a child. I shudder not only at the very thought, but even at the sound of the words. Spoil so easily fits with words like rot and stink and ruin. The horror of the notion terrifies me: That I could introduce a new person to the physical world and then somehow spoil either the child or the world or both.

I love and am excited by the potential of a child—I guess the unspoiled potential—for greatness, for heretofore unachieved relative perfection. In that enterprise, I would want only to help, not hinder. I would want to be like the wise and doting gardener, not the parasitic fungus that wilted the growing buds, or the huge, old tree that hogged all the sunlight.

I wonder how many of us who employ the phrase "spoiled child" can offer an accurate definition of the term. I have heard it all my life; used it, too, perhaps loosely. I may have used it cruelly, slanderously. It seems so heavy-handed a judgment. Do you spoil a child the way you spoil tea when you add both milk and lemon? Is the spoilage permanent, irreparable? And could you do this through generosity?

Most commonly used, the phrase meant a child whose parents lavished gifts upon him. Somehow, because of their untempered indulgence, he became insufferably demanding or cruelly unappreciative of their sacrifices or viciously competitive with less fortunate (or less spoiled) children. He would then grow to be insatiable in his adulthood appetites, and therefore unhappy; or self-absorbed in his relationships, and therefore incapable of love; or small-minded and mean, and therefore a menace to his society.

I think I agreed with those observations until I became financially able to lavish; although, years back, when I could not afford a particular gift, I frequently plunged headlong into debt to get it. Given the resources, I suppose I am dangerously capable of lavishing. If I ever get to the point where I can lavish lavishly, I might do that, too.

I did notice that a presumptuous and often obnoxious attitude appeared to develop in children who were granted their every request, but I began to question whether the gifts created the attitude or the motivation behind them. Some gifts are designed to shut you up. Some are meant to shut your mother up. In this case, I've decided after months of stomach-twisting self-examination that I am happy with my motives.

I bought Jed a boat. Not a toy boat for the bathtub; not a battery-operated, remote-control boat for the little pond in the park; not a model of the USS *Constitution* for his bookshelf. I bought a sit-in, oars-in-the-water, maybe-someday-outboard-motor-powered, ride-down-the-canal-and-out-into-the-bay, serious, official B-O-A-T boat. All right, so it's an inflatable, but it has a wood floor and a wood transom, and if ever I mount an outboard motor on it, I'll have to register it with the State Motor Vehicle Department. So, it's a boat.

Don't tell him.

I'm sure he suspects it, anyway. His longing for a boat was so powerful that it became another inhabitant of our house. It personified itself. We've talked. We've shaken hands.

Hi. I know you. You're my son's wish for a boat, aren't you? You're taller than I expected. Stronger, too. You're crushing my hand. I won't tell you that you won't come true, but I'm not going to say that you will. You have to understand, my payback in these annual generosities is getting to see wonder and surprise reflected in his face. If he goes from suspecting your realization to expecting it, I lose some of the thrill. Sorry.

I wavered in my resolve at a Christmas party Saturday night, in a house whose deck overlooked the prettiest section of the Amityville River, which rippled for me in the moonlight. A neighbor asked if I had finished my Christmas shopping. I had, but I delivered the answer with an involuntary sigh of such anguished uncertainty, I then felt compelled to explain it. Emphasizing Jed's age, I told her about the boat and wondered aloud if I'd been unwise, maybe giving too much too soon, maybe risking spoiling him.

"He lives near the water; he should have a boat," she said flatly, her vowels curled by a childhood in the rural South. "I could drive a truck with five forward gears and two reverse gears, and that when I wasn't 9 years old."

There it was, simple as nature. For me to buy a little boat for my young child was natural. I wished I'd done it for the girls when they were little. It would have been natural then, too. Later, while carrying an ice bucket out to the deck for replenishing, I stopped and gazed at the water. I love that bay, I thought. And I love that boy. I'm introducing them to each other.

YEAR TWO

No Looking Back

Sometimes, like when I steal an opportunity to gaze at my boys as they sleep or eavesdrop on their rapidly maturing conversations, I suffer remorse over how selfishly I argued against our conceiving them, ashamed I might have skirted their existence.

That confessed, there are other times, like, when my wife and I have two, up front tickets to a Billy Joel concert, and we have exhausted all possibilities for an available babysitter; and, as concert time approaches, so does the possibility that we may not be the attendees. We may have to give the tickets to someone else, someone with a sitter, or without kids. At such moments, I remember how passionately I longed for the relative freedom I thought I saw on my life's horizon, as my girls approached midteens and required less scrutiny by surrogate wardens.

In those days, I fantasized that my wife and I soon would be able to travel at whim, dine out at random, accept overnight invitations impetuously, take Sunday rides whenever the weather extended an invitation, sleep late on weekends and nap with decadent abandon.

I had first become a father at the age of 22. In my retrospective view, I had proceeded directly from adolescence to parenthood and had no experience as an adult male without dependents. Therefore, in my arguments 10 years ago against continued procreation, I maintained that from the moment-of-entry into our lives, a new child would postpone our ultimate liberation for a minimum of 15 additional years; that our occasional liberties would depend on the availability and cost of child care; that we would have to procure babysitting assistance just to lead an approximately normal work life; forget the likelihood of freely enjoying each other's exclusive company or that of our adult friends. I said a baby was not just a baby but a long-term, full-time job.

I argued passionately and lost, but only the debate. Against my own stupid judgment, I won a lifetime with four fine children instead of two. So, all right. I'm a lucky fool.

However, was I so wrong? Have we not lost sleep over who would watch the kiddies? Have we not acquired stomach problems, developed headaches, argued unnecessarily, stormed away from each other, compromised reluctantly, paid small fortunes, skipped meals, declined invitations and felt global-weight guilt over the issue of babysitting?

I am not much of a concertgoer, but two years ago I attended Paul Simon's "Graceland" concert, and this Christmas, I jumped at the chance to see Joel, whose lyrics I hold to be similarly poetic, whose musical compositions I consider masterly and whose delivery I find remarkable.

Our full-time Child Care Provider was gone for the holidays. My wife made a series of calls and announced that the local babysitters were either booked solid, off skiing with their families or grown out of babysitting and into fancier, clerking jobs at the mall.

I sighed impatiently, involuntarily employing the wrong body language. I couldn't even bite my tongue; I would have had to have bitten my whole body. I knew the line I had crossed. I knew what was coming and couldn't stop it.

"Then you find someone!" she snapped. "Why is it always my responsibility to come up with a sitter?" I fell mute. I have been down that road enough to know that I have no answer. None exists.

"Do you think your mother would watch them?" she asked finally, "if we brought them to her house?"

My mother. Grandma Doe. Why hadn't I thought of that? She used to delight in watching the kids. She would cook her famous pot roast and dark gravy for dinner, with mashed potatoes, stewed tomatoes and corn. She would read to them, as she'd read to me. She let them wail away on the little, electric organ in her sewing room. She sang to them, and with them, and then tape-recorded their songs and played them back. I guessed that we must have stopped asking her to babysit sometime after Danny was born, when he became too burdensome. Now, at 4, Danny was delightful. The three of them would enjoy themselves. Perfect.

I called. Grandma Doe accepted. We dropped off the boys and enjoyed the concert. It snowed during the concert. When we returned, both boys were asleep, Danny on a blanket on the floor; Jed on the couch. I looked at their limp bodies, one impossibly long and sprawled, the other short and made, it sometimes seemed, of old sash weights. I remembered why we had stopped dropping them off at Grandma Doe's: picking them up.

I wrapped Danny's blanket around him, hauled him out to the car and dumped him onto a seat just as I slipped in the snow and hit my knee on a Belgian block. I covered him with his coat and returned for Jed, who required forced insertion into his winter jacket. Holding aloft his seemingly boneless arm, I tried four times to cover it with his sleeve, but the arm kept dropping back out. I changed tactics. I turned him upside down and pulled the sleeve up around his arm like a sock. Worried about Danny, frustrated with the reluctant arm, I grew more forceful, until my mother and my wife yelled that I might break him. I responded awfully, growling. I slung Jed's corpse over my back in a fireman's carry, muttering angrily and already feeling bad for it.

"I don't want to do this again." I said, making the two women feel even worse. I still owe the apologies.

Really, Really Mad

For the longest time, I used controlled anger as a disciplinary tool. I am only now beginning to wonder about the wisdom of its application.

As usual, I took my lessons in these precincts from my father, frequently calling up scenes from my past that I kept stored like videocassettes in the attic of my mind.

When, as a boy, I crossed the behavioral boundaries that were most important to him—if I lied, if I spoke disrespectfully to my mother—he moved with a suddenness and a certainty that now seem expertly designed to render his reaction forever unforgettable and, thus, extremely educational.

One particularly vivid scene has me standing in the doorway between the living room and the tiny kitchen of their 1949 Cape, apologizing to my mother, as ordered, for my fresh mouth. I apologized, but with an abrupt tone of sarcasm designed more to pry open than to salve the original wound.

Having vomited my contrition ("All right! I'm sorry!"), I stormed down the hallway and through the door at the end, which I slammed behind me, for emphasis. I prostrated myself on my bed and would have cried in humiliated rage had I not then heard a wooden kitchen chair fall backward and bounce onto the linoleum floor, its occupant having stood up too hastily to politely push it back or steady it.

I froze on the bed, and then listened further as my father stomped down the hallway. As he passed the bathroom, his footfalls shook the contents of the medicine cabinet audibly. With the thunderous rhythm of mortar rounds approaching in a perfect pattern, he stormed toward my door, which then blew open and crashed against the wall.

Silence reigned for a long second. Then, in a voice whose origins bubbled from some molten rock in the earth's core, and breathing heavily between each utterance, he spoke:

"Now. Go back. To the kitchen. And. Apologize. To your mother.

"And.

"This time.

"Be. Sorry."

I stood, very humbly. I discovered that I had shrunk. I was smaller by about two and a half feet. He, on the other hand, had grown. His chest took up the entire doorway; his wavy, black hair brushed against the ceiling.

Every time thereafter that I felt tempted to apologize sarcastically to my mother, or to slam a door behind myself to punctuate my dissatisfaction, I managed to suffocate the temptation.

Interestingly, my memories of the sounds of his disapproving anger loom far clearer than any images of it, such as, for instance, the image of an angry glare in his eye. I can recall no vision of an angry glare, and have long suspected that there may not have been any, because there may not have been any anger. It may have been an act. But it was a memorable act, and when I became a father of people who perpetrated similar crimes against Truth or their mother, I tried to act similarly and thus be just as memorable.

And I succeeded. My oldest child recently recalled how I once terrified her when I stormed up the stairs behind her to emphasize my disapproval of her parting sarcasm. I remembered the incident, and I remembered that I was not angry, but was acting. At the time, I wanted her to know that she had crossed a line that she ought not to cross again, and to remember how I felt about her crossing it. I did not want her to feel terrified, though. At least, I don't think I did.

As she told the tale, she laughed, just as I laugh when I tell mine. I could not laugh, however, at her memory, at least not very convincingly. I tried a sheepish chuckle, but I found myself not as proud of my scaring her as I was of my father's scaring me. In fact, I still feel pretty bad about it, and I wonder whether it accomplished much beyond being unforgettable.

Last week, a neighbor visited with her 3-year-old boy, and I watched as my Danny demonstrated the toy cars and plastic racetrack he got for Christmas. The two boys squatted on opposite sides of the oval track, each aiming to get a car whipping around to the other.

Worried that the 3-year-old's hand was not sufficiently prepared for the coming impact of the fast, little, metal car, I knelt and asked Danny to wait his turn. He ignored me. I asked louder, employing his name. He ignored me. I bellowed, "DANNY! I SAID: WAIT!"

His body jerked involuntarily, shocked by the timbre of my voice. He looked up at me with the saddest and most permanently wounded expression I had ever seen on any face. His eyelids slowly closing as he rose, he stood silently and walked away, toward the stairs.

I felt like a murderer.

Also, I was stuck. Having deprived the 3-year-old of his playmate, I had to demonstrate, myself, how he should press down on the car, roll it backwards to crank its mechanics and release it on track.

That done, I slipped away to find out where my sad Danny had gone. I found him in his brother's room. Jed was seated on the floor, leaning against his bed, playing Nintendo. Danny was seated next to him, his head resting on his brother's left shoulder, his arm draped over the right. I approached and whispered, "Dan?" Pouting, he pulled in his shoulder, as if to fend me away.

Talk about memorable.

Sense and Sensitivity

I don't know why I insist on applying sense to situations that cannot endure it, don't call for it, are only complicated by it and more often than not suffer for its intrusion.

I agree that I'm probably being sexist, as well, but I also suspect that illogical insistence on the use of sense is more a father's flaw than a mother's. Men seem less able than women to let go of the square peg that does not, despite dimensions that ought to make the fit a certainty, fit into the square hole. The circumstance would inspire my wife to say, "If it doesn't fit, it doesn't fit. Move on to the next task"; whereas I would say, "It has to fit. All the laws of physics require that it fit, and I am going to stay here until I make it fit, because its not fitting doesn't make any sense."

Imagine: sense as an enemy.

My experiences as the son, husband and brother-in-law of mothers tells me that mothers are better able to abandon sense in the interests of a higher goal; say, peace, or, the gathering of children to the dinner table at roughly the same time, or, allowing for the effects of biochemistry on the emotional stability of a 4-year-old under a bacteriological siege.

My Danny has bronchitis this week. He thus awakens in the morning in a world whose rules and systems differ from my own.

Danny is not inclined to make much sense in the morning, anyway. The floppy disc in his brain needs to whirl around for a while before he can boot up and tap his own memory. But under the influence of general physiological misery, he is particularly slow to agree with my definitions of reality and manage himself without harming anybody. Add to this mixture an artificial antibiotic and a codeine-based cough medicine, and sense becomes a stupid and unattainable notion. With my years of experience as somebody's father, I should know this.

Tuesday morning, Danny entered consciousness in the middle of a dream, and so was overheard asking a question of his Montessori classmate, Gina, before he could pry open his eyes. When he did open his eyes and saw that his body was not where his mind was, and that he was in my presence and not Gina's, he began to cry. The crying inspired a cough, which evidently hurt, and the pain inspired more crying.

I tried to comfort him by hugging him and telling him that his mother was downstairs and had brought a surprise back from the 7-Eleven store (where she drives for coffee each morning, dressed fashionably in a flannel nightgown, a raincoat and slippers).

Danny did not want the comforting hug and yanked himself away. He did want the surprise, however, and so shuffled down the stairs, holding onto the rail and crying over his still-sleepy brain, his sore throat and the esthetic shock of seeing my big nose and mustache where he expected Gina's delicate beauty. "I want a Twinkie!" he howled.

I figured we were in trouble already. My wife draws what I consider odd boundaries around junk foods. Packaged crumb cakes meet with her begrudging approval, but the likes of Twinkies or similarly goo-injected delicacies are judged too junky. This time, by some intuitive miracle, she had made an exception. "I have Twinkies for you, honey!" she said.

I was relieved to hear it.

Danny then approached his brother, who was dressed for school and seated at the kitchen table, eating his own Twinkie. Dan reached up, ripped Jed's Twinkie out of his hand and ran away, crying, "That's my Twinkie!"

Jed, of course, tore after him, punched him between the shoulder blades, wrenched away the disintegrating Twinkie and returned to his place at the table. Danny then lost his mind entirely. His woefully stupid parents responded by trying to apply sense to the situation.

"Look, Dan," I said, brandishing the unopened package of Twinkies formally designated by us as the exclusive property of Daniel Philip Lowe, "Mommy got these Twinkies for you! These are yours! That Twinkie, the one that Jed has, that's Jed's Twinkie. See? He's already eaten half of it."

"NO!" the boy howled in rage and anguish. "That's MINE. JED has my Twinkie!"

"Dan," I said brilliantly, "calm down for a minute[!]. Look. This package is not even opened. It's all yours. Fresh, new Twinkies . . ."

"JED has MINE!" he screamed. "That's MY Twinkie!"

"No it's not, Danny it's mine!"

"Jed, please, stay out of this."

"Dad! He came down here and took it right out of my hand!"

"Jed! I know. He's crazy."

"It's NOT Jed's. It's MY TWINKIE! I'm NOT crazy!"

"I'm sorry. You're not crazy. But you are acting crazy. I'm offering you unopened Twinkies. Two of them. Brand new. Yours. And you're insisting on eating his. It doesn't make any . . ."

"It's NOT his! It's MINE!"

We were dealing with a maniac. I looked at Jed in the kitchen. I knew just what I was going to do, and I knew the argument I was going to get.

"Jed, do me a favor. Give me your half-eaten, half-crushed, tattered, ugly, no-good-anymore Twinkie, and I'll trade you this fresh, new, unopened package."

"Dad! That's so unfair!"

"Jed! 'Fair' we'll deal with another time. Right now, I'm just trying to make sense!"

Out of Their Mouths

I had to confront a language problem in my house. I had been avoiding facing it, mainly because, once again, I was torn between my intellectual and emotional selves. But my sons were testing my emotional tolerance, and severely.

When their bedroom door was closed and I was standing near enough to hear through it; or, when they huddled just outside the dining room window, playing in the "fort" that their imaginations had discovered beneath a hoop skirt of boy-level, pine tree branches, my boys and their young pals talked freely, as if no adult in the world could ever overhear their musings. On those occasions, when I did hear them, I alternately laughed at their chatter and then cringed at their word usage.

Conceptually, their notions were wildly funny. They invented concoctions of disgusting ingredients, and they mixed gigantic objects with comparatively small host body parts, and in hilariously imaginative, comedic ways. They made themselves laugh hysterically, and their hysteria made me laugh.

Esthetically, however, they were on these secret occasions what my mother would call, "foulmouthed," and the words that tumbled from between their sweet, innocent lips inspired in me involuntary shudders of anticipatory humiliation. My imagination instantly created a scene wherein some person whose respect I cherished asked, incredulously and with a tone of revulsion: "Were those your boys I just heard talking that way?"

"Er . . . ah . . . umm. No."

Scatology dominates my sons' scientific interests and seems to be their favorite subject, overall. I have tried to be as understanding of this interest as possible, lest I encourage in them such needless embarrassments as I still suffer, myself, presumably from the lingering results of swift, severe condemnations—both parental and clerical—of my boyhood curiosities about people's parts.

I determined somewhere along the line that as long my sons conducted their linguistic experiments in the privacy of each other's company—notwithstanding my spying—I would pretend to be as out of earshot as they thought I was. I would permit them the range of silliness that I suspected was probably normal for male humans of their respective ages, and that I remember being denied me, with the foreboding weight of eternal damnation as an ultimate consequence, and house-arrest as the immediate one.

I have long been intrigued by the mysteries of forbidden language: combinations of consonant and vowel sounds, or printed symbols of such combinations, which societies judge to be offensive. The reasons for offensiveness always are murky. If a word is offensive because of the concept it represents, for instance, do we condemn contemplation of the concept? And where is the logic to support the existence of an acceptable synonym for the same concept? If the sound of the consonant-vowel combination is the offender, what logic supports inoffensive use of the same words?

Riding on an ass.

The bitch Doberman. The bastard prince. Hind tit. Cock of the walk.

Words—sounds which have meaning because we have agreed that they do—can be offensive only if we agree that they are. If someone refers to me, especially in a crowd, as a furbish darn-lab, I am apt to be as unoffended by the comment as I am uncomplimented, no matter how sincere the author.

Manure, urine, penis, anus and buttock are some of the subdivisions of subject matter that appear to have seized the imaginations of my sons and their colleagues.

Again, as long as the boys stayed sequestered with their semantic forbidden fruit (my mother would say filth), I tolerated it. But they escalated, as if to test my limits. They always do.

And, when I saw and heard one of those sweet, boyish faces utter the monosyllabic, Anglo-Saxon substitute for copulation, I lost all my tolerance, all my logic and most of my self-control. Why? I don't know.

Why, suddenly, should my otherwise cogent analysis of society's syntactic intolerance suddenly disappear from my brain and be replaced by an emotional reaction bordering on rage? If I could have found the patience to explain, and if someday I am asked to explain, I will say that some rules exist because they exist. I will say, "Some words are offensive because people are offended by them, and you are not allowed to use those words."

Worse, I will say that ". . . yes, I use some of those words, myself, often very effectively, but sometimes for absolutely no reason at all. And, I who use them am in fact still telling you, my sons, that you must not use them. I do recognize my unfairness. It's too bad."

I should have said that.

Instead, I grasped two, tiny shoulders, shook them until some eyeballs spinned, and shouted into a face: "NO MORE BAD WORDS!" followed by a typically stupid father-type question: "YOU HEAR ME?" followed by emphatic repetition: "NO MORE BAD WORDS! GOT IT? NO MORE! NOT IN YOUR ROOM! NOT IN YOUR FORT! NOT EVEN IN YOUR THOUGHTS!"

I stormed away, cursing (under my breath, of course).

Ski-Wee to Jaws of Death

In January of 1960, after the holiday break, one of the boys in my high school freshman class returned to school with the deepest tan I had ever seen on a Caucasian. It did not occur to me that he might have vacationed in another climate; nobody in my experience could afford to think such thoughts. So, I concluded that he had been stricken with an exotic disease.

A few days later, his browned skin started to flake and peel. I feared he might rot to death before spring. I tried to muster the courage to offer my sympathies, but I lost my nerve every time I approached him. One afternoon, I overheard him talking about the joys of skiing down a snowy mountain, the bright sun burning his face at the same time the bitter wind was freezing it.

He wasn't dying. He'd been skiing.

I stared at him all through Introduction to Biology. I had seen people skiing down a mountain, but only on television shows and in newsreels at the movies. I had also seen magazine and newspaper cartoons depicting skiers whose arms and legs were broken, so I surmised that skiing was a sport designed to damage rich people. I was neither rich nor interested in breaking my parts, so I never sought to participate.

Twenty-five years later, on a wintry Friday morning, at a condominium ski facility in Vermont, and mainly at the insistence of a brother-in-law who was both a condo salesman and a member of the local Ski Patrol, I took a half-hour ski lesson. After the lesson, I allowed a T-bar-type lift to drag my body up a small hill, all day long, so that I could fall my way down, all day long, until I was convinced that I could ski without harming anybody, especially myself. The most important lesson I learned about skiing was that falling did not hurt. Getting up hurt. The instructor had advised me to use my stomach muscles to pull myself up, and I didn't have any stomach muscles. I had to bend my legs sideways and hoist myself by the ski poles. By day's end, I felt like I had been hanging by my wrists.

But my son Jed was 3 years old at the time, and I can remember wistfully entertaining a fantasy that someday he and I and maybe his mother—if I could talk her into it—and maybe one of his sisters might ski some slope together as a family, later to relax by a fire, forgetting, together, about bills, deadlines and spelling tests. My daughter Colleen, propelled by her independence and adventurousness, already had signed up for charter bus trips and learned to ski with her high school friends. Her older sister had shown less interest in the sport than even I had, and my son Danny did not exist yet, so it was a distant sort of fantasy. It was made all the more desirable, though, by my secret worry that, 10 or 15 years down the road, I might not have the stamina to keep up with my son in many other sports.

At the risk of confessing to sexism—and I am no macho man—I do feel differently playing athletics with my sons than I felt about playing with my daughters. I enjoyed tossing a baseball to T.C., still do enjoy it, and I always was proud of the way she handled a baseball glove. But I never fired a ripping grounder through the grass at her, the way I would to Jed, nor did I lean very hard into a bounce pass to Colleen, as she ran up the driveway for a lay-up. I suspect I will pitch and pass to the boys with more vigor, I guess because I want them to be ready for the inevitable competition with their peers, and probably, too, because I want them to know that the old man is no sissy.

I went skiing about twice a year from 1985 to 1990, during which time Jed grew to the age of 8 and we were joined by Danny, now 4.

During this year's February break from school, we joined a whole posse of people from town who trekked to Mt. Snow in Vermont, rented condominium apartments and shared cooking chores to defray expenses. We enrolled Jed in a Ski-Wee program for a day, and I reintroduced my wife to an activity she had last enjoyed in high school, when she lived in Chicago, presumably with kids whose faces were tanned in the winter.

I figured I could impress Jed with my skiing prowess for a few years, at least. I can ski well enough after five years to be able to show my son a decent time, I thought. In five years, Jed will want to ski more challenging trails than I, but meantime, we'll have some nice family outings, where I will still be the boss.

On our second day, I took Jed aside and tried to determine how much he had learned in a day. He followed me down a tiny learning trail. He then followed me down a five-mile-long beginner's trail whose tributaries were called "Deer Run" and "Easier Way Down." He then followed me down two intermediate trails called "Ridge Run" and "Sundance."

"What did they teach you in a day?" I asked. I kept skiing harder and faster. I would stop to look back up the trail for him and find that he was standing behind me.

"Dad," he asked, holding the trail map, "when are we going to ski 'Jaws of Death'?"

"I don't ski anything named 'Jaws of Death.'"

"Christian's Aunt Linda says it's not that hard."

"Jed, Aunt Linda is an experienced skier." Wait'll I get hold of her! "I, however, am a sissy. You ski 'Jaws of Death' next year, with her and Chris. I'll be in the lodge."

Extended Family

It is 365 days since my T.C.'s wedding. The year shot by faster than any of its rivals in the history of recorded time.

(Nearly everyone in the family agrees with me on this except Danny, for whom a year represents a quarter of a life. I am sadly confident that in due course, he will come around to our way of experiencing the passage of time, i.e., easy go; easy go.)

Now, we are merely waiting, hanging around in the foyers of our minds, biding time, frequently telephoning each other with no useful information to share, no pertinent questions to ask. We indulge in psychic loitering. Our collective hopes, needs and curiosities regarding the future of our family hover above us, as if in a spiral of holding patterns over T.C.'s swollen belly.

The pending new person already has been sonogrammed at over 7 pounds. If he/she embraces punctuality as a trait and arrives on the appointed due date, our new member is guaranteed to be a child of healthy, entry-level heft. If she/he plucks from the DNA tree my propensity for being on time—or T.C.'s, or her sister, Colleen's (all of us arrived on earth weeks after our reserved dates), this birth could occur under the next astrological sign. Given the projected growth rate of apprentice humans in the ninth month of gestation, T.C. might then give birth to the equivalent, in length and girth, of a second grader.

I feel for her. I also am glad I never had to bear any of my children. I have not visited T.C. as frequently as I ought, because in my jaded eyes, she is huge. I have not been the father of a huge, pregnant daughter, and I've so far been incapable of getting used to it. When I move to hug her, I feel like we're approaching each other from opposite fenders of a Volkswagen. I'm afraid I'm knocking the sideview mirror out of whack.

During this anticipatory period, rankings in the family and in the extended family are realigning. Some are blurring. The half-relatives, the steps, the grands, the step-grands and the great-grands all are meditating, if only for seconds, over what is the significance to them of this approaching scout from the next generation.

My mother looks rapturously forward to the birth, until she begins to gag on the phrase, "Great-grandma . . ."

Colleen, who, after an initial period of doubt, enthusiastically

.embraced the role of older sister, then much older sister (the designation, half-, vaporized after the first brother-sister embrace) shall be an aunt. Aunt Colleen. How will she feel, in 1994, as the aunt of a 4-year-old and the sister of an 8-year-old?

The boys will be uncles. Uncle Jed. Uncle Dan. Jed, pushing 9, seems ready. He is a remarkably attentive older brother, already, more often insisting that his friends put up with his brother's company than leaving poor Danny behind, crying in the driveway, as the pack of older boys bicycle out of Dan's perimeter of permitted travel. Jed will likely be a role-model, an older friend, a generous and doting young uncle. Danny doesn't know it, but he is in for a disappointment. For weeks, as he has exited the house on the way to pre-school, Danny has been thrusting his fist into the air in anticipatory triumph and declaring: "Five more weeks 'til Uncle Danny!" "Four more weeks 'til Uncle Danny!" "Three more weeks . . ."

We all considered the gesture terminally cute and marveled at his enthusiasm for a birth. However, after a brief and accidental conversation last week, I realized that Danny fervently believes that on the instant of the nativity of this niece or nephew, "Uncle Danny" will become a 6-foot-4 man, licensed to drive Daddy's truck and stay out well past dinnertime. Danny doesn't care about the baby so much as he wants to skip childhood and become a property owner. However, he will be Jed's age when the baby is his age. I have a good feeling about that.

My wife's position intrigues me, and I often wonder (and doubt) if reversed circumstances would reveal such generosity and strength in me, as it has in her.

She has known and loved the girls since they were 6 and 7 years old, respectively. They never called her "Mom," to the unspoken relief of all three of us in the guardian category; but when called upon, she performed so unselfishly as a surrogate that their Mom regularly conversed and consulted with her—still does—and far more confidently than with me.

They—my wives—became strangely connected when the boys entered the picture. My wife was now the mother of my daughters' brothers; my girls were her sons' sisters. Moreover, my ex-wife automatically became the mother of my wife's sons' sisters. Egad.

Like it or not, our tents all were suddenly tethered to the same stakes. The popular joke, for men of my station, is to suggest that

I don't mind being a grandfather so much as I mind being married to a grandmother. Ha, ha. My wife considers herself as much this new child's grandmother as if T.C. were her own daughter. My ex-wife is the grandmother, as T.C. is her own daughter.

That leaves me to wrestle not only with the notion of my young, innocent and unqualified self as a grandfather, but as a man permanently connected to two grandmothers.

I don't recall applying for the job.

Perfect Baby, with a Problem

T.C. called Tuesday evening at 6 to say that she already was in Good Samaritan Hospital and that they were going to induce her because, what the hell, she was five days past due and had gestational diabetes and the baby was only going to get bigger, anyway, not better, so sometime on Wednesday she was going to give birth to my grandsomething; and what did I think?

I began by saying, "Uh." I don't recall contributing much more value than that to the conversation. I suppose I thought that events were moving along pretty briskly, but they were moving too briskly for me to know that I was thinking it. I think I also thought I was not ready, yet, and I hoped she was. I wished her well. I then thought I would walk up to the restaurant on the corner and order up a concoction that at least would help slow the involuntary tapping of my fingernails on the kitchen counter.

She called again several hours later to say that the process had accelerated and that she had summoned her husband back to the hospital at the very moment he had entered their house. The finger-tapping resumed.

My ex-wife called several hours after that—somewhere in the neighborhood of 2:30 A.M., March 28, as I recall—to say that I was the grandfather of an 8-pound, 10-ounce boy with huge hands, Kevin William, and that he seemed to having a slight problem inhaling when he cried, though he looked as near to perfect as any baby in the entire history of the world.

I lay awake all night thereafter.

I somewhat distractedly addressed a gathering of retired telephone company employees the following morning and was thus late in arriving at the maternity ward of Good Samaritan

Hospital, where my wife and my ex-wife greeted me, surrealistically twin-like in height, hair color, yellow hospital gowns and disturbingly worried faces. The baby was being transferred to St. Francis Hospital, they said.

I felt the day turn upside down.

I know about St. Francis Hospital. Its reputation suggests that it is easily the best place on the planet to be if you are a child with a serious heart problem. So the simple, declarative sentence that told me Kevin's destination bore two profound truths—that he was going to be in the best place, and that he had a serious heart problem.

Much of the rest of that day, and the next, and this one, for that matter, is still a blur of speculation and the most damnable uncertainty I have ever encountered, fraught with conflicting reports of holes in hearts, inadequate oxygenation and a balloon angioplasty; but the bottom line, so far, is that inside this beautiful little boy's chest is a heart whose great vessels are somehow transposed, which is to say, in the simplest terms (and the only terms I so far have been capable of wielding) that he has a fat pipe where a slender one should be, and a skinny pipe where a fat one should be, and that they are crucial pipelines designed to transport blood to and from his heart.

We would learn in a day or so that a complex and sophisticated surgical procedure to correct so bizarre a defect not only existed, but had been pioneered by a doctor at St. Francis, into whose hands Kevin's fragile parts were to be entrusted. I would then learn independently and quite accidentally that this surgeon also made a specific practice of sleeping in the recovery room with those innocents upon whom he practiced his considerable skills, until such time as the patient stabilized to his demanding satisfaction. I remain as comforted by that endearing characteristic as I am awed by it.

But we did not know any of this Wednesday morning, and I cannot imagine how the knowledge might have mattered at that moment, anyway. We all were too busy struggling with the seemingly unspeakable idea that T.C. and her husband, Bill, were going to be separated by miles and institutions from their son, Kevin, before he was 12 hours old and essentially before the rest of the family had even made his acquaintance.

I recalled how devastated my wife and I felt nearly nine years ago, when Jed's two-day-old face turned the color of furnitureantiquing stain, and we had to leave him behind in the hospital until the jaundice was corrected. However common it was, the subject of jaundice had been generally left out of our Lamaze classes, and leaving the hospital without our baby had never entered our minds, at all.

Here, by comparison, was my T.C., awaiting a highly trained team of pediatric, cardiac-care specialists—two technicians, a nurse and a cardiologist—who were on their way to rush her brand-new, first baby miles away, to a heart hospital whose very prestige ironically made the mystery of the baby's condition all the more ominous.

The team arrived, and a comforting and almost-ebullient nurse named Terry entered the room and asked who the parents were. The question and her subsequent behavior placed the rest of us in the room, me, Bill's mother and my mother, in our rightful places as grandpersons less entitled to informational courtesies than were our children. It was a new role—fifth wheel—and I have yet to come to grips with it.

They listened intently as the nurse explained what tests would be performed at St. Francis and why she therefore had no answers to any questions about the baby. Bill then followed the ambulance from West Islip to Roslyn, which I considered heroic. I tried to imagine myself alone at the wheel of my own car, tracking the path of my newborn son to a world of high-tech, sophisticated, invasive uncertainty, wondering about the possibilities and feeling so perfectly powerless to help. I don't how he managed to turn the first corner.

In his absence, with the baby and the monitors and the IV and the paraphernalia and everyone else gone, I moved to kiss T.C. good-bye and suggest, however unrealistically, that she try to get some sleep. Her demeanor up to this point had ranged from mildly puzzled to almost naively optimistic. I leaned over, and she collapsed into my shoulder, sobbing. I joined her. My baby.

Brief Touches, Memories Forever

Two weeks ago, I joked that I didn't feel qualified to be a grandfather. I said I wasn't old enough.

I'm old enough, now.

NOT AS I DO: A FATHER'S REPORT

My grandson . . . The phrase paralyzes me for whole, long minutes; it shuts down my mind like a light switch . . . My grandson, Kevin, was born at Good Samaritan Hospital on a Wednesday and transported that afternoon by ambulance to St. Francis Hospital. There, some of the most unselfish egos in the cardiology trade tested, examined and meditated over him before deciding on Friday to place him on a jet bound for Children's Hospital in Boston, because his chances for survival were a little better, there, in the largest pediatric cardiac surgery department in the world.

One of Kevin's parts was slightly defective, as if his architect had daydreamed over the drawing board for just one, crucial second. Of the two trillion possibilities for engineering error, Kevin's problem was in his heart. In order for his already incredibly complex system to continue functioning outside the womb, his heart had to pump blood into his lung, which would oxygenate the blood and ship it back out for redistribution to the rest of him, keeping him alive. The process required pipelines—a way in and a way out. The pipes were switched, so that the blood was not going to the lungs; would not, therefore, get oxygenated and would not keep him alive for very long at all. He required a surgical procedure called, "transposition of the great vessels," a pipe switch. Moreover, the vessels were supposed to be roughly the same size, and one was half the diameter of the other, a particularly sticky complication that ultimately inspired the transfer to Boston, where an Australian-born surgeon named Richard Jonas had been performing such near-miracles with a success rate that at some point must have angered Nature for thwarting its plans.

My son-in-law, Bill, flew to Boston with the baby and a team from St. Francis, including a cardiologist named Jerry, and a nurse, Lisa, who Bill swore operated beneath a halo. The next day, my wife, my ex-wife and a very uncomfortable T.C. (After all, Kevin's birth weight was 8 pounds, 10 ounces) piled into my Suburban, and we drove to Boston.

We first saw Kevin Sunday night, in a sixth-floor, intensive-care ward. He was unconscious, his body wired to a posse of blinking machines. He was painfully beautiful. I touched his toes and kissed a bare spot between two pieces of white tape on his arm. While a nurse was explaining the apparatus, I heard a double beep and looked up, startled. The nurse quickly warned us to not be alarmed by the sounds; she said the slightest movements in the room tripped the sensitive monitoring machinery. She reset the machine. It beeped again, and then another machine beeped. Other nurses rushed into the area while our hostess nurse ushered us out. Over my shoulder, I thought I saw Kevin's skin tone taking on a bluish hue.

His heart had stopped, we learned after an hour and a half of waiting-room, neurological agony. During that awful time, we began meeting our fellow relatives of imperiled children, most notably John Conlin, a transplanted, Queens-bred man from somewhere near Albany, whose heroic attitude toward the hour-to-hour, coin flip of cardiac care changed me profoundly. Conlin's 6-year-old son, John, was in for his third, crucial, dangerous, high-risk, open-heart surgery. "Get ready," Conlin said to us after he saw the terror in our eyes. "This is a roller coaster."

How prophetic. After hours of surgery the next day, Dr. Jonas told Bill and me that he had run into an unexpected snag, a half-inch hole in the aorta. To avoid cutting muscle tissue in the heart, he had patched the hole with Dacron by working through a valve, unfortunately the one in the vessel of diminished size. He said it was like fixing something through a keyhole, and that the next 48 hours were critical.

Kevin made it through the 48 hours, though not without a handful of heartstopping crises. He looked bloated, puffy. When I visited the ICU, I held onto his little toes.

Mainly because of our boys, my wife and I returned home for the weekend. Bill and T.C. stayed, and Bill's parents visited for a while. One day, T.C. told me by phone that Conlin's boy was playing in the hallway and might go home for the weekend. The next day she said that Kevin's condition had improved, worsened and then improved again, and that Conlin's son suddenly had to go back for more surgery.

I daydreamed constantly about falling asleep on the couch with a sweaty little face pressed against my cheek, and the cheesy smell of baby vomit on my flannel collar.

Kevin died late Tuesday afternoon, during a risky catheterization procedure designed to widen the smaller vessel and allow more blood through his system, which was not getting enough. I hated that I was home and T.C. was in Boston, but she seemed to handle the loss better than I, anyway. They let her hold Kevin for a while. I'm glad. I wish I'd been there for that. I worry only about how she will feel next month, or the next.

I asked her about John Conlin. She said the boy was playing in the lobby, again. I felt very relieved.

This is a new and terrible feeling, grieving so desperately for somebody I knew only by his soft, tiny toes.

Losing and Finding

The aftermath of a numbing family tragedy is a weird and curious chapter in the life of a man.

In the few weeks since the death of my daughter's 13-day-old son, I have been as depressed and as joyous as ever in my life— maybe more than ever—and alternately as angry, serene, patient, short-tempered, wise, stupid, strong and needy; as self-absorbed and as generous; as energetic and as weary as ever, at any time, in all my years.

I have awakened wishing I had not, and then, on the very same day, taken limitless delight in viewing a squadron of cormorants in flight over the bay. I have worked harder and faster and accomplished more in less time than ever before, but I've gone fishing at a moment's notice on a heavily-scheduled Monday, and without telling anyone. So, I'm behind schedule with every task, and I don't even like fishing that much.

With my grief-stricken daughter, T.C., I have managed to be present and as (helplessly) comforting as possible during all the crucial moments, the morally mandatory times; and then as evasive and distant as my conscience would allow, between those times—what with no ideas of any value to offer nor enough patience and fortitude to stand around being useless, except to be standing around.

I was awed by her composure at the funeral, but frightened by it, too, unable to escape the belief that unreleased grief festers, until it eventually emerges in a more powerful and uglier form. But that night, after she had comforted dozens and played hostess all day, she fell apart. Paradoxically, the depth of her misery gladdened me. Paradoxes seem to have dominated the period.

I've actually laughed at the memory of the moment I learned

of little Kevin's death. My son Danny delivered the news as I walked in the front door of the house. I had talked long-distance to T.C. from work, when the cardiologists at Boston Children's Hospital were about to begin a procedure that they identified as "risky." T.C. said that we would know how the baby fared by the time I arrived home from the office.

It happens to be the boys' custom, on hearing my entrance, to race to the front door to see who "gets Daddy" first, a tradition I know to be sadly temporary, and one whose vivid memory I plan to cherish as much I cherish that of my girls racing similarly to the back door of another house years ago.

Jed is usually faster than Danny but more careful about damaging himself on such obstacles as kitchen chairs and the garbage. Danny will risk a concussion to win. Also, Jed has matured so that he just wants to get to me; Danny still enjoys being swooped up and hugged. He threw himself at me, arms opened wide, smiling with happy abandon and an evidently unbridled eagerness to deliver the important news he had just overheard in one side of a telephone conversation. As the two of them thundered toward me, I heard: "I get Daddy first!" "No, I get Daddy first! Daddy! Daddy! T.C.'s baby died! T.C.'s baby died!" I lifted his 45 pounds to my neck, and he hugged me and patted my back.

Someday, I'm going to tell him, "Don't equivocate so, Dan. When you have important information, try to just get to the point and say what's on your mind."

Later in the week, when Danny realized that someone he did not know was missing, we discussed some of his preschooler, theological theories. On his own, Danny has concluded that God is "in the world," which makes God diametrically opposite from the Teenage Mutant Ninja Turtles, who appear to be "in the world" though they are not (thank God). With God in the world, "Baby Kevin" would be all right. I said it sounded pretty good to me.

Any temptation on my part to indulge my grief was mitigated by a succession of rapid-fire obligations and emergencies. Jed's ninth birthday had been looming on the horizon and suddenly was looming in our faces. My wife, on whom I overdepend rather irresponsibly for the planning and administration of these annual insurrections, had schemed an overnight party for Jed and eight of his friends, a merry band who represent as many sizes, temperaments, ethnicities and religions as their head-count but who are unified by their passion for Nintendo games and, we were stunned to discover as they shouted "YESSSS!" while watching "Tales from the Crypt," parts of the female anatomy.

The boys—little Danny included—had been shouting these "YESSSES" at a computer baseball game called RBI. We alien adults hovered outside the room, enjoying the sounds of their triumphant playing, though the hour was getting late and I was growing tired and bored with the task of periodically policing the hall. My wife noticed at one point that the sound one, particular "YESSS!" made seemed to carry further than its predecessors and was accompanied by more jumping and high-five slapping than any of the electronic, grand-slam, home-run "YESSSES" she had heard earlier in the evening.

We broke into the party room and saw a bosomy belly dancer on the screen, threatening to twirl her tassels. My wife abruptly turned off the set. "I didn't think this would happen so soon," she said, leaving me to command the pack to suddenly become fatigued, to relax and to drift off into slumber, or what I called the Fat Chance Department.

A Day at the Races

Jed's first track meet was scheduled for Saturday. I had volunteered to stay home with little Danny while my wife played the part of "Jock Mom," as she called it.

We know that eventually I will have to be "Jock Dad," and we know that I am and have been avoiding the role. For several reasons, my wife patiently indulges my procrastination: She knows that I accept how inevitably Danny will grow into eligibility for organized competition, robbing me of my excuse to stay home; and she actually enjoys being Jock Mom, so far. She attended all the swim meets last summer and whooped and howled as Jed struggled toward the end of the pool, while his goggles leaked chlorinated water into his eyes because he hadn't put them on until the moment the starter fired his cap gun.

This year, as before, she, not I, signed the boy to his soccer league contracts and his winter CYO swim team obligation. She interviewed him extensively about his apparent disdain for Little League, until she was certain that he simply did not want to play Little League baseball (and was not, therefore, yielding to some incipient abnormality, displaying the signs of a pending cowardice, or depriving himself of a memorable experience merely to devote more time to his Nintendo skills).

I attended two swim meets last year, some soccer games and no practices of any kind. I always have lacked patience for these affairs. I know it is a major fault, and selfish, and unfatherly; but having to loiter around steamy pools or buggy fields at meets and heats and field days sets my dentures against each other with a hypertensive vengeance powerful enough to drive me back to tobacco usage.

I must not complain about any of it, because my feeling is so manifestly wrong, and alien to the accepted principles of proper American fatherhood. I cannot complain about the disorganized nature of some of the events, because they are disorganized by parents vastly more generous and devoted than I, more enthusiastic, more doting and more parentally involved, who donate their spare time and energies for the delight and development of my children as well as their own. So, I keep my mouth shut and tacitly volunteer to distract Danny, who is too young to join, too enthusiastic, himself, to stay off the field and not interfere in the competition, and too impatient, as well, to hang around while his brother gets all the game time and the attention.

It rained Saturday. All day. The track meeters quickly rescheduled the track meet for Sunday.

The weather warp threw all the weekend plans awry and placed me in the worst position I could imagine for this specific weekend: I had agreed to serve Sunday afternoon as a so-called "celebrity" judge/taster in a pizza competition at a pizza fair designed to raise funds for the March of Dimes. I had offered to take the boys with me, as a combination apologetic-and-self-punitive gesture, designed to make up for my transparent avoidance of Saturday's track meet. My wife accepted my contrite offer and made plans for herself, for Sunday. Now, with the track meet on Sunday, I had to take Jed to the track meet, where I would be bored to death, and then race with him to the pizza fair, where he would be bored to death, unaccompanied by his brother or any other kids he knew.

Jed and his pal, Kevin Kretz, were entered in four events for third graders, one of which, a 220-yard relay race, was immediately scratched because of a shortage of team members. Evidently some families couldn't accommodate the sudden scheduling change. I envied them. The boys also were to run in a 40-yard and a 60-yard dash, after they competed with other third-graders at the long jump. We waited through 90 minutes of relay races before we heard instructions for the boys to gather at the long jump pit; then stood for a half-hour of fourth-grade long jumping before we learned that our boys already had missed the third-grade jump. How happy I was to know that we had lingered two hours for no reason.

The other two races ended in minutes. Jed, who is fast, never had competed on a track before and was clearly distracted by the other runners, so he did not perform nearly as well as he had expected. How delighted I was, now, to have stood around for 2½ hours to watch my son become disappointed and saddened, before I then would drag him off to a boring pizza fair and destroy what was left of his sunny Sunday. By this time, I had clenched my dentures loose and was also facing the prospect of returning to my other favorite activity, visiting the dentist.

Kevin and his two older brothers, Danny and Patrick, asked if they could accompany Jed and me to the pizza fair. Slyly, I agreed, thinking I would distribute the boredom to include my friend's sons, and thus lessen the impact on my own.

Somehow, the day turned. At the fair, I bought the boys a sheaf of tickets to a series of 25-cent contests and events. The other boys' father appeared and bought even more. They frolicked with such delight that when I wanted to leave, I could not. They won enough prizes to open a store, and, when we finally trudged back to the car, Jed said to me, "Dad, this was the best day of my life!"

Naturally, I accepted full credit for it.

Waking Up

Following some presumably probing conversation about current sociological theory, my wife and a co-conspirator have concluded that members of our family should gather together in the morning and enjoy breakfast in one another's company. The plot to convince, invite and include me already is afoot, as if I were the only member apt to be resistant.

I have heard of this sort of ritual, family breakfasting. I've even seen its liturgy depicted in old films and in quaint paintings, mainly by artists from New England, whose settlers, I am told, first developed the habit after a successful, autumnal, outdoor luncheon for their own families, as well as the families of the people they planned eventually to massacre.

However, during the three stages of my life, I have garnered precious little experience taking regular meals, regularly, with other members of my respective families. I thus never cuddled up to the constancy of such uniformity, never missed it and therefore am not sure I can be any good at it, or reliable.

I easily can be convinced that the custom has great value; to children, most specifically; to a marriage, to community stability, in general. But diamonds have great value, and I have lived happily without them, too.

When I was a boy and the only child in the household, my father's job as a village police officer required him to work for about a week, each, at three different, eight-hour shifts.

When he worked midnight-to-eights, my father would arrive home in the morning after I left for school and usually was asleep when I returned. We dined together, sometimes, when he worked eight-to-fours, although the job often kept him busy through dinnertime. When he worked four-to-twelves, he slept late in the morning. I climbed the kitchen counter, found a bowl and mixed my own Cheerios and bananas. My father ate lunch while I was at school; he left for work at about the time I arrived home, and he often managed to stop home for a half-hour dinner, although my mother and I were not to count on him, especially not at any reserved time.

Sometimes, in those days, my mother and I ate dinner together. Sometimes, she and my father ate dinner together while I was granted the advantages of daylight savings play time; and, sometimes, my mother ate alone and called me into the house when my father arrived, so he and I could dine together. I've clam-raked the bottom of my memory and still cannot find one unsatisfying recollection of any of those meals, whether I ate unaccompanied or in a crowd of three.

When my adult children were young, I worked whatever

hours were available for whichever jobs I was juggling—often during the dinner hour—and I slept whenever an occasion presented itself, frequently during the rest of the family's breakfasting.

In recent years—say, the last decade or so—I developed habits of taking lunch alone at or near work, forfeiting breakfast altogether and accepting whatever was the consensus of the family for dinner plans, even when that meant accompanying them to fast-food, chain restaurants. I decline to eat any of the food, however, because it hates me more than I hate it.

We are a family of working people, especially during the academic year, when the younger children are either attending school or preparing to leave for an organized activity. We who shared cooking chores before the boys arrived now take meals from any source, and merely to prevent starvation. When our contractor friends finished enlarging our kitchen, I pointed out that we now had much more counter space for pizza boxes and Chinese food take-out packages.

So, this should be an interesting experiment, taming Daddy's culinary habits to conform to the children's presumed needs for gastronomic stabilization and ceremonialized, family bonding, especially considering the habits they have developed and thus will have to break or twist to accommodate the New Way.

My wife, for instance, must drink coffee in the morning, and the coffee must come from the local 7-Eleven store. She is specifically addicted. If the Southland Corp. ever goes belly-up, my wife will require institutionalized detoxification. Until now—or, until the inauguration of the New Breakfast Deal—her custom has been to awaken before everyone else and drive to the store, entrusting the slumbering children's safety to her slumbering husband's reflexes.

Inspired by some cosmic knowledge of her diminishing proximity, Danny will awaken soon after her departure and whine sleepily but with increasing dissatisfaction for her, until she returns. Knowing that, she has developed a habit of buying a box of small doughnuts. When Jed learned of the new custom and complained of the imbalance, she began buying Twinkies for him.

A newspaper editor, she spends much of her morning reading newspapers and prefers to do so undisturbed. To ensure the required peace, she rewards the boys' prompt washing, eating and preparing for school by promising them Nintendo game time while I shower.

So, I plan to suggest that the best way for us to breakfast together is to rise, dress, drive to 7-Eleven and hover between the newspaper rack and the video games with our coffee and doughnuts.

Everything but Father's Day

The blackboard hanging on the wall near our back door bore two entries:

June 11—Danny's Field Day

June 12—Jed's Field Day

It was Sunday morning, Memorial Day weekend. My in-laws had arrived earlier to spend the day. My wife and Mommynon (Explanation: When Jed's infant mouth was beginning to associate certain syllabic combinations with specific people in his life, he tried to navigate its parts around the phrase, "Grandma Marion." The inverted contraction, "Mommynon" limped out from between his lips and so charmed the assemblage, it became her new name, even in Florida.)—anyway, my wife and Mommynon were upstairs, yielding to their shared, genetic predisposition to rescheme the redecoration of the entire house. Danny, who didn't know better yet, had accompanied them.

In one of the few conspiracies that my father-in-law and I join together, we jokingly assumed that they were imagining the placement and design of vast, unnecessary dormers and stairways, fantasizing about wings filled with fireplaces and new bathrooms for the testing of color schemes of tiles, window arrangements and wall-hangings.

We, however, were talking about important stuff: business and the economy, subjects that have dominated a half-century of his life and that he, in a very real sense, has dominated in return, during a fairly spectacular career. I always try weakly to pretend to understand his passions for propriety, decorum, pinstripes and lowered interest rates, but I rarely am successful at the enterprise. Sometimes I manage to construct a vaguely credible, analytical paragraph by fastening together a few empty clauses, after the fashion of many business executives I have met. Eventually, he catches me at it. Unlike my business-executive acquaintances, I cannot switch to obsequiousness when I run out of thoughtful offerings. We don't have a business relationship.

Suddenly, my father-in-law rose from his chair—tired, I assumed, of my insufferable ignorance. He hiked up his trousers, surveyed the kitchen, fixed his attentions on the blackboard near the back door and approached it with curiosity, purpose and some ceremony. He picked up a piece of chalk, aimed it at the space beneath Jed's Field Day and scratched onto the slate: June 17th—Father's Day.

Uh-oh, I thought.

He then turned and announced that since he and Mommynon would be spending Father's Day with us, he wanted to be sure that his daughter remembered the approaching occasion as well as she would remember the boys' respective Field Days. I smiled at his news bulletin and said I understood his concern. Were it not for Father's Day, I told him, I would be shirtless. So, Father's Day was important to me, too, I said. I kept working at sustaining the smile as he further announced that my niece (his granddaughter) and her husband would be driving up from South Jersey to spend Father's Day at our house, too, as he had invited them to. (They raise show dogs and are likely to bring along a favorite.) I broadened the smile and in an appropriately high voice sang my surprised and delighted, "Oh! No kidding! Great!"

Mommynon returned to the kitchen followed by Danny and my wife, who, having caught the tail end of her father's conversation and matched it against my glazed look and frozen smile, suggested that I take Danny for a boat ride, as he was becoming restless. ("Probably overexcited," I said, "by all the talk of pillows, fabric and wallpaper.")

Danny and I made for the door and escaped.

Sooo! I thought. Father's Day. Sunday morning begins this year with the sound of car doors slamming in the driveway beneath my bedroom window. People arriving at 10 A.M., already showered, shaved and dressed. We'll eat. We'll talk. We'll take a walk. We'll eat, again. The boys will try to play with their friends, but we won't let them. We'll barbecue. We'll eat, again. We'll talk.

Why do we do this Father's Day business? Okay, to pay special attention to the father. That's me. The idea is to make me feel better about my role in the family. I have a better idea. Don't pay special attention to me once a year. Pay normal attention to me when I say, "Take your wet sneakers off the kitchen table," or, "Stop accumulating parking fines in the campus lot."

I wandered to the home of my neighbor and friend and doused him with my (however adolescent) lamentations about Father's Day. I chose him because his wife once had arranged a family walking tour of an arboretum as his Father's Day activity, forcing him to pass up an invitation to watch a Mets game from a corporate box just behind the Mets dugout. After that, he said he hated Father's Day, dreaded it. He said it was easily the worst day of the year for him. "I have to look all day as if I'm enjoying whatever my wife wants us to do."

"Why do they call it that, anyway?" I whined. "Why don't they call it 'Family Day,' or retitle it as a sequel, like, 'Mother's Day II?' Either that, or let me wake up, late on Sunday morning, and see a note on my wife's pillow that reads: 'Happy Father's Day! Your new shirt is on the kitchen counter. A 16-ounce bottle of Orangina has been chilling all night in the refrigerator, and we filled the gas tank in the boat. We'll be back around 8:30 tonight. Go for it!'"

Boys, and Dads, Will Be Boys

I felt bad that Jed had to wait months for the launching of his Christmas present—a deep-blue, 8½-foot-long, U.S. Marine inflatable boat—but I would have felt worse, had I been forced to wade into winter's water temperature to retrieve the thing. I made him postpone using his gift for so long that the gap probably stretched to Herculean limits such patience as a boy his age can muster.

He waited through the winter, past his birthday and into late spring for his maiden voyage. Worse, the Saturday morning I chose for its perfect weather conditions arrived with a menacing social cloud hovering over it, as far as he would be concerned; we were supposed to leave at noon that day to visit friends in Sag Harbor. I thus would be giving Jed a taste of sea captaincy and then whisking him away for a long ride in the car and an afternoon spent mainly with adults. I wondered if he would store the moment in his memory under the category, Torture. (Later, unable to endure the fear of his lifelong disdain, I deflated the boat and wedged it into the back of the Suburban. Jed rowed around a glimmering Sag Harbor lagoon until dusk, while I watched, guilt-free and proud.)

My son-in-law had procured a small trailer so that we—and eventually, Jed, himself—could walk the yet-unnamed boat to the end of the street and shove it into our creek, the Amityville River. After we foot-pumped the air compartments and hefted the boat onto the little trailer, we (Dad, Jed, Danny, Jed's friends, Pat and Kenny) listened patiently as my wife applied sun block to her boys and a litany of rules to the occasion: that Jed wear a hat, Danny wear a life jacket, Kenny call his mother for permission and Patrick stop at his house to tell his parents what he was doing; that they be careful; that they not row past a certain landmark in either direction; that they remain seated in the boat; that they not horse around and that they have a good time, of course.

I knew that I was duty-bound to repeat, re-emphasize and adhere to those regulations, but I was feeling more the boy than the man at the moment and probably would have joined the chorus that whined, Aw, Ma! had my sons been tactless and impolitic enough to whine it. Instead, they adopted fiercely serious expressions and nodded their obedient assurances of compliance. I nodded with them, as we tried to mask our eagerness to get on with the launch.

From the stir we caused lumbering to the end of the street, followed by a pack of young boys and a gaggle of seniors out strolling from the nearby adult condominium community, you'd have thought we were launching a submarine. One kind condo-dweller was so thrilled by the spiritual ramifications of the scene, he recorded every step with a 35-mm camera and later delivered the prints to my mailbox. I, of course, had forgotten to bring my camera, as is my custom.

In order to get from the road to the water, we had to drag the boat over a section of grass and sand, all of it generously garnished by the neighborhood flock of Canada geese. Fifteen years ago, a newspaper executive who had moved to the area from New York City telephoned me, nearly speechless with excitement, whispering into the receiver that he was at that very moment watching a Canada goose pace across his backyard, a rare sighting, indeed, at the time. That goose must have been scouting for future generations of settlers, however. For now, 15 years later, the lawns in our area are an enviable kelly green, but very squishy. Our streets are crowded and stained, and the air above them is pungent with the freshest fertilizer.

The boys—thinking, but then, not thinking—had removed their shoes for the boat ride and began to howl in disgust at the notion of slogging barefoot through goose doo on their way to canal mud. Little Danny's body froze at the instant his toes encountered the legacy of the geese. He would not take another step, and he abhorred the step he already had taken. I had to carry his stiffened, crying body to the water's edge before I could drag the inflatable to meet him.

Once freed from land, Jed performed masterfully at the oars, surprising me happily on the one hand but robbing me of the pleasure of teaching him, on the other. Other boys had beaten me to imparting rowing skills. Jed tried admirably to maintain dignity and decorum as he disappeared behind an island in the river, but, knowing him as I do, I detected a soaring spirit in his posture and his smile.

The following weekend, he and Danny visited friends on the other side of the island. My job was to watch them. I wanted to be angry that they had taken the liberty to stop, debark and play, but I did exactly the same in my boat. I thought of lecturing Jed about it later that evening, but he stopped me, cold, saying: "Dad, I can't believe how great it is to have my own boat and be able to visit my friends. Dad, this boat is the best present! The best!"

When they were asleep in bed, their mother included, I slipped down to the canal, climbed carefully into the little inflatable and pushed off in the gentle breeze. I rowed out toward the bay, and a swarm of gnats.

Clammed Up

Twenty-two years ago today, early in the morning, my first wife nudged me awake with the very-anticipated but nonetheless surprising news that her water had broken.

The phrase represented more of a mystery to me then than it

does now, for I was 22, myself, and mainly faking my way into adulthood. Water did not break; some other apparatus must have broken.

My job, however, as I analyzed the requirements of the position, was twofold: not to question another gender's knowledge of its own physiology, and not to panic.

I thus did not debate the idiom. I did panic, though, in a way. I argued for immediate admission to the hospital. I tried to argue with pure logic and no emotion, in what I held to be a manly sort of fashion. For some reason, it was of paramount importance to me to appear older than my age and therefore less ignorant, unsophisticated and terrified than I actually was.

I could not have constructed a whole sentence with the information I knew about childbirth, but I wanted nobody to know that. I wanted everyone to believe that I could handle life's most monumental milestones as if I were emotionally impervious to their impacts and implications, as if I had been through it all before. I knew that the faster I got her admitted, the less likely I was to get caught at being afraid and ignorant. (How ironic is this life; I now make a respectable living publicly confessing what a dope I've been.)

My arguments prevailed, even over the protestations of her physician, and by 8:30 or 9 that morning, I was holding a paper bag containing my wife's street clothes and instructions from a nurse to go home and wait by the telephone until the doctor called, a role for which I felt qualified and ready.

I was a cigarette smoker then, as if ignorance required a badge, and, after I had made the appropriate telephone calls informing interested parties of our status, and our pending status, I smoked and paced in the living room of the house we had managed to buy in spite of my starting teacher's salary.

I worried about the oddest contingencies. My father-in-law had planned a neighborhood barbecue for that Sunday, and I was to be his co-host in one culinary enterprise, the opening, garnishing and distribution of raw clams. I was the acknowledged family expert at clams (also, clam dip, cocktail sauce and barbecued chuck steaks), and I took the assignment seriously. Together, my father-in-law and I had visited my favorite clam vendor the night before and purchased 10 dozen little neck clams, which I then deposited in a cooler and covered with ice cubes. Who, now, would open these clams, I worried, if I could not attend the party because I was waiting by the phone for the announcement of the birth of my first child? Worse, who would make the cocktail sauce?

The phone rang (telephones rang in those days) at about 12:30, and somebody at the other end rather unceremoniously pronounced me the father of a baby girl, my T.C., whom he described as healthy and beautiful, having arrived at 12:19 P.M., weighing 8 pounds, 13 ounces (Later that day, I would pass on the misinformation to two nuns from the nearby parochial school that my new daughter weighed 13 pounds, 8 ounces and then wonder why the sisters' eyes popped so.) The voice on the phone said that I would be able to see my wife and baby at 3:30 P.M.

Three-thirty? I thought. What about, say, right now? I did not ask, though. I did not question nor protest. It was a different time. I was a different man, actually more an old boy than a young man. Under my life-conditioning, birth was wholly within the province of women and doctors.

Three-thirty seemed sadly distant, but it would give me time to rush to my in-laws' house and open the clams, which also would serve to show my immediate world how unaffected I was by an occasion so ordinary, to me, as my elevation to fatherhood.

The guests had begun to arrive already. I quickly mixed the ingredients for cocktail sauce. I set up a table adjacent to the garage and graciously accepting greetings, congratulations and questions about my wife and the baby, I nonchalantly opened clams, discarded shells, scooped dollops of cocktail sauce and arranged plates containing about 10 or 12 clams apiece, blissfully satisfied that I was successfully concealing my unbridled excitement.

At around 2:30, my father-in-law and his next-door neighbor, both smiling wryly, asked if being so nervous always made me so hungry. I said I was neither nervous nor hungry; I was fine. Smiling wider, my father-in-law noted that only 12 clams were left in the cooler and said that no guest had eaten any—not one guest; not one clam. Still befuddled, I asked, "Well, who ate them?"

"You did," he said, laughing.

"I ate NINE DOZEN clams? That's impossible!"

"It's not, apparently. We all watched you. Congratulations, Pop!"

Cycle of Life

I think my first two-wheeled bicycle was blue. I know it was short. I know it had training wheels. I remember my mother scurrying down Hamilton Street alongside me, grasping the back of my seat with her right hand and heroically trying to rest her left hand on my handlebar, without disrupting such control as I was trying to exercise over it.

I remember how triumphant and liberated I felt the moment I thought I had gotten the hang of negotiating the machine, and how frustrated and angry I felt when I tried to begin again by myself, without a push. Whenever the pedal in the up position descended under the pressure from my right foot, the pedal in the down position ascended on the opposite side of the bicycle, driving itself painfully into my left calf and stopping the forward progress of the bicycle. The stoppage left my novice, young self struggling to balance a two-wheel vehicle without the gyroscopic assistance of forward motion. So, I fell down. I vividly remember how I eventually coped with this problem. I walked the bike to a rock, a mound of grass, or a rare curb, so I could arrange the pedals just right and push off without parental assistance.

Years later, I ran alongside my daughters' bicycles in the driveway that ran alongside my first house. It was a two-runner, concrete driveway with a bumpy mound of grass up the middle, and a half-dozen huge cracks and/or depressions in the concrete. I would trip in the bumpy mounds of grass and lose my grip on their bikes, and they would wobble down the concrete runner a yard or so, until they hit a crack or a depression in the concrete, and then they would fall down. They fared better when we moved the operation to the nearby parking lot of St. Martin's School, and I yielded the tutorial role to their mother.

Jed learned bicycling late in life—I think he was 5—and without my assistance; in fact, without much assistance at all. I had tried to teach him, once, the way my mother had taught me. He had spurned me, probably for my insufferable lecturing, and demanded that I simply rebolt the training wheels to the bike and leave him alone. Crushed, I complied. Weeks later, as I was leaving for work, he begged me to remove the training wheels again, but also to continue going to work. I started to caution him against bicycling off alone. But in a very polite and calm way, he pretty much repeated the request that I shut up and leave. He later prevailed upon a friend's mother to walk him 10 paces down the block, and when I returned home that evening, I passed him on Perkins Avenue. He was leaning over, holding onto the handlebars, his feet perched, pigeon-toed, on the bar between the seat and the front-wheel fork, trick-riding.

Last week, Danny asked about his bike, which had been loitering about for a year, its flat, rear tire gathering garage-dust between two dented training wheels. We gave him the vehicle for his third birthday, but he preferred to follow the older boys around on a skateboard. Bicycling never meant much to Danny until he saw little Katy McGrath tool down her drive-way on her pink two-wheeler, sans training wheels.

On a sultry, summer evening of a day that Danny Lowe had spent throwing himself repeatedly into a neighbor's pool and then splashing about vigorously for hour after hour, until he had sapped all of his strength, energy, judgment and patience, I arrived home and, ignorant of his condition, presented him with a fixed bicycle with no training wheels. I wonder if he would have cared at all had Katy McGrath not reappeared at that moment, blithely pedaling along, wearing a dress.

Inspired by sex-war adrenaline, Danny made for his bike. I began the old lecture, warning him about being overconfident, begging him to be patient, exhorting him to try to head for a lawn for the purposes of stopping-without-losing-much-flesh, and promising him that, despite the heat and humidity, I, his hero Dad, would run alongside him every step of the way.

He mounted the bike. I shoved once. He pushed away my hand and promptly rode down the street. As he sped past Katy McGrath's house, he stood up on the pedals and tried to pop a wheelie, by lifting the front wheel off the pavement.

Neighbors came out of their houses. Jed and his friends appeared out of nowhere and cheered him on. My wife arrived home and wept at the sight, and then Danny tried to stop, presumably to soak up the applause.

He hadn't figured on stopping, so he fell.

He tried to start, again, by himself. But whenever the pedal in the up position descended under the pressure of his right foot, the pedal in the down position ascended driving itself into his left calf and stopping the forward progress of the bicycle, so he fell down. To cover for this humiliation, he stood in the middle of the street, crying desperately and wailing, "JED SAID SOME-THING! THAT'S WHY I FELL!" Dumbfounded, but wise, Jed left the territory for an hour, until Danny got the hang of it.

Welcome the Wanderer

I already was in bed Wednesday night when Colleen called collect from a pay phone located on some street corner in Boulder, Colorado, to tell me the scheduled time and the number of the flight that she would be arriving on tonight at LaGuardia Airport.

I envy her the summer of 1990. I wish I had enjoyed one similarly when I was her age. Having spent the last two months traveling, hiking, tubing rivers, canvassing various sections of Colorado soliciting donations for Greenpeace and intermittently attending Grateful Dead concerts, outdoor jazz nights and impromptu jam sessions, she said she now suffers two powerful longings beyond the privations caused by personal bankruptcy: She desperately misses her brothers, and she feels that if her eyes do not soon scan a large body of salt water, her brain surely will burst and her head start spinning until it unscrews itself from her body.

I was charmed by the former and said I understood the latter completely. I told her a story I probably had told her before. (We do that, fathers. We repeat ourselves constantly. Our young children love it; our adolescents loathe it; our young adults find it mildly-amusing-to-occasionally charming; and, based on my own behavior toward my parents, our adult children try not only to tolerate it but to appear as appreciative as if they were hearing the stories for the very first time, every time.)

I told . . . retold . . . Colleen that years ago, near Las Vegas, I had encountered a couple who invited me to visit their house for a nightcap. They were southwestern artists; she was a descendant both of native desert peoples and invading European settlers.

Intrigued, and thinking we would be driving around the corner and into a development, I accepted the invitation and then rode in the car with them for more than an hour, 60 or 70 miles into the desert.

The house was as spacious as an elementary school, its wide corridors guarded alternately by huge wooden sculptures and grand western landscapes, all individually lighted as if in a museum. The wide-planked, wooden floors were intermittently covered by bright, Native American area rugs. Blankets of like patterns were folded over the backs of enough sofas to furnish a college lounge.

While the husband prepared the drinks, the wife escorted me out onto an enormous deck that wrapped around the house. Approaching a railing overlooking what appeared to be hundreds of miles of flat dirt, she gazed out into the night sky. She heaved a contented sigh and said, "Doesn't it make you feel free?"

I grinned as enthusiastically as I could, under the circumstances. I said, "I guess I understand how it would make you feel free, but the truth is, it makes me feel trapped. I feel as if, no matter how far I ran from here, I still would be here. I feel free when I can stick my toe into the stuff that is simultaneously touching the coasts of Ireland, Madagascar, China and India. I suppose I could adapt to a good river, if I knew the mouth was close by, but I really am most comfortable within bicycling distance of an ocean or a bay."

"Isn't that interesting?" the woman had asked. "Last year, my husband and I drove to San Diego. It was the first time in my life I had really seen an ocean, believe it or not, as much as we've traveled. I walked down a long pier to look at the boats—and it was lovely, no question—but when I turned around, it felt as if I was looking at the entire North American continent, with me sort of stuck, at the end of the land. I felt trapped, actually, now that you mention it."

I told Colleen she was a coastal person. I said I didn't think it happened to everyone, this romanticized, emotional attachment, this assimilation of place, and that I didn't think it ultimately would render relocating impossible, just spiced, now and then, by reverie and an intangible longing.

I said that for a reason; I knew how much Colleen despised Long Island, especially after she discovered that the proprietors of self-serve service stations upstate—and now, she knew, out of state—allowed motorists to pump their gasoline before they demanded payment for it, just as if they expected people to pay for the gas and did not cynically assume that everyone on earth was a thieving creep.

I continued, saying that I found place-identification an endearing characteristic; psychologically healthy, esthetically poetic and possibly physically rejuvenative; that I suspected T.C., Jed and Danny were similarly afflicted; and I promised to scoot her across the bay to Gilgo Beach, for a fix, at the first opportunity.

I hesitated to tell her about her brothers, preferring instead to watch her see the changes their summer had wrought. But I couldn't resist.

"The boys will knock you out," I said. "Jed has nearly finished a safe-boating course and swims like an eel. He's won ribbons in races. Danny does flips off the diving board, swims the length of a pool and rides his two-wheeler over curbs."

"I'm ready to come home," Colleen said.

Hired Hand

The very idea bothered me from the start, and on several levels. Nobody in my background ever had live-in help, unless from an ailing grandparent who had no other place to live. I had even felt embarrassed the first time I paid another man to mow my lawn, fearing he would think me elitist, condescending or plain lazy. Hiring a nanny almost seemed a level beyond that, an ancestral betrayal on the one hand, a parental abdication on the other.

However, my wife and I had plunged headlong into a modern dilemma. The boys were 2 and 7 at the time. Their physical and emotional health depended on the reliable, daily presence in the house of a responsible, loving adult, most preferably a parent. But we worked a standard work week at jobs so personally fulfilling that neither parent was willing to disengage professionally; and our up-to-date marriage was so egalitarian, neither entertained a dream of suggesting that the other quit.

We so far had gotten by with the steady assistance of wonderful friends and relatives, but the personal relationships always were so strong, we suffered stomach cramps whenever we had to think and act like employers. I never aspired to be anybody's boss but my own; it takes all the management skills I can muster to manage myself. My wife worried that any criticism we might offer would shatter a personal relationship and end a convenient caretaking one. We needed a different arrangement.

An agent told us of a 22-year-old woman from Iowa who had been working for a year as a nanny on Long Island and was looking for another situation. We arranged to meet her in a park within walking distance of her job on a day that she had some time off. There, Tammy introduced herself and told us her qualifications and her needs, with a confidence that suggested that she had suffered some inconvenience for indulging her more natural inclination to be cooperative and uncomplaining. She wanted to care for and work with children, not a house, she said. She also declared that she was very religious, and she wanted to know about the proximity and accessibility of a Lutheran church. She somehow made clear to me that she could balance being an employee and a surrogate member of the family, and would prefer and even needed the dual relationship, which she also thought would be best for the children. I liked that. The boys scampered with us through the park as we talked, and she seemed to like them and relate to them immediately, especially Danny. Jed was old enough to be quietly shy; Danny young enough to be uncontrollably cute.

Somewhat reluctantly, and to provide her with civilized living space, I moved my newly claimed office-den from a former bedroom off the kitchen to a corner of the basement (which turns out to be a cooler, quieter and more private place to work, plus nobody minds that I'm a slob down there); and Tammy moved in for the summer of 1988.

Two and a quarter years shot by. I remember how comfortably right I felt almost immediately about our decision, when I would arrive home early and find Tammy and one or both of the boys on the floor fashioning a village of houses and stores out of cardboard boxes; or reading stories from books that she had helped them select from the childrens' section of the library; or when my neighbors and close friends would gush about our good fortune after they had spent some of those summer weeks home on vacation and had watched Tammy and the boys together.

She wound up referring to us as her second set of parents. We did, in fact, fall easily into assuming aunt-uncle roles, as Tammy agonized over choices and details of, say, continuing her interrupted college education, or as she wrestled with the complexities of the relationships she enjoyed with young men she had met at church. Two or three times, we hosted her friends and relatives who visited from Iowa; I took them for boat rides, accompanied them to a Mets game, all the while feeling humbly complimented by the familiarity with which they addressed me, as if the whole, extended family in Vinton, Iowa, felt secure and happy that Tammy was in such good hands—while we were enjoying the same security regarding Danny and Jed.

She danced at T.C.'s wedding, listened to rock groups with Colleen, befriended parents of the boys' classmates and some of our own neighborhood friends. She taught us about walking beans, on the farm, and we showed her how to eat blue-claw crabs from the bay. When we accompanied T.C.'s imperiled baby to the Children's Hospital in Boston, Tammy took care of the boys and the house for almost a week. Later, she wept with us at the baby's funeral.

With dreams of teaching in a parochial elementary school, she registered this summer for fall classes at Iowa State. On Wednesday, Danny Lowe reopened for the fifth time a knee wound from his foolishly acrobatic, bicycle curb-jumping. Tammy held him close as he wailed tearfully in her arms, until he calmed enough to suddenly throw his arms around her neck and cry, "I don't want you to leave!"

She cried with him.

Hanging Tough for Kindergarten

Life's first full-time, full-fledged, take-the-bus school morning had an interesting effect on my youngest child. I studied his expression intently while we waited for the minibus to pick up him and his brother. I even ran back into the house and rummaged through the closet to find my camera, hoping to capture the dilemma in his eyes.

An only child, I then meditated all day over fraternity's mixed blessings.

Throughout the summer of 1990, Danny Lowe told anyone

who asked that he was 5 years old. Once, while waiting for a ferry to Hyannis, Massachusetts, from Nantucket Island, Danny boldly announced to an older, much bigger boy, that he was 5-and-a-half. The boy was 7.

Bored with standing on the ferry line, Danny challenged the boy to, "See if you can get me," goading him repeatedly: "Come on! Get me! See if you can get me." Finally, the boy lunged. Danny darted to his right, but the boy had good reflexes and a long reach. He reacted quickly to Danny's evasive maneuver, and his open left hand managed to intercept Danny's left upper chest with an audible slap. Danny's brazen expression returned to his younger-than-5 pout, as he buried his face in my thigh and tried to hide his tears.

I felt bad for him, but I could not resist the impulse to say, "Dan, what did you expect? You told him to get you! Guess what? He got you." Exactly the postgame analysis Danny did not want to hear.

Worse, and really stupidly, I then drove a figurative stake through his heart by asking, within earshot of the other boy, "And why did you tell him that you were 5½, anyway?"

"Because I AM!" insisted my now doubly humiliated son.

I had forgotten that Danny Lowe rides, runs, jumps, dives, swims, fights, and plays Nintendo, always as the younger brother by five years of Jed Lowe, and as the youngest boy by two years in the neighborhood pack. He thus has devoted an enormous percentage of his life's energies to proving himself worthy of the attention, affection and respect of taller, more physiologically developed, potential competitors. I am not always aware of it, but I suspect he is. Always.

I recalled watching one night recently as Dan and two of his 6-year-old pals, Tommy and Eamonn, frolicked in Tommy's family pool. Each of his friends stood taller than Danny, Eamonn by a head. All three seemed happy and comfortable jumping into the water, splashing around, laughing and playing, but Danny's behavior had a more frenetic edge to it. When the boys jumped into the pool, Danny dove. When the boys executed a dive, Danny scampered to the diving board and did a full, forward flip. When the boys answered a challenge to swim a backstroke, Danny plunged in and swam the butterfly, the hardest possible stroke, and one that his brother really could not swim until this year, at 9.

I remembered another occasion, too, when my friend and neighbor, Eamonn's father, called me aside and said, "I don't like telling on kids, but I have to tell you: Danny just out-thicked me. I saw him and Eamonn across the street, with their bikes, crabbing off the dock. I said to them, 'Boys, you're not supposed to be riding bikes on this street.' Danny says, 'I'm allowed!' and I know he's not. So, I said, 'Well, Dan, I know you're not allowed to be across the street, near the canal, without a grown-up present.' Again, Danny says, 'I'm allowed! I can.' I know otherwise, but what am I going to do, call him a liar? So I said, 'Okay, if you say you're allowed, I'll believe you; but Eamonn is not allowed. I'm going to have to ask both of you to go back across the street, and to not ride bikes on this street. Otherwise, Dan, you won't be able to play with Eamonn.'

"I figured I had him," said Eamonn's father. But he looks up at me, eye-to-eye, with the exact same look that I gave people all my life—other kids, teachers, principals, bosses—and he shrugs and says, 'Okay.' He turns his back and walks away, back to the canal, by himself."

I sighed. "I figured the next 15 years were going to be rough," I said, "but this seems like an early start."

This week, however, on the first school morning, freshman kindergartner Danny Lowe wore a more somber face than I was accustomed to seeing. He alternately sat on a rock on the corner, fingering the strap on his backpack, staring at the street or, when he stood, he absentmindedly grasped a part of himself that polite males ought not to grasp in public, let alone in stadiums and coliseums, where they too frequently do. I recalled a physician telling me about four years ago that when a boy that age clutches those parts in that fashion, and answers that he does not have to go to the bathroom, he is exhibiting a profound lack of self-confidence.

So my Danny was scared, but, bolstered by the presence of his brother, who would ride next to him on the bus, and true to his developing defiance, he would not even reveal it except involuntarily. He remained a 4-year-old boy wearing a 5-year-old's face. I felt strangely proud, but it made his mother cry.

Posse Rescues Ratso

Saturday mornings, the other residents of my house like to get up early. I suspect a genetic dysfunction.

The boys, whose arousal on school mornings requires force, scramble out of bed on Saturdays as if responding to an alarm, while my wife dons sweats and sneakers and prepares to walk briskly for at least a half-hour, all around the village, until she alights at the coffee counter of the 7-Eleven.

Not wishing to discourage their ambitions, interrupt their activities or eavesdrop on their conversations, I generally roll over, apply a pillow to my exposed ear, and resume the activity for which I believe Saturday mornings originally were designed.

Last Saturday, just as the soothing, cool side of the pillow was enveloping my weary head, I heard a young person's slightly panicky voice say, "Mom, Fuzzy got out of the cage! He's loose in my room."

I moaned.

I long ago stopped entertaining ambitions to share my home with other forms of life, save for an occasional plant. First, I (happily) discovered myself to be philosophically opposed to the ownership of a living being, especially one who resisted the relationship.

Mainly, I don't like the smell of most captive animal forms. I don't like their sounds, either. I especially don't like the messages I translate in their eyes, which range from: "Give me food" to "Get out of my part of the house" to "I just made a mistake that is going to make you fiercely angry when you discover it."

So far, I have successfully dissuaded my sons from even asking for a dog. I have done my utmost to conceal my delight over my wife's severe allergic reaction to cats; and, until recently, I employed procrastination, auditory and memory lapses and general paternal vagueness to evade the issue of pets—the question of a turtle was my last victory. I answered, "I don't know" and "Someday, maybe" and "I'll think about it" until the queries ceased.

All of a sudden, I lost on the hamster. My wife and older son somehow blindsided me when my powers were dimmed. I think Jed said, "Mommy said I could have a hamster if I did well in school. So, can I?" I think my wife then said, "I didn't say that. I said it would be all right with me, but you would have to ask your father."

I think that I then looked at my wife and said, "Why would you tell him that? You know I think of hamsters as rats. You know you think of hamsters as rats."

I think Jed then said, "Please, Dad?" with the classic, plaintively interrogative tone required for desperation begging. "Please, Dad, please? I'll take care of it, myself! I'll feed it! I'll clean the cage! I promise, Dad. Please?"

I think I said, "You weren't around, yet, to know your sister Colleen's rabbit, were you? Old Gratefully Dead?"

I think my wife said, "That's not fair!"

I don't think I then said, "Oh, all right!" but other people evidently thought I did. Within an hour, Jed and my wife were carrying a caged hamster upstairs to Jed's room, Danny following along excitedly, asking what was the hamster's name.

"Fuzzy," Jed answered.

"Mud," I mumbled.

During the week, while the boys were in school and my wife was at work, I secretly visited the hamster, silently challenging it to exhibit a characteristic that might weaken my resolute disdain or dull my animosity. I tapped gently at the cage door with the nail of my forefinger, and the hamster made for the finger with speed and vengeance. Good! I thought. You're a nasty little rodent. We'll get along just fine, hating each other.

He (or she—I haven't asked and don't intend to) grabbed at the cage with tiny paws, twisted his beady little head to the side, smushed his little nose between the bars and chomped at a vertical cage bar. The thought of biting into a piece of metal made my teeth itch, so I left the room, muttering aloud, "You just stay in that cage, Ratso."

So now, on a bright Saturday morning, he was out of his cage and into my house. I pressed the pillow against both sides of my head as I heard Danny and his friend Eamonn bound up the stairs, followed by Jed's pal, Kevin. I heard Jed instruct the posse to put socks on their hands. I had to admire his instinct for precaution. As I listened distractedly to the sounds of four boys armed in white socks scurrying about the room in pursuit of a tiny, tan rodent, my hatred became mushy and turned into mirth. Envisioning the scene, I bet on Eamonn making the good grab. Eamonn is the worm-and-bug king of the neighborhood, which delights his mother. And, at only 6, he rivals my expertise at capturing blue-claw crabs off the dock. Jed calls him The Amazing Eamonn.

The thumping sounds of the chase continued for 20 minutes, until I heard squeals of, "We got him! We got him, Mom! Mom, you can come back in the house now!"

"Who got him?" I yelled.

"Eamonn got him!"

Three Adults, Two Kids, One Car

Alone in the car, the cruise control set at 60 miles an hour (5 miles above the state speed limit and 10 miles slower than the rest of the traffic), I can make the road trip from Amityville to the State University of New York at Plattsburgh—64 miles south of Montreal—in 5 hours, 45 minutes.

Passengers slow the trip by 15 minutes per adult, 25 per child, according to calculations I base on a coefficient-of-bladder formula.

I had been preparing myself mentally for this trip since late summer, weeks before Colleen actually returned to school. Elements of the visitation conspiracy hatched by Colleen and her stepmother included our taking off on a Friday morning, accompanied by Jed and Danny and my mother. (That's 1 hour, 20 minutes additional, plus another 15 minutes for my wife, for an anticipated total trip time of 7 hours, 20 minutes.)

Laden with clothing and paraphernalia Colleen either had forgotten or had left behind to ensure our trip, we would visit Colleen at her apartment; my mother would stay with Linda DelBel, her friend of decades; Danny and Jed would sleep overnight at least one night with their sister; we would enjoy each other's company all day Saturday and then take a leisurely drive home Sunday, cruising the perimeter of Adirondack State Park, where freshly dying foliage would dazzle us with its brilliant anguish.

We departed at 10:30 A.M.; stopped twice for tea and sundry functions, and we arrived at the Comfort Inn on Route 3 in Plattsburgh at 5:50 P.M. Friday, exactly according to formula. We enjoyed a reasonably happy time, save for the nights. The inn rests in the path of a U.S. Air Force runway that appears from the periodic roar to be the launch point for the Strategic Air Command.

Perhaps it was that brain-rending thunder that frayed my nerves for the drive home, exacerbated by the knowledge that driving toward New York would be much less pleasant than driving away from it; but somehow, I knew by dawn's torrential rainfall that I would be less tolerant southbound than I had been heading north. I protest that I am a patient man, but the evidence almost always betrays me.

Anticipating difficulty, I arranged the seating in the Suburban specifically to keep the boys and me separated beyond arm's length. Two-thirds of the passenger seat amidships collapses for cargo, and I collapsed it for the placement of games, pillows, a bag of sandwiches and a cooler containing bottled water, Orangina and grapes, although I opposed the inclusion of grapes. They too easily could become projectiles, I declared, and our sons are obsessive throwers. My most hateful passion about long automobiles trips with children centers around the nerve-shattering danger of objects flying inside the car.

On the way up, despite every effort to deprive the boys of any tossable toy, I was struck in the back of the head by a foil ball they had rolled after dispatching with their bologna sandwiches. I glanced menacingly at my wife, inserted a Billy Joel album into the tape deck and turned up the volume until I saw my mother wincing in pain, while my wife lectured the boys about the danger of messing with Daddy's fragile sanity by throwing in the car.

For the ride home, I arranged for my mother to ride up front, next to me, so my wife, stationed in the remaining one-third of the middle backseat, could entertain the boys and enforce the rules. They were seatbelted into what they call the way-back, the third three-passenger seat. Everybody operated under strict orders to use the motel bathrooms to the best of their abilities prior to departure.

Intimidated, presumably, by the notion of command performing, Danny lied about his results, so we had to make our first extra stop after only 10 minutes. Interrupted by two more stops, they colored for an hour, played quietly for an hour, giggled happily for an hour, tortured each other for an hour, whined for an hour, and fought and complained for an hour.

Danny claimed gastrointestinal trouble not 25 minutes after what I thought would be our last stop. I don't know what community we were in, but the service station proprietor spoke no language common to us. The men's room was inoperative and the women's room had no doorknob, only a round hole. I felt a steel rod growing from the top of my spine into the back of my head, and I gripped the steering wheel for the next hour.

An object hit the back of my head just three-quarters of a mile from home. I snapped. I pulled over, got out and opened the back door. Quickly, both boys cemented themselves to the opposite windows, so I could not reach them. Wildly, I threw paper cups, grapes and candy wrappers all over the car, all the while bellowing madly about throwing things.

We rode in deathly silence to my mother's house. I carried her bag inside. Alone with her in her living room, I apologized for the outburst. "I lost it," I said humbly. She touched my cheek. "I'm surprised you didn't lose it hours earlier," she said.

Mothers are like that.

A Goal Achieved

Thanks to a stroke of unusually good luck, someone scheduled the J&K Bakery team's Sunday soccer game at almost the same time as the La Mansarde Restaurant team game; and then arranged for both to be played on adjacent fields. The fields were separated by a single section of bleachers, whose top plank offered a simulcast, bird's-eye view of both contests—the 5–6-year-olds and the 9–10-year-olds.

Dutifully, I had attended previous soccer games played at opposite ends of the park and, worse, at opposite ends of a warm afternoon whose brilliance pleaded for my indulgence in boat rides or end-of-season, chaise lounge trial tests. But, with this scheduling bonanza, I could watch two sons from one bleacher and not lose an entire Sunday to a game I never played or cared about.

The social pressure in our community for both mothers and fathers to attend every soccer game surprised me. If you failed to show up, someone at the next game was sure to ask: Where were you last week? as if soccer meant Sabbath.

Moreover, I remained mostly unconvinced about what benefit such fervid parental audience-participation offered the field combatants. My memories of the year or two I played run-of-the-mill, B-level, Little League bore only a few games observed by one or both parents, and I recalled that their presence made me feel pressured to perform way above my mediocre abilities and ambitions. (I had set two goals for myself: Spit like a real ballplayer and don't make a fool of yourself.)

I guessed that my current attitude about my sons' sporting endeavors was not a very good one. I tried—probably halfheartedly—not to convey it to the boys, but my pained body language at piling into the car, and then my rejuvenated eagerness to depart the field upon the final whistle, probably leaked the secret that I felt less euphoric than imposed upon by their participation.

Danny's game was to start a half hour before Jed's, and on a field about half the size. Danny recently had been declared just barely eligible to play with the 5-year-olds, because we had documented that he would become a 5-year-old before January. In his first game, which everybody knew was his first ever, he had stunned the crowd of parents with a running and kicking performance that inspired comments ranging from "He's a natural" to "Who's the ringer?" I like to think that I am above beaming proudly over accomplishments for which I deserve no credit; but I am not. I beamed shamelessly for hours.

In his later field appearances, Danny's performance was unspectacular, partly because it was unspectacular, and partly because everyone's expectations had risen. Also, Danny suffered lapses. Sometimes, he ran and kicked for the pleasure of it, forgetting that he shared the field with a ball, let alone opponents. He kicked over here; they and ball were over there.

So, when the La Mansarde game began on the larger field behind me, I stealthily turned away to watch Jed, whenever the opportunity arose. Jed's coach once was Colleen's classmate, long before Jed existed. Colleen called her Sir, after Charles Schulz' comic strip character, Peppermint Patty, and I remember her chasing a softball as far as I could hit it, then catching the thing, every time. A New York City cop, now, she wore an orange soccer jersey with "Pep. Patty" printed across the shoulder blades, so the name must have stuck. Between quarters, while her charges were sipping water from plastic Ninja Turtle bottles, she kicked a soccer ball to herself in a manner that had me searching for an invisible tether. Then she booted it from midfield into the net. I thus gained confidence in her familiarity with the rudiments of the game.

I sensed a problem, however, when I overheard her promise Jed that he would score a goal that day. It seemed an over-confident vow and one that surely would result in profound disappointment. Through three quarters, however, alternately assigned to defense and offense, he nearly scored two goals. Still, I was less impressed with that than I was with the way his feet danced with the ball; the patient and deliberate way he faked and controlled the play. Suddenly, he was a boy I had not noticed before, growing in ways I would not have predicted.

With 30 seconds left in the fourth quarter of a game tied at 22, he suddenly dribbled and danced the ball through an impossibly thick crowd, and then deftly tapped it into the net. My eyes fixed on his huge smile, as his teammates hugged and high-fived him. I tried to remain properly aloof and sophisticated, but my biochemistry went haywire. I thought I would explode from the contagion of his joy. I howled.

The game ended. The teams met and dispersed; and the bleachers emptied, but for a profoundly stunned me, woozy from my euphoria; still savoring the moment. I looked down and saw him walking toward me, alone. I stepped to meet him and hugged him, pressing his sweaty head into my chest, saddened, slightly, that he seemed taller.

Unmasking Halloween

I hid out for Halloween. I stayed late at work, pretending to be agonizing over the fashioning of a paragraph, and thus left the whole deal up to my wife; driving the boys to parties, finding appropriate costumes, trick-or-treating, all of it.

I feel a little sheepish about my passive noninvolvement in the festivities, but not so ashamed that I wouldn't try to get away with it, again. I am on record as hating Halloween.

I don't like the color combination of black and orange. I think the dead are best left that way. I know too well that excessive candy renders my younger children hot-wired for circuit breakage, and I am sufficiently discomforted by the existence of real beggars that I cannot imagine why anyone would encourage his or her children to play at begging.

However, in the face of national peer pressure, I also am too cowardly to discourage my children's participation in the coercive, door-to-door, give-me-treats-or-I'll-deface-your-property tradition, which leaves me suffering ambivalence for several days before and after the designated holiday.

I also hate costumes, a personal problem whose origins I have not fully probed, mainly because the available evidence regarding my disdain is unflattering. The most revealing moment of truth hit me about six years ago, when a friend, Donna Reid, insisted that my wife and I attend a Halloween party. I declined the initial invitation as graciously as possible, offering up one lie or another about bogus prior engagements. Donna persisted, and afterwards prodded my wife for weeks, prying at her guilt gland, until my wife began to pry at mine.

Finally, and very privately, I confessed to my wife that while I wanted to go to the party, I would feel unbearably uncomfortable showing up at a costume party without a costume; and I absolutely and adamantly refused to show up anywhere in a costume. The dilemma left me no choice but to absent myself from any costume parties. I apologized but would not budge. I suggested to my wife that she dress up as a widow and attend the party alone, as a seasonably macabre jest. In fact, in keeping with the tone of the holiday, she could tell our hosts whatever gruesome fib she wished, for instance that our babysitter hanged herself at the last minute, and that I, Husband-of-the-Year, had volunteered to fill in.

She claimed to understand my agony. She offered sympathy for a while, but then asked me to attend, anyway, first as a personal favor to her; then as a major, self-sacrificial statement of my devotion; then as a test of our marriage. I would not go.

On the night of the party, a babysitter arrived. I shook my head in despair. My wife descended the stairs wearing an oxford cloth, button-down shirt; tan, khaki pants; deck shoes and a tweed jacket. A slave to habit and an admitted, sartorial disaster area, I wore—wear—oxford cloth, button-down shirts; tan, khaki pants; deck shoes and a tweed jacket. She also had donned a tweed cap, one of mine. I wear a tweed cap. She also wore a store-bought mask, consisting of fake eyeglasses with bushy, black eyebrows; a huge, pink nose in the middle and a bushy black mustache underneath.

My face.

I, who had refused to wear a costume, was confronted with the costume I wore all the time. "I figured we could both go as Ed Lowe," she said smiling; winning, again.

Jed seems to have inherited my antipathy for regalia. Heroically, my wife had spirited the boys to Toys R Us the night before Halloween and purchased the last available Spider Man costume for Danny. (A size 14, it was eight sizes too big. Danny looked more like Cocoon Man.) Jed wanted to go trick-or-treating, but he could not abide any of the costumes, not one.

On Halloween morning, the arguing and whining was almost too much to bear. Jed, who last year had dressed as a skateboarder, which required his wearing what he wore anyway, had settled on a black sweatsuit, loosely indicative of a Ninja costume, though without the hood, mask or bandanna depicted in the thoroughly tasteless and awful Ninja-related VCR movie tapes he and his friends so frequently rented. Remembering a protective ski mask I had purchased at Bromley Mountain one year, when I thought the wind-chill factor might peel my face off my head, I arose and rummaged sleepily through old suitcases until I found it and wrapped it around his face, all the while congratulating myself for this, my fatherly participation in Halloween.

Later, when he took to the streets, he did not wear the mask, only the sweatsuit. Masks were nerdy. Costumes were nerdy. Trick-or-treating was nerdy. Only shaving cream was cool. Jed's three co-conspirators were similarly un-costumed, except for the shaving cream in their hair and the cans of shaving cream in their respective arsenals.

"Who are you going as?" my wife asked Jed's friend, Kevin.

"Nobody," he said. "But I have shaving cream!"

I sort of liked that.

My Sons' Other Moms

Through my work, I recently learned a subtly terrifying story about a toddler who may have been molested by an adult in whom the child's parents evidently misplaced their trust.

The story haunted me. Distracted by imagined comparisons, and then the death of a noble friend, I alternately sympathized with the child's parents and rejoiced that, through no effort of my own, I had so far escaped their particularly sickening brand of anguish. I've been very lucky.

I don't know why I never became very involved in the selection of persons to whom my wife and I would entrust our children while we worked. I should have. Though I have guessed badly about other people and thus suffered some minor betrayals, I still fancy myself a fairly perceptive judge of humans, and I know that my wife values my opinions. Yet, I frequently evaded that crucial responsibility, except to voice my praises or objections after my wife already had settled on her choice.

It is and has been her most watertight complaint about our partnership: my passive abdication of certain parental concerns, as if somehow they were divisible by gender. "Why am I the only one who worries about dinner?" is one of her refrains for which I have no sensible answer. "Why is it only my responsibility to arrange for a babysitter, even when the babysitter is your mother?"

Sometimes I counter (feebly) that I worry instead, and alone, about the frequency of oil-filter changes and tire mileage, but I don't press the argument, because its foundation is softer and deeper than bay mud. The true answer is that there is no reason. She happens to be right. I don't worry about dinner until I'm hungry, or until the kids say that they are. I don't request or require that my wife worry about it, either. She just does, and I just don't.

As partners in an infuriatingly modern marriage, with its dual careers, ex-spouses, step-relationships and mixed ethnicities, we still are children of intensely traditional unions of men and women. We both claim to be struggling to free ourselves from whatever we consider potentially dysfunctional about the orthodoxy of tradition, but there is no denying that she struggles much harder than I do; I suspect because tradition gave her gender a longer list of domestic tasks than it did mine.

When the working-couple child-care dilemma loomed over her—us—for the first time, nearly a decade ago, my wife drove herself to abdominal pain worrying about how she would find someone with whom she could feel even moderately comfortable leaving her precious, newborn son for 8 to 10 hours at a time, five days a week. I was not much help, except to suggest that since we lived in a small town in which I had spent all but the first two weeks of my life, we ought to first tap such possible resources as existed immediately around us before we began soliciting professional help through unfamiliar agencies and the potluck of newspaper advertisements.

Eventually, my wife made such arrangements with a mutual friend, Donna Reid, a woman whom I had known since we shared desks in school. She was my cousin Mary's lifelong closest friend, who since childhood had referred to my own parents as her Uncle Eddie and Aunt Doe. Her most frequent dinner and party companion was an intensely affable, slightly daffy, 400-pound marine mechanic, Bob (Foo) Davidge, whom I had known all my life and with whom I would have trusted my children, too, though not any salable dry good I might own.

A single parent, Donna had raised a daughter and a son to a secure, happy and proud adolescence, despite the total absence of paternal support—financial or otherwise; moreover, despite the unintentional but unrelenting efforts of governmental support systems to humiliate its applicants as a prerequisite for assistance.

Donna would not be humiliated, nor would her children. In her direst times, she withheld her electric bill and her rent payments to make sure her kids returned to school in clothes as bright, crisp and new as those of a surgeon's children. Rather than live in quarters beneath such dignity as she felt her children deserved, she constantly badgered realtor friends and relatives for information and offered herself as a house-sitter for people who might be vacating their homes for all or part of a given year. The family of three moved around a lot, but never into squalor, and sometimes into splendor.

Jed was an infant, almost a decade ago, when Donna truly became his second mother for six years. He called her Donnie, and they were crazy about each other. Knowing how easily it would redden my cheeks and inspire me to stammer an explanation, she would playfully introduce me to one person or another as the "father of my baby."

During the years she cared for Jed, and then Danny, too, she studied and earned the credentials to become a hospital lab technician. All the while, she fought breast cancer, as well as she could, until this week.

Boys at Play

I am learning, after all these years, to take sibling spats less seriously.

My neighbor and I were chatting and listening to music in my house during one of the last balmy days of a particularly balmy autumn, while our boys—my two, his one—played in the side yard; first with a football, then with a Wiffle ball, then with leaves, then in a tree, and finally, with each other; as they pretended with characteristic innocence to be hand-to-hand, foot-to-head, combat Ninja fighters.

Blithely, they crushed each other's imaginary sternums, as if they were fashioned out of chopsticks and gum. (Once, we thought we would discourage games of mass murder by refusing to buy plastic replicas of automatic rifles for our children. It didn't work; they found high-caliber, automatic sticks and branches. Maybe kill-play is in our genetic code.)

Suddenly, Danny's 5-year-old vocal chords stove through a Steely Dan chorus that I would have considered impenetrable, especially since I was demonstrating the amazing power of two, new, stereo speakers at the time.

I used to think, quite prejudicially—and more so in my first and more traditional marriage and fatherhood—that only mothers possessed the inner-ear sensitivity to discriminate between children's varied vocal tones and pitch, especially during a din that would otherwise mask the sounds of an unmuffled diesel. But through my experiences with our boys, I have discovered that auditory expertise can be acquired merely through repetition—simple practice. A parent who manages to be present often when the children are hovering between playing and fighting, or when they are playing at fighting, soon learns that howls of certain notes and decibel levels are designed to ward off continued torment. They, thus, are voluntary and require no parental intervention. Other wailings, their notes higher and sometimes garnished with a bubbly sound from the back of the performer's throat, are more primal and involuntary. Their messages invariably stem from true need, ranging from that for an adult referee to the more horrific requirement for immediate emergency services.

My neighbor and I looked at each other and nodded affirmatively, as if to say, "Yep, that's a real one." Danny's high, long, sustained, repeated scream required a visit.

Deliberately, but not even at a trot, I rounded the southwest corner of the house and saw through the white pickets that Danny and Jed were on the ground, together, their pal Eamonn standing off to the side, watching with distant curiosity. Jed, kneeling over his younger brother, was close to crying, himself, and was pleading desperately: "Danny, if you don't stop, you're gonna get us both in trouble!" Dan was writhing on his back, holding his right buttock.

"All right! What happened?"

Jed's face contorted as if he were about to join Danny in crying. I had seen that act too many times before. Now, I knew the sequence: Danny had perpetrated some aggressive nastiness on Jed; Jed had retaliated in kind, and probably with more strength, accuracy and/or enthusiasm. Danny had then erupted, attracting the attention of me, Trouble Incarnate, and now Jed was joining the Chorus of the Stricken, knowing that I would yell louder at him than at Danny, because, I would say, I refused to accept retaliation as a reason or an excuse for inflicting pain or injury.

"Jed BIT me!" Danny screamed, before resuming the howl.

"WHAT!" I bellowed, in a half-faked, half-genuine rage. I had thought we were way past biting.

"But he bit me!" Jed cried, now shedding real tears, as if suffering suddenly from a buttock bite.

"What does THAT have to do with anything?" I hollered at Jed. "You don't bite people! There are no circumstances that change that! Whatever he did, it has nothing to do with what you're supposed to do or not do! The damned HAMSTER bit you, Jed! Did you bite the HAMSTER back?" Jed cried.

"And YOU!" I yelled, turning my attentions to the more demonstrably stricken. "You BIT your brother?"

Danny turned up the volume of his howl, a familiar tactic for fending me off. Eamonn's father rounded the corner behind me, gazed through the fence at his son's agape face and asked, "What did you do?"

"Nothing," Eamonn said.

"You two, upstairs!" I ordered. "To your rooms!"

I followed them up, slammed their doors behind me and stood in the bathroom, watching Eamonn and his dad toss the football in the back yard. I waited three minutes, then addressed Danny. "When you are ready to stop crying and apologize to your brother, you can come out of this room and go to his," I said in an artificially deepened voice.

Then, I opened Jed's door. "If Danny comes in and apologizes to you, you are to apologize to him. Then you can come out and try to act more like a civilized human being" [playing at slaughtering each other, I thought, without grinning].

The same Steely Dan song was still playing when the boys happily rejoined Eamonn outside.

New Hope

Hovering ominously above us in the December air, a nagging trepidation regarding the final holiday season of 1990 has haunted some family members.

A season so thoroughly swathed in the joy of nativity—specifically the birth of a son, no less—was bound to present emotional difficulties for my daughter, T.C., and her husband, Bill, whose son, Kevin, would be approaching 9 months old, now, had he lived.

I happen to be blissfully unfamiliar with the holiday blues phenomenon that we read about annually in the pages of newspapers and periodicals. I experienced one relatively unsatisfying Christmas in my life, and I cannot recall its details without the help of a witness, who remembers my waking up at 4 A.M. and lapsing into a half-hour fit of uncontrollable sobbing. Evidently, I had realized in my sleep that I would be spending Christmas without my daughters for the first time since the dissolution of my first marriage. I'm told I bolted upright and exclaimed, "Oh my God, no!" and proceeded to fall apart.

Long ago, some involuntary protective impulse in my psyche fogged the memory of that outburst, and I must have thereafter chosen not to strain myself trying to restore it. I don't know whether I cannot or will not, but I am satisfied and happy that I do not.

More recently, though, I wondered—gratefully in the absence of any experience—by what measure such momentary grief would have been multiplied had I lost a child permanently, as my own daughter has. Also, I wondered about my role in helping escort her through this potentially depressing holiday period. I assume that talking about the subject is more helpful than evading it, but how and when? And for how long, and in whose company? Protracted discussions of that nature have a way of wandering down conversational cul-de-sacs, leaving participants directionless, silently disappointed in their performance and wishing they were elsewhere.

Aided by my talent for procrastination, the frenetic nature of the pre-Christmas season has otherwise distracted me from indulging in more than a moment's seasonal sadness, myself. This year, while I characteristically put off shopping until the last possible days, I have decided to worry instead about Colleen's car, for instance, which languishes inoperative in a cold driveway in Plattsburgh, while she scrambles to complete course requirements and rehearse theatrical productions and procrastinates calling a mechanic—just as I would. I also fret over Jed's hamster, which again has taken leave of its cage and apparently is vacationing at various, ad hoc, rodent resort spots throughout the house. I worry, therefore, about the future integrity of the telephone wires. I worry about where the hamster goes to the hamster bathroom. I worry what happens if the hamster doesn't survive this trip. Who will find him and where?

Meanwhile, when I do worry about T.C., I have to admire the way she has been taking care of herself. Whenever she feels the urge, she visits her son's gravesite, which I suspect is healthy. She also enrolled in night courses at the State University and has busied herself writing sociological term papers about bereavement and, more recently, about the residual effects of divorce on the children of a marriage rent asunder.

When she decorated her house for Christmas, she hung stockings for her and her husband and then placed between them a small gold ornament, engraved with Kevin's name and birth date. The gesture honors him as a departed member of the family, but because of its subtle size, the acknowledgment is not maudlin.

T.C. telephoned one morning last week at 7:30 A.M., just as the boys' bus driver had politely honked her presence and catapulted my nerves into panic mode. My wife was upstairs, looking for Danny's jacket; I was downstairs, looking for Jed's shoes. The boys stood at the foot of the stairs, staring blankly at their backpacks and gym bags, as if trying to imagine what purpose they might serve, so early in the morning.

T.C. chirped an incongruously cheery hello, while I silently cursed the timing of the call. "How are you?" she asked in a singsong voice. Remembering my fears about her emotional fragility, I refrained from answering with sarcasms, such as, "Are you kidding?" or "A little preoccupied, thank you," and instead said that I was fine. She asked me to ask my wife to pick up the extension. In the next few seconds, I yelled upstairs, placed the receiver down, hustled the boys out the door and realized why T.C. was calling. My wife already was on the phone when I yelled up my best guess: "Is she saying she's pregnant?"

"No," my wife answered, as I lifted the receiver.

"We're due in August," T.C. said.

Later, dizzy with confusion, I wept again. We were restarting the emotional roller-coaster ride, this time taking much less for granted, but also, we would glide through the Christmas season on new hope, which seemed like a perfect fit.

The Years of Stupidity

Paternal idiocy, an unavoidable affliction but curable, requires for its eradication tremendous paternal patience and, quite inconveniently, time—much time; heaps of it; months stacked atop months. Years.

I don't remember anymore when or with what symptoms idiocy strikes the fathers of sons, but I am certain to learn anew, beginning around four or five years from now. I recall that my own father became helplessly wrongheaded in 1962 and got progressively imbecilic until late 1967, when miraculously he began to return to my senses.

Fathers of females are usually stricken with mental paralysis in their 13th or 14th year of paternity, when, coincidentally, their daughters approach their 13th or 14th years of life on the planet.

I must have begun to blither and babble in tongues sometime around 1982 or '83. I don't recall feeling so much like a jerk, but the symptoms evidently are so insidious that no father recognizes them as fast or as clearly as his daughter. I only understand now what a buffoon I must have seemed. My daughters knew almost instinctively that my opinions had aged overnight, like rank cheese left on the picnic table over an entire summer vacation.

They saw my point of view become veiled in ignorance, while I could not discern any change whatsoever. When I struggled in the quicksand of my stupidity to understand where and how I had erred, I only sank deeper and became stupider. I even took on a stupid pallor. My clothing became frumpy. I wore my hair too long for too long. My explanations and, much worse, my lectures, extended to insufferable lengths, became more repetitive and more dreadfully boring and irrelevant.

My values fossilized, and my fatherly tactics decayed and began to stink. Gestures I had considered involuntary and benign metamorphosed into cruelly critical sarcasms.

When I tried to explain or apologize, I somehow meddled, instead, always making matters worse. When I turned dolefully away from the arguments, escaping in frustration and helplessness, I abandoned. My compliments were embarrassments; my suggestions, humiliations. I didn't offer my daughters my trust in sufficient quantity, but I didn't demand enough of them, either. When I tried recovering from either of these errors, I found myself suddenly demanding too much, too soon, too late. I lived in extreme worlds, running from one wrong end of the right-wrong spectrum to the other. I even drove the wrong routes to selected destinations. I answered the telephone wrong.

When troubled, during those years, my girls sought solace and advice from their mother and their stepmother; and got it, too. I learned their deepest secrets, heartaches and dilemmas second-hand, like a cabdriver or a haircutter. My opinions, my support and my affections traveled through intermediaries to their destinations.

Weary, confused and with exponentially waning enthusiasm for the job, I stopped trying to attain, achieve or display wisdom and retreated to an effort to be consistent in one, primary characteristic: I would try to help whenever summoned. That was it.

In the weeks leading to the permanent disappearance of 1990, I began receiving evening telephone calls from both Colleen and T.C. and afterward was stunned, each time, to realize that I had spent more than an hour on the phone with each of them, four nights in a row.

At first, I suspected that they were calling me because of the inconvenient unavailability of my wife or my ex-wife, especially because of the subject matter. T.C. seemed to want to test me with the profoundest theories about her future, her ambitions for her marriage and, eventually, her family.

We also explored the biology of childbearing with a tender frankness that I had feared she would forever restrict to her gender.

Colleen spoke not only of her triumphs and trials within the undergraduate curriculum and of her feelings about faculty and colleagues, in general, but about one or two specific young men, in particular.

I found myself exploring with her the fragile relationships between men and women, the exquisite agony of uncertainty and the soul-callousing pain of betrayal. She read me a letter she had written that rendered me as dumbfounded for its wisdom and clarity as it was humbling for the courage and trust she exhibited in sharing it.

My wife seemed as bemused as I, when she learned that I was so late to bed because of these protracted conversations with my daughters; but it made her smile.

Me, too, in a shrugging and sheepish sort of way.

"What do you think it is?" my wife asked.

"I'm not sure," I said, "but I suspect I may be in recovery. I may finally be coming out of my stupid years. It's a stage, you know. We all have to go through it."

YEAR THREE

Valiant Men in a Crunch

The boys were lunching on the floor of the den Saturday, managing also to distribute their attentions pretty evenly to petting the damned hamster, watching the damned television and goading and kicking each other, all of which meant that I soon would be vacuuming the den for the second time since morning.

For a valiant while—I thought valiant, anyway—I vehemently opposed the scattering of crumbs in any room other than the kitchen. I would howl when I encountered the offense, never really examining why I considered it disrespectful to our home, in general, and to their mother, in particular. But when I was not at home, my wife would allow the children to take itinerant meals. She then would claim sole possession of one or two peaceful moments in the kitchen, in the company of a cup of tea and a graham cracker. She seemed as unperturbed by the inevitability of randomly scattered, particulate food matter as I was bothered by it.

A hidden truth interrupted the eruption of my rising anger during this most recent violation, and I found myself feeling slightly ashamed and even tempted toward apology, though I did not yield to the temptation. Blurted confessions and apologies may be cathartic, but they too often have consequences as repetitive as they are unpleasant.

My opposition, I suddenly realized, to children's eating and spilling food in rooms other than the kitchen was directly related to the extent to which I accepted responsibility for vacuuming those rooms, and, conversely, to my abdication of most responsibilities for tidying the kitchen itself. I wanted the boys to restrict their eating to the kitchen so I could then freely ignore the crunching of the evidence beneath my feet. The kitchen was her problem. I, thus, was being a Visigoth, again.

In a household as infuriatingly modern as ours, we wrestle constantly with unfair assumptions about the respective roles of family participants. Probably a little smugly, I have considered myself an especially yielding combatant in the debate, pointing with evidentiary pride to my longtime voluntary association with the vacuum cleaner and, in earlier times, ripe diapers.

Because American social history tilted so much of the unfairness in favor of my gender, however, I almost am required to be smug and boastful about such rudimentary cooperation, just to avoid some of the debilitating discomfort of being in the wrong all the time. If I accepted every egalitarianist argument and behaved accordingly, I would be noble and exemplary and so utterly miserable that I would quit the house and, no doubt, take up residence with a man, with whom I likely would split all the chores but feel far less conciliatory about it.

To make myself feel less defeated in this life, I have constructed several quite plainly sensible arguments for the physically stronger member of the family to embrace the furniture-moving, machine-toting responsibilities associated with vacuuming floors, for instance. I stop occasionally at the kitchen's threshold because of a symbolic need to not surrender so completely. When nobody is around, I hoist all the chairs and vacuum the kitchen, too. I'm not bragging; I'm clinging.

Conditioned in my youth—and largely by women—to cower and flee from aromatic diapers, too, but then reconditioned by Lamaze births and the invading force of reason, I constructed an analogy that defeated any argument against diaper-changing by persons who might on another day willingly snake a toilet, gut a bass or eat head cheese. The argument was unnecessary, but repeating it made me feel better. I similarly rationalized my participation in dishwashing by describing to all who would listen our Jack Sprat system of labor division: I hate dirty dishes, I would say, and she hates squeaky-clean ones. So, she fills the dishwasher, and I empty it. Nobody needed to know this or hear about it, but repeating it helped me explain to myself why I behaved differently from how I was conditioned to behave.

My wife seems to have embraced the notion that she and I can best change the world's institutionalized unfairness through our example, showing our sons a different matrix of possibilities than our parents showed us, thus changing the presumptive attitudes of the next generation, rather than fighting each other for turf. I like the idea for its generosity and patience. It forgives me for being boorish once in a while, appreciates my efforts to reform and gives me some credit for helping improve the species. My sons already have a lifetime of seeing their mother go to work every day. They have visited her office and watched men and women enter and exit with questions for her to answer and problems for her to solve. And they have seen both their parents at the stove and dishwasher—true, one more frequently than the other—or folding the laundry, or vacuuming the floors.

I hope they become good men. To that end, I shall require them to vacuum the den this week.

Close to Home

Members of the committee on ambiance and entertainment for the Long Island Barkeepers' Ball were debating their preferences for black rather than white tablecloths when the U.S. Armed Forces began blowing up Iraq.

Oblivious to the news, we settled on black. We said we would trim the time for the honors and the charity presentations to a half hour from last year's hour, and we gladly agreed to let the head of the entertainment troupe preside over the rest of the timing of the evening.

Two hours later, having skipped dinner, and having uncharacteristically listened to a cassette tape in the car rather than a radio program, I wandered into a West Islip restaurant reputed to offer a particularly hearty clam chowder. I ordered a cup and learned from another patron that the country had gone to war somewhere between the tablecloth decision and a discussion about balloons.

Saddened more than I would have anticipated, I watched the bombing on television while waiting for the soup to arrive. I was not expected home until late, and I felt a steadily diminishing inclination to turn away from the television. I finished the chowder and ordered a second cup. I learned the word Scud and judged it appropriately monosyllabic and near-as-possible to revolting in sound and structure, suitable to its meaning. Conversations about weapons and tactics erupted here and there, and I mainly nodded at such information and theory as they contained, until one particular analysis stuck in my brain like a dart.

A man had said that the real purpose of conventional weapons in a war was not so much to kill as to maim. He reasoned that maiming and wounding people created more chaos and required the diverted attention of more ancillary personnel than did merely slaughtering members of the opposition, willy-nilly. Given the historic (and evidently naive) inclination of even the most warlike humans to be distracted and disturbed by their comrades' anguished wailing, he estimated that the calming, removal, treatment and subsequent comforting of one freshly dismembered soldier would require the ministrations of 10 more healthy enemies, whose mercy and compassion would thus subtract them as combatants.

So, if you were to kill 10 people, you would reduce the enemy's capabilities by only 10. If, however, you were sufficiently deft in your warring to blind, dismember and disembowel the 10, inspiring them to scream in unimaginable pain and terror with all the force of what remained of their lungs, you would do your country tenfold the service toward eventually terminating the conflict and allowing the striking up of the parade band.

I had never heard such a theory before, and its sense was as clear to me as its horror cosmic. My species' capacity for reason had become a bottomless embarrassment.

The boys were asleep when I got home. My wife said that they had watched the televised warfare, too, and had decided, especially in my absence, to bunk down on comforters arranged next to each other on the floor of our bedroom.

Honored by the security they applied to my proximity, I sat in a wicker rocker and stared at them in the soft, blue glow of the flickering rocketry being replayed on Cable News Network. My attention was momentarily interrupted by some superbly tasteful guitar work that accompanied the image of a red sports car rounding a bend on a dirt track, and I began to suspect that an army of ironies was about to lay siege to these days of my life.

Danny slept on his right side, his sturdy little left arm resting across his brother's left cheek. Jed's right arm, ending in long, slender, even elegant fingers, was draped lazily over Danny's ribs. The skin of their cheeks appeared smoother than usual, their long, black eyelashes longer.

I could not possibly be alone in how I feel, looking at them, I thought. Other men must feel exactly the same, looking at their children.

War talk had dominated the week. Danny, now about a year older than I was when the Korean War began, seemed to pay little attention to any of it, but the barrage of words, images and ominous news program jingles, apparently composed to evoke feelings of doom, had worked their way into Jed's otherwise pacific nervous system. My wife said that he earlier had asked if any chance existed for the members of the opposition to bomb us. She said he had been glued to the television and seemed deeply troubled by the mere notion of bombing. I shuddered and looked at his face, again. The enormity of war sucked the sense out of the room.

The next day, he helped me with a task his mother had invented for us. She had bought a large, yellow bow for the front door, and we replaced the Christmas wreath with it. I told him that, long ago, I had read that the color yellow represented two qualities. It was the color of hope, and of madness.

Walking to Trouble

Evidently, I am old enough to walk.

After considerable prodding, but convincingly in the noble and generous interest of prolonging my time on Earth, my wife persuaded me last autumn to join her in one of her thrice-weekly morning constitutionals of approximately three miles. I admired the care she took in calling the activity taking a walk, judiciously avoiding the terminology that would automatically deter a devoutly slothful man, words such as workout or exercise. So, I further yielded to this aerobic seduction and accompanied her a second and then a third time, and then a fourth, fifth and sixth.

Just as I began to fear a habit forming, Christmas arrived, and my wife presented me with what she called walking shoes, as if to symbolically render my cooperation no longer voluntary, but a permanent element of our marriage. The walking shoes bore a strong resemblance to sneakers, but with frills that suggest some sort of graduate degree. I found their brightness a distraction, as if little gray and white animals were continually running out in front of me, but my wife insisted that my comfortably tattered, brown deck shoes would eventually cripple me if I used them for (and here, she paused) taking walks. The prognosis seemed a tad severe, but since I already owned the walking shoes now, I promised to walk in them. They required tying, which was more work than I customarily devoted to protecting my feet, but I endure the labor as a statement of my gratitude.

An interesting and pleasant by-product has emerged from this joint venture in strainless exercise: We find ourselves alone when we walk, unencumbered by household obligations and uninterrupted by calls from the office, homework questions, pet escapees, spilled cereal or war news. We saw that we could converse, and we eagerly took advantage of the opportunities, discussing matters from the mundane to the eternal, theorizing, analyzing, reminiscing and prognosticating.

Thursday's unseasonably warm fog drew my walking shoes and my eyes to the Amityville River, where the gray moisture softened the edges of all the waterfront images and gently faded away those in the distance. Inspired, as always, by the serenity, I talked dreamily about the boys and how much I hoped I could infect them with my hopeless infatuation with the water. Its proximity comforts me daily. When I seize an opportunity to indulge even the briefest boat ride, I feel as if I am escaping into an ancient still life. My privileged inclusion in its artistry inspires and restores me in the ways that I suspect vacated cathedrals resanctify the faithful. I want my children, and for that matter anybody else I can influence, at least to know the availability of such a strengthening and pacifying romance. My wife, whom I have influenced as well, knows that; cherishes it, in fact. So we fell smoothly into a discussion of our recent water-related history and of our options for the future.

We recalled with grand affection the radiant glow on Jed's face Christmas morning, 1989, when he descended the stairs and saw the 8½-foot, bright blue, U.S. Marine inflatable boat incongruously absorbing an ocean of floor space in the living room. The only family photograph I display near the unholy mess that is my newspaper-office workstation shows Jed that following summer, proudly and deftly rowing his craft, his little brother perched behind him, near the bow of the boat.

Last summer, we enrolled Jed in a safe-boating course offered by the Coast Guard Auxiliary. Although I thoroughly hated the chore, I sat in the unconditioned summer air with him, listening to lectures about the principles and the apparatus of boating safety, the rules of the road, the unwritten (and too-often unperformed) requirements of common courtesy and the systems and procedures invented to quell emergencies. Eventually—and though he, too, hated the chores—he studied his workbooks and memorized his regulations, endured and passed his test and won the award that would permit him in the eyes of the federal government to operate a motorboat as of the occasion, this April, of his 10th birthday.

Since then, of course, he has badgered me for an outboard motor, and my wife and I have wrestled with our fears of the various costs—in money, worry and work—of such an acquisition. Should we restore the old 10-horsepower motor that my son-in-law offered, or is that too powerful a start for this captain? How do we prevent theft; must I detach the motor each time he uses it and lug it from the dock to the car to the house, when I so fervently loathe lugging even the laundry baskets upstairs?

We were wrestling with these perplexities when we walked by the dockside evergreens behind which I had hidden Jed's boat. It was gone.

The Band Was Just Too Good

The emotional capacity of an artist probably compares favorably with that of a lunatic, and doubtless strikes members of both their families as exhilarating one moment, and exasperating the next.

I try not to claim to be an artist. Fearing the self-characterization too presumptuous, I line up for public categorization with the practitioners of other crafts. Whenever somebody accuses me of artistry, however, I am charmed, satisfied and honored beyond expression. So, I must suspect or need that identity, if secretly. I certainly am no scientist, nor any kind of businessman. I rarely look for a bottom line; I look instead for depth and breadth and often cannot describe or explain what I encountered in the search.

But I am blessed and cursed with the temperamental extremes that accompany whatever energies drive a man to seek fulfillment in endeavors more subjective than objective. I am impetuous, and I frequently ascribe gigantic, personal importance to serving impulsive needs that must seem absolutely frivolous when I try to communicate or share them. Still, I try to share them, especially those from which I draw pure, simple joy.

Two of the more ostensibly frivolous of my private passions are being at Gilgo Beach and listening to the Jim Small Band. I have been indulging the one for more than 35 years, the other for about 10. Mostly, when I tap into these life delicacies, I am alone, but I have tried to share my enjoyment for one or the other with my children, among others, and in the case of Colleen, to share both.

Three years ago, when our relationship was not yet as strained, distant, confusing and painful as it ultimately would become before it began to develop an adult form, I visited Colleen at college. Hesitantly—I suppose because the change in state law regarding the drinking age had not yet been seamlessly matched by the change in custom and practice in all college towns—she asked if I would join her and some friends at a bar later that evening. She said she had discovered a band she wanted me to hear, the Perry Nunn Band, if I remember right. I said I would, but for some stupid reason I tried to hide how wonderful I felt that she had asked. Worse, I succeeded.

The place was typically crowded, but with great faces and broad smiles, and I was very pleasantly surprised by the reception I got from each of her girlfriends, as they shook my hand exuberantly and said, "You must be Colleen's dad! It's great to finally meet you!" Evidently, my daughter had revealed much more affection for me than to me, and the discovery gave me back some hope.

I told her that Perry Nunn was fabulous, and I meant it, but I also begged her to save me a Thursday night the next time she returned home. Every now and then, I confessed to her, on a Thursday night, when I am still awake and everyone else in the house is not—and especially when I feel real good or real bad—I walk a half mile to the Dakota Rose and listen to the Jim Small Band perform an hour's set. I said that the band's relaxed precision and easy excellence had never failed to amaze and then restore me. I had sought them out when my youngest son was born and when my father died. Knowing how deeply she appreciated a wide range of music, but particularly fun and funky jazz and rock, I promised that she would feel the same. I swore it, guaranteed it.

The plan backfired, for a while.

Toward the end of last summer, on a weekday afternoon, when the parking lot at Gilgo Beach was nearly empty, I spied a bearded face—vaguely familiar but out of context—and suddenly realized it belonged to Phil Riley, a singer-guitarist with Jim Small. I told him the story: that I'd brought Colleen to see and hear the band, and that they were so good, and she so overwhelmed, she felt I had belittled her. "Sure," she had said, "I bring you to see Perry Nunn, so you blow my brains out with this. Great. Thanks a lot."

Riley laughed. On an impulse, I guess, he yanked an acoustic guitar out of his trunk and sat atop a picnic table. We fiddled with songs I hadn't played or sung since my girls were little. Riley said he had not been to Gilgo before—wasn't even sure why he drove there that day—but he liked the place. I said I understood, probably better than anyone.

During the winter recess last month, on a Thursday evening, Colleen asked if I thought I would be up late enough to take a walk to the Dakota Rose. I beamed. I said I would nap if I thought I required it.

Later, on the way, we chatted and marveled at what an unseasonably warm and beautiful day it had been, though windy. Colleen said, "Yeah, the ocean was beautiful today, the way the wind blew back the tops of the waves." She had driven to Gilgo Beach at about 2:30. I laughed. I told her I had been there, too, from around noon until just after one o'clock.

When the Jim Small Band had finished their first set, Riley walked over to say that he and his wife had driven to Gilgo Beach at around 1:30; where was I?

I still laugh aloud when I think of it.

Good Night, Sweet Prince

When our boys seem particularly restless (we use the word, wired) late in the evening, my task is to lie down with them until they fall asleep; a dirty and disgusting job, as they say, but somebody has to do it. My enthusiasm for the duty usually is mitigated by how heroically I have to strain to prevent the calming effects of the working conditions from robbing me of consciousness, first.

Their periodically frenzied state depends on factors as diverse as their attendance that afternoon at a birthday party, their discovery of the hidden boxes of Girl Scout cookies, their having accompanied us to an impromptu, extended dinner with the neighbors or, especially in Jed's case, their dinnertime viewing of televised scenes from a war.

In that specific instance, we further conceded to allow them to choose their own slumber site. Indulgently, I suppose, we have provided each boy with a room with bunk beds. They never yet have volunteered to sleep separated from each other, and we no longer look forward to the day when they choose to, but, given the extended latitude of options, they still try to insist that they sleep with us. Correctly guessing at my reaction, they no longer risk revealing their preference aloud. Instead, they wait until I am performing my ablutions in the bathroom and then crawl into the bed next to their mother.

I have become almost pathological in my protestations over the notion of sharing my half of the marital bed with an aggressive boy and an apprentice adolescent. Wednesday night, when I saw their forms buried under the covers next to my wife, I yanked two comforters out of the closet and spread them on the floor at the foot of our bed. I grabbed pillows and a blanket off the bunks in Danny's room and applied those to the floor, too, howling all the while.

"We're living in a house containing five bedrooms," I bellowed, "into which we have installed five single beds, a queen-sized bed and a convertible sofa; and the four of us remaining inhabitants are going to sleep together, in one bed? Are we nuts? Are we on drugs? Have we lost all connections to our brains? And does anybody here believe that we might actually sleep, what with Danny's horizontal, nocturnal cartwheels and Jed's gangly legs draping over everyone?"

Quietly, they slithered out from under the covers and descended, puppy-like, to my ad hoc arrangement on the floor, Danny wearing a pout of abject gloom, Jed adopting a more mature expression of disappointed resignation.

I took my place next to Danny, who promptly switched off his frown, snuggled close and began kissing my face. I held him in my arms until two whole minutes later, when he snored directly into my ear. While a 10 P.M. television news program whispered overhead, Jed fidgeted, cleared his throat repeatedly and held his hands high into the blue light. He seemed to be counting and recounting his elegant fingers, which I always will remember as the first physical characteristic to absolutely amaze me upon his exit from the womb. I reached over with my left hand and grasped several of those miracles, and with uninvented rules we played a strange, tactile game, entangling our fingers.

Suddenly, the bruised and swollen face of a black man identified as Rodney Glenn King appeared on the TV screen and wrenched Jed's attention away from the dark. He turned over, prone, and watched as the next clip, a videotape taken by a Los Angeles resident, showed what the voiceover identified as Los Angeles police officers surrounding a man rolling on the ground, beating him with sticks, and with almost homicidal fervor. I knew Jed now would be awake for another hour. His nearly mystical sensitivity to other people's pain has long astounded me for its seemingly limitless depth. He began his inquiry immediately, his eyes fixed on the scene. "Who were they? Why were they doing this? What could the man have done to deserve this?"

"Well, they were cops," my wife and I stumbled to explain, and it seemed quite clear that they were not very good at it, and that they were demonstrably racist cops, as well.

"I hate cops," said my gentle boy.

"Whoa! Hold on, hold on," I said. "Not all cops are like that. Remember, Pop was a cop. Can you imagine him doing that?"

"Pop was?" Jed asked, nearly breaking my heart.

"Jed, you don't remember?"

"I thought he was a chief."

I laughed with relief, and elaborated, reveling in the opportunity to re-tell him of his grandfather's compassion and honesty, his strength, generosity and sense of fairness. Worried that Jed would be witless with fatigue at school Thursday, I glanced at my watch as I spoke, and then jumped to my feet when I saw the date, March 6, six years to the day since Pop died. I quickly put on shoes and excused myself to my wife and son, with apologies. Another generation's nerves needed soothing this night.

My mother and I sat in her den and watched a Frank Sinatra retrospective on public television, until late.

Ecumenical Agonizing

The long weekend of family ecumenism began on Holy Thursday. Its culinary celebrations would include samples from two-thirds of the world's colliding holy periods, Ramadan excepted.

My in-laws arrived that morning from Florida, in anticipation of the Passover seder scheduled for our house the following evening, Good Friday. My mother-in-law would prepare that ancient ceremonial supper for a seating of no less than a dozen celebrants, possibly more. Predictably, she arrived with extra luggage containing her favorite pots and pans, including the enormous, bucket-handled contraption she insists is the only vessel that can render her chicken soup precisely delectable, which, in fact, it does.

Within scant hours—and this actually happened—my mother, Dolores, bumped shopping carts at Finast with my mother-in-law, Marion. Marion's cart teemed with boxes of matzoh, heads of cabbage, jars of horseradish, dozens of eggs and briskets of beef. In the opposite marketing carriage, Dolores wheeled about a huge leg of lamb, accompanied by potatoes to mash, corn to cream and fresh asparagus for which I would mix a simple sauce of mayonnaise and Dijon mustard, while Dolores cooked Easter dinner Sunday, at our house.

More in-laws arrived Friday, adults all. Everyone scheduled for the Friday night session was staying until Saturday afternoon. Saturday evening, neighbors less familiar with the cuisine of Pesach were joining us to feast on guaranteed leftovers, plenitude being paramount among Marion's passions.

It struck me hard that for a resident boy at our house, someone whose school had loosed him for spring break and who ached only to test his pre-summer stamina by playing with his friends until he no longer could stand nor hold up his head, these four days would amount to a trying experience.

Grownups swarmed, all either talking about, preparing, consuming, wrapping or discarding food; all insisting on order, quiet, etiquette, cleanliness, sartorial propriety and minimized automotion; all publicly examining, comparing and critiquing the skin, facial construction, posture, talent, performance, triumphs, faults and probable girlfriends of the two youngest members of the gathering, who finally put their feet down on the issue that most bothered them: being kissed by anybody wearing lipstick.

My deepest sympathies took up residence in the hearts of my sons. I recalled vividly more than 35 years ago having to dress in a gray, glen plaid suit, accessorized by a fedora, no less, to attend Easter Sunday dinner at my aunt's house, where my maternal grandparents lived. I loved my grandparents. Mamie would crumple a faded, softened dollar bill into my palm, stroke my hair and make me feel beatifically special; Tom Pop taught me dominos, played checkers and invited me to listen with him to the Brooklyn Dodgers on his Zenith. But I hated the suit and the sitting around, and I hated, hated, hated the fedora.

Beyond secular sympathies, I wrestled privately throughout the weekend with my escaped convictions, my periodically reworked thoughts about the indoctrination and separatism requisite to a successfully organized religion. As co-parents who had abandoned orthodoxy but who struggled with deep affection for family traditions, my wife and I had tacitly compromised by clinging to the latter only. The highly ritualized seder was no ordinary holiday dinner, however, and I wondered throughout the readings about the cumulative effects on my children of religious indoctrination.

Jed, standing beside his Conservative Jewish grandfather (who aches to see the boys bar-mitzvah'd as badly as my mother wishes them baptized), read his four questions with a confidence and dignity that had me beaming. But then the assemblage took turns reading aloud the grisly history of a deity who first permitted his fondest admirers to be miserably enslaved for generations, then personally slaughtered the firstborn of their entire enemy nation without so much as a perfunctory interview.

In the interest of cultural balance, was I to take the boys aside in the next days and recount the story I had learned in my boyhood, wherein bureaucrats pressed thorns into the head of this same God's son, tortured Him all day, hammered spikes into His wrists and fastened Him to boards for vertical, public display? The literature of the great religions, though poetic and profound, seemed preoccupied with unspeakable bloodbaths.

Secretly, as I spooned purple horseradish onto a cake of gefilte fish, my mind writhed over these eternal mysteries, until I determined I had to at least find out what Jed thought of this sacred meal. First chance I got, I put my arm around his waist and asked him. He smiled and said, "When do they get to the part where Poppa hides the matzoh, so me and Danny can go find it?"

Thus taught, I later hid a half dozen Easter eggs for Sunday morning.

A Love Story, Times 10

Hopelessly conditioned by, of all oddities, the decimal system, I search for meaning in multiples of 10.

I know I am not alone in this arithmetic addiction. Friends of mine have turned or will turn 50 this year, and they already are behaving as if the seconds before that midnight are so fateful as to inspire fantasies of retirement, divorce, religious conversion, suicide or at the very least, one hell of a party.

James Edward Lowe, my third child, my first son, the first infant to whom I so effortlessly referred as my baby, stands this weekend on the precipice of the 10th anniversary of his birth, his first life-multiple of 10. For no other reason than the numerical, I therefore have spent the last fortnight alternately reminiscing about him and marveling at the passage of time: how a traffic light can seem so interminable and a decade so fleeting.

Memories flash by in snippets and clips.

Thanks to my ultimate acquiescence to the Lamaze approach to childbirth, I was not pacing at home or in a hospital waiting room when this too-rapidly-aging boy sucked his first lungful of delivery-room air. Instead, I watched it swell his chest cavity and listened in awe as he bellowed it back out. I then held him in my arms for the first 45 minutes of his life, possibly the most spectacular 45 minutes of my own. The resultant magic between us often seems eternal.

I remember some silly details. I deliberately wore sneakers for traction, fearing that I would slide on the highly polished hospital floors. The nurse ordered me to slip sterile, paper booties over the sneakers, so that I slid on the highly polished hospital floors anyway.

He was jaundiced. However statistically routine, it was a new concept for me and his mother, and we were horrified beyond reason that we had to tear ourselves from the hospital, leaving him behind to bask under fluorescent lights. The disadvantage converted to a benefit for me, though, because I handled an evening and then a 2 A.M. feeding every night. Draped in a yellow paper hospital gown, surrounded by the blue dark of an empty nursery, I got to stay as long as I wished, cradling my baby until my arms and shoulders ached.

We already had decided that if he were not an Emily, we would nickname him Jed, at my suggestion. I did not want any more Edwards in my life, having spent my entire juniorhood responding in concert with my father whenever my mother called out our name. She would yell, "Ed!" from one end of the house or yard, and we would drop tools or toys and come running, one of us always the unbeckoned.

I was determined not to relive that annoying phenomenon.

Convenient to my purpose, my wife loved the name James, but she did not like what so often became of it: Jim, Jimmy, Jamie. So, smugly considering myself imaginative, even brilliant, I invented a compromise: name him James Edward and call him Jed. She liked it, and we did it. Now, however, when my wife yells "Jed!" or "Ed!" from one end of the house or yard, neither of the summonees discern the absence or presence of a distinguishing consonant sound at the beginning of the bellow. We both come running.

Jed requested—and in fact expects—an outboard motor as an acknowledgment of our joy over the occasion of his 10th birthday, his blue inflatable boat having miraculously returned from the clutches of whoever stole it two months ago. Despite all my customary ruminations and doubts over the wisdom, risk and affordability of such an indulgence, he will get an outboard motor, because I love him, and I trust him, and because I want him to feel such exhilarating liberation as I do when I take my leave of shore.

Of course, in granting this gift, I truly will have inaugurated the process of his eventual separation, his step-by-step attainment of independence. At once wistful and proud, I suppose, my wife and I will watch him pilot his boat away from the dock. I recall watching a pair of swans lead their adolescent cygnets out the mouth of the Narrasketuck Creek. The hen, mother of the youngsters, held back, reluctant to follow her mate eastward while the cygnets swam off to the west. The old man honked brusquely, insisting that they separate from their young. Tough role, the paternal.

I found Jed paging through a copy of one of my favorite volumes Thursday, a cloth-covered gift edition of Peter Matthiesen's *Men's Lives*, containing poetic black-and-white photographs of baymen and commercial fishermen from the East End of Long Island, the Bonackers, including members of the Lester family, men and families I had met, in fact. Jed asked me about a quote from one of the men, who said that he had to go down to the water every day, if only to look it; the salt water was in his blood.

"Are you like that, Dad?" Jed asked. Surprised, I looked at him and answered, "Yeah, Jed. I am."

"I think I am, too," he said quietly, paying me back double for the outboard motor.

Absence Makes the Heart Ache

I cannot recall ever having left home alone, as a child, for any extended period of time. My wife can. For eight weeks each summer, she attended sleep-away camp. She always spoke rapturously about the experience, until I began to erode her euphoria with my infernal opinions, in an attempt to prepare her for a time when she would be the mother of children whose extended absence, I knew, she would not comfortably endure.

I have no guess as to where the knowledge came from, but I simply knew that as a full-time working woman, who continually enjoyed or endured alternating moments of triumph and frustration over the constant juggling of career and family responsibilities, she would lapse into psychological self-flagellation if she were to dispatch her kids to summer camp.

After all, I would; and I am not beguiled, as she is, by wonderfully pleasant memories of the camp experience. Nor am I burdened by ancestral messages obligating me to try to give 100 percent of my energies to both careers. I come from relatively sexist stock, and while I try to remain open to enlightenment and behaviorial alteration, I do not ache about my failures as does the modern American working mother.

However, though I long for even a brief spate of days wherein I am under no obligation to drive children someplace, or observe them performing at some organized activity, or intercept them at a certain time lest they feel abandoned, I cannot abide the notion of sending a young dependent away for longer than an overnight stay with a friend. I suspect I would have considered sleep-away camp a form of banishment, myself, as wholesome as I hear the experience is. As a boy, I wanted to be home whenever I was liberated from school. I wanted to say goodnight to my mother and sleep in my bed, or at least in a bed near the room where she would sleep. I wanted to hang out with my neighborhood friends, even if we were only going to mope about steamy summer lawns, whining that we had nothing to do. (You want something to do? my mother would tease, I'll give you something to do. Clean your room.) I preferred nothing to do to a daily, obligatory appointment at a dusty baseball field, whether I cared to play baseball that day or not.

My 10-year-old son has been on Fire Island for five days with his class from the Maria Montessori School in Seaford. Five days is enough, thank you, and I want him back. I am certain that the experience has been exhilarating, educational and maturing, because any such experience would be, anyway, and also because I am confident that the people who preside over this particular school will make certain of it. They display an institutional affection for a child's sense of wonder, constantly encouraging and nourishing it, while insisting that the child, himself, take responsibility for his own growth. Once, this past winter, the director of the school caught Jed outside his class, standing in the corridor, staring out a window at a slow, windless, heavy, wet snowfall. She approached him from behind, gently rested her hands on his shoulders and said, "Peaceful, isn't it." Together they watched the snowfall for whole minutes before resuming their respective workdays. I am more encouraged and satisfied by the memory of that moment than by all the materials, test scores, evaluations and school shows I have seen, because I know that my sons spend their days with people who appreciate both my sons and their days.

So, I am eager to hear of the wonders of nature on Fire Island, and I am certain that Jed will have been changed by the experience of even so little time as five days away from home. In fact for him, five days probably seems a great deal longer. My memories of vacations with my parents have magically converted four- and five-day trips into what seems like whole summers of time, driving to the Adirondacks, the mountains in upstate New York, visiting such attractions as Ausable Chasm, Fort Ticonderoga, Frontier Town and Santa Claus Village. Perhaps in time, this Fire Island deal will grow similarly in his memory, and I hope it does. But for now, I want him back.

Colleen, my wanderer, was not much older than Jed when she arranged to spend two weeks living with a family in LeBourget, France, as part of a twinning program of cross-visitation between that Paris suburb and the village of Amityville. I was torn in half by my admiration for her courage and independence on the one hand, and my trepidation over her comfort and safety on the other. She over-soothed my discomfort by calling home frequently, collect.

I was 17 when I first left home to spend what turned out to be only one semester in a college in Belmont, North Carolina. My father accompanied me on my first airplane flight, and his, and when the time came for us to bid each other good-bye, I extended my hand for him to shake. He talked about it for decades. He had expected a hug, wanted one, and I broke his heart with my pseudo-adult gesture.

Well, I want a hug, and I'm not accepting any handshake as a substitute.

Meeting May's Challenges

I once looked forward to the month of May. I loved its brightness, its embracing warmth and rich colors. Deprived by some genetic warp of any immunity to spring fever, I spent many of my earliest Mays staring out classroom windows, meditating, wondering what the squirrels were thinking when they halted for 10 seconds between darting leaps and touch-and-go scamperings. In high school and college, my second semester performances always fell short of the mid-year grades, all for the dreamy distractions offered by the month of May.

I never fell in love in May, but I ached to, annually, for years. Once, on a spectacular May day in the distant past, a colleague corrupted my formerly fierce work ethic with a suggestion that still lives in the foyer of my memory as the prologue to a perfectly exhilarating day. He said, Let's skip work, walk around the city and watch the coats come off, and we did.

Somehow, appointments and obligations have stealthily invaded my Mays, like termites who feed on time. Now that I am the father and father-figure to a handful of humans, a veteran of the paragraph manufacturing trade, a senior apprentice at the podium (with nothing of value to say but enough audacity to say it, anyhow) and a scribe under contract to a publisher, my May—formerly my jump-start to a blissful season of sloth—seems to have become less and less mine.

Both Jed and Danny elected to attend a baseball clinic for the first two weeks of May, offered by their physical education teacher at the only hour of the day convenient to his schedule and theirs: 7 A.M. I know that other people already have completed 15 percent of their daily tasks by 7 A.M., but I am rarely conscious at such an hour, and since the inauguration of the clinic, by midafternoon I feel as if a burglar has invaded my circulatory system and drawn away half its content. Also, the boys' rejuvenated enthusiasm for the sport requires that I ferret out my own glove and play catch whenever the other boys in the neighborhood are eating dinner, completing homework assignments, attending church, or visiting the dentist's office. My throwing arm aches a little, and my ego, too, when I overthrow or undercatch, but I like the duty and accept every invitation, even when I am short on time to finish another assignment, such as a book manuscript which an otherwise unimpassioned editor suddenly wanted in mid-May instead of late June. In fact, I like the whole avalanche of tasks and assignments that have fallen across my path this May, but I am scrambling with increasing enthusiasm to reach a duller month.

My cousin, Mary, with whom I summered for the bulk of my infancy, toddlerhood and adolescence and now see less than once a year, decided this April to marry this May, in the chapel of the University of Virginia, where her husband reigns as a world-class constitutional scholar. Orphaned in her 30s, she bestowed on me the high honor of serving as the father of the bride. I accepted the assignment, though it meant that I would have to relinquish three May days to the trip and, even more nerve-wracking, read aloud a Shakespearean sonnet to a congregation of academics sprinkled with Rhodes scholars, including the groom and best man.

Miraculously, the wedding date wedged itself between longstanding, prior commitments to address gatherings of people whom I fear I could disappoint just as easily by showing up as by forfeiting. They included students of schools, an Intergenerational Conference at the Port Washington Public Library, members of a church organization, a chapter of the American Association of Retired Persons and the Mary P. Myton Literary Society, whose prudent program chairman locked in a luncheon date two Januarys ago.

In the epicenter of this activity, I had to evacuate Colleen from her apartment near the state university campus in Plattsburgh. With speaking engagements on Wednesday and Friday night, I had Thursday to travel and stock the Suburban, and half of Friday to return, shave, shower, dress and appear. I called Colleen to make sure she packed her belongings.

I first reached her a during the throes of an end-of-semester panic attack. Overdue to present a slide show for an independent study course she had all but neglected, she was alternately writhing over a pending linguistics final and wailing about a theater-history exam that required no intellection but plenty of rote memorization, for which she claimed to be dreadfully psychologically unready. She also said her car was ailing and her finances ill-equipped to heal it. I next reached her on Thursday. She had aced the slide presentation, memorized the history of the theater and maybe beat the linguistics test. The car remained a problem and she thought she might have everything packed by the time I arrived.

I told her she ought to learn to schedule her time better.

No More Excuses

Jed asked me to hang something in his room. I didn't know what, yet, but the detail didn't matter. I already was beginning to feel incompetent, neglectful and anxious. He had asked twice before, and I had wormed my way out of the work by suggesting that his timing was bad. I claimed pompously that more important tasks and obligations stood in line ahead of hanging something in his room.

Now, I was trapped. We all had eaten dinner, removed the dishes, cleaned the counter and the table; Jed had finished his homework; Danny was in the den playing his recorder, not interrupting, not distracting any one of us. I had no appointments. Nobody was ringing the doorbell, and the telephone was hanging uncharacteristically mute on the wall. I glared at it, thinking, Sure. Now you're silent. What about when no one's home and I'm in the bathroom?

"Okay pal," I said with fervor in my voice and doom in my mind, "let's go look at this project." I followed him forlornly up the stairs. He showed me a cheap-looking basketball backboard with a orange rim to which he already had attached a white net about five feet long.

In the middle of the backboard, half-concealed by the pro basketball team stickers Danny had randomly pasted over it, was the name of the product: Dirty Dunk. Jed wanted it hanging from his closet door. He would place a laundry basket under the net, and thereafter he and Danny would aim their clothes rather than just fling them with the kind of carefree caprice common to the other inhabitants of the house.

A Nerf ball backboard from two years ago adorned their other closet door. That job had called for minor assembly. The product came accompanied by a little plastic bag containing six, small, wood screws and two door-hanging brackets, which I had to fasten to the backboard's back, using three wood screws for each. I bought an electric screwdriver for the job, charged it for a week or so and eventually draped the bracketed backboard over the door. I admire it triumphantly each time I see it.

The Dirty Dunk backboard evidently had arrived alone, without equipment or instructions. Two plastic holders protruded from its top, each with a large hole in the middle. Apparently knowing me better than I thought he did, Jed raised his brow and his left hand, in which he held for my examination one galvanized roofing nail that he had found.

"Dad?" he said plaintively, as if to suggest that even I might discern a potential relationship between the nail and one of the holes in the plastic backboard holders and the closet door. He then placed the nail in the hole, as if to show me that its wide, flat head would not pass through the hole and therefore might secure the backboard against the door.

I shook my head in disagreement. Even though he had found our hammer, missing lo these recent years, the job would require a second roofing nail. I thought it more likely that I could successfully search the house for two wood screws, unearth an electric hand drill from the garage or the basement (having long since forgotten where I put the electric screwdriver), find one of the stashed extension cords from Christmas, drill two holes and drive the damned backboard into the door, forever.

"Dad, you said a curse," said Danny.

"I'm sorry, Dan."

The search and preparation maneuvers required two trips to the basement and two more to the garage, then one more down to the kitchen for a stepstool. But, in the bottom of a red, wooden tool box that my wife's ex-husband left behind 16 years ago, I had found two used wood screws suitable for my plan. My red plastic case of drill bits contained only one bit, and its delicate diameter would make holes for the passage of screws much more slender than my fat old wood screws, but I determined to press on, anyway, having started the torture and already become angry with myself. Perched atop a kitchen stool, I drilled two tiny holes that were destined to present large problems when I tried to drive the old screws into the holes, while Jed struggled to hold the backboard against door. I pressed the electric drill against the first screw, and for the first eight or nine tries, it slid out of the groove as it began to turn, which elicited involuntary, monosyllabic comments and judgments from me that inspired Danny to interrupt the proceedings with infuriating and humiliating frequency.

"Dad, you said another curse."

"I'm sorry, Dan."

Shirt soaked, perspiration dripping onto the lenses of my glasses, teeth clenched, I drilled and slipped, drilled and slipped, widening the grooves in the screws and warping the head of the driving bit, until the screws were mostly in and I had apologized four more times to Danny.

"Jed," I said. "I'm sorry. I don't do this well. Other dads do this. You want me to make a paragraph for you, invent a rhyme, play a song, draw a cartoon, sing, recite, all kinds of useless entertainment, I'm yours. This, I'm no good at."

I swear: he placed his hand on my arm and said, "Thanks, Dad."

The stupid backboard works, too.

Dates Got Away

I need a better calendar in my head; or I need to carry a calendar in my pocket; or I need calendrical surgery on whichever quadrant of my brain is in the business of filing dates, collating them and holding them up in front of my face, whenever I am about to agree to appear at two places at the same time.

I know my own birthday, but twice in my life, on that occasion, a relative has surprised me with the information that it was my birthday, because I didn't know what date it was at the time. I have been extraordinarily fortunate with most of the birthdays I am supposed to have committed to memory, in that they are so numerologically memorable. My mother and my mother-in-law were born on one-twenty. Repeating the coincidence to hundreds of uninterested people has branded the date on my brain. My oldest child, the very pregnant T.C., entered the earth's atmosphere on seven-seven; Colleen followed thirteen months later on eight-eight; Jed was born on four-twenty-two (which is close enough to four-four to become safely lodged in my memory next to seven-seven and eight-eight); my wife a month later, on five-two-two; and Danny came within four days of emerging from the womb on eleven-eleven. Somehow I manage to remember that he was born on the fifteenth, instead.

My father-in-law was born in autumn, a long time ago.

Recently, (I don't remember exactly when), I accepted an invitation to attend a luncheon at the Explorer's Club in New York, hosted by my alma mater and designed to present CBS News correspondent Charles Kuralt with the Marist College Lowell Thomas Award for broadcast journalism. I've attended this dignified insurrection annually since the award's inception nine years ago, for no other reason than that the school's president keeps inviting me and I keep being flattered by the attention. The date of this year's luncheon was announced late, because Kuralt never stays in one place very long. The awards committee nearly had to throw a net over him as he blew through town. I had received my presidential letter two weeks before the event saying on what precise date the honoree would get his plaque. Characteristically, I did not pay much attention to the date. Nor did I remember that it bore any resemblance to the date of the last day of school for Danny and Jed; the day of their annual talent show; the day Danny would be awarded a certificate for completing three years of the primary Montessori program and effectively be graduated from kindergarten; the day the boys would be honored for whatever achievements they had forgotten to tell their parents about; the day I was not supposed to miss, especially since I had reached a plateau in my trade where I could dictate my own schedule and not miss such milestones as I missed when my daughters were little.

More stupidly, I continued to not remember the conflicting dates and continued to fail to prepare my family, or myself for that matter, for the felony I had destined myself to commit. One Saturday morning, as a smug, old hand at parenting, I answered the telephone and blithely counseled the mother of a student in Danny's class against feeling guilty for having purchased a costume for the Bumblesnout routine rather than having made one, herself. Like my wife, she was a full-time businesswoman burdened with a genetic predisposition to think she should perform all the details of two full-time occupations at the same time. After I had reassured her and hung up the receiver, the phrase at the same time rattled my memory cells, and I fumbled around the kitchen distractedly for my luncheon letter. I found it and saw that I was scheduled to be at two places at the same time.

In previous years, I ached watching the boys as they so reluctantly appeared on stage at the annual end-of-year festivities. Jed looked terribly shy and lacking in confidence until he was 8 years old. Danny, though not so uncomfortable on stage, seemed distracted and fidgety.

This year, fogged with guilt, I learned from my wife what I had missed. Five-year-old Danny and his heartthrob of three years, Gina Thomas, performed like seasoned stars in the Bumblesnout show (they called it Bumblesnot, of course). He remembered all the lyrics, my wife beamed, and he and Gina, who used to be the little babies, kept it all organized, shepherding the younger players around like parents. Next, at the invitation of the seventh and eighth graders who ran the talent show, Danny, the only participant under 10, performed a recorder solo flawlessly (though he then ran off the stage and refused to reappear, even when begged). And then, said my wife, as I slumped lower into the chair, after Jed won a prize for raising the most money in the jump-rope-a-thon, and Danny won a prize for jumping the most jumps in his class, they announced that only one kid in the school had scored higher than 85 per cent in the President's Physical Fitness program: Jed Lowe.

Well, I shrugged. I feel very proud. And, if it's any comfort, I also feel like an idiot, but a proud idiot.

Lessons in Fragility

With the exception of an introductory explanation, I have tried for 63 consecutive reports on fathering to keep separate the stories I write about my children and myself from the fact that I write them at all; to more or less ignore that I have accepted an unusual side job, sharing details of my family life, plus my paternal prejudices, uncertainties, triumphs and tragedies, with a million people. I lose sleep now and then over the role, frequently wondering how arrogant is a man who suspects that an audience would be remotely interested in his alternating spasms of anger, foolishness, wisdom, impatience, amusement, guilt or heartbreak. Where exactly is the line between true and false humility; or the one that separates a proud father from an insufferable braggart?

Worse: How selfish is a man who regularly makes intimate details of his children's lives as public as a televised fireworks display? Several times during the past two years, I have seriously miscalculated what reaction I might have anticipated from my daughter, Colleen, to my public revelation of such ruts as existed in our relationship. I thought she would feel complimented; she was furious. My sons are young yet, but at 10, Jed already has revealed a keen and delicate sensitivity that I might quickly refashion into a lasting resentment if I am not careful about his rights to privacy. And having chronicled T.C.'s wedding, her subsequent pregnancy and the birth of my grandson, I wrote myself into the responsibility to fashion his obituary, as well.

I realized two days ago, thanks to readers, that I have been avoiding the pregnant T.C., and in a cowardly way.

I received a phone call from one Hillary Buzen, whose daughter and son-in-law were the leading characters in another story I told in May, basically about young people being trapped in circumstances. Her daughter, Stacey, had been married last February to Gary Stapleton. Hoping someday to become an FBI agent, Gary subsequently joined the Marines, attending various training camps and schools until he was assigned to study cryptology in Georgia, where Stacey joined him. She eventually became pregnant with twins. But in April, the Marines gave Gary a medical discharge, because the strapping 24-year-old could not keep his weight below a certain minimum requirement. That left the couple unemployed, completely without health insurance coverage or any hope of getting it, and in a high-risk pregnancy with high costs on the horizon. An outraged Hillary Buzen wrote a letter railing against a world that could so betray her daughter, and I exercised my option to spread her fury around for public examination.

"I don't know exactly why I'm calling you," Hillary said, "but I remember reading about your daughter. I needed to tell you this. I'm the one whose daughter is pregnant with twins and no coverage?"

I said I remembered.

"Well, a week ago Monday, she went into premature labor. She gave birth this past Tuesday, after 22 weeks' gestation. Two tiny infant girls, Lauren and Ashley, one 10 ounces, one 13½. One died shortly after birth, and the other lasted another 15 minutes. We were fortunate that they let us hold the babies. This was Newton Memorial Hospital. They're so sensible, now, letting you hold the babies, touch them, kiss them and say your hellos and good-byes. She was so gentle with them, playing with their little hands, talking about their eyes, about how they must have gotten their big feet from their father's side. It gave you a chance for the babies to be real.

"Your kids continually surprise you with how mature they are," she said, bringing to the surface vivid memories of awe and admiration at my own daughter's behavior last spring when her infant was dying. "At one point," Hillary said. "Tracey and I walked down the hall and were looking through the windows into the nursery. Another couple was there, and they said, 'Oh, which one is your baby?' I turned away with a lump in my throat the size of an apple, and I heard her say, 'Oh, none of them are mine. I just like to visit the nursery to look at all the babies.' It amazed me that she thought to protect this couple from feeling awkward." She paused. I told her I knew how she felt.

"It still comes in waves, every now and then," I said, evidently summoning one, so that I paused, becoming strangely connected to this person I had not seen and might never meet. We chatted for a while and I hung up and opened the first piece of mail for the day, from a woman in Centerport.

"Dear Ed: A follow up on my note in December thanking you for your column about T.C. and Bill's coming baby. I spoke of how my son, Goeff, and his wife, Donna, had also lost a baby last year and were expecting again. Their son, Brian James, arrived June 17 at 9 pounds, 5 ounces and healthy healthy healthy. You were right, the rejoicing over this birth was stupendous because we all realized how fragile life is. I now await with confidence the birth of your grandchild."

Grateful, I folded the note. I last saw T.C. on Father's Day. I squirmed uneasily until we parted ways, I guess because I'm scared.

An Uneasy Membership

Membership and I have not coexisted comfortably for many years. I am ever uneasy when someone officially lists me as a member of an organization, group, committee, church, party, gender or race. When circumstances have required my adult membership, I have tried almost consciously to not be a very good member, nor a very obedient member, nor a member always respectful of the requirements and ceremonies charted in the constitutions, by-laws and canons of memberships. Obnoxious though I suspect I am for it, I try to be just another member, unenthusiastically compliant, mainly invisible. I never identify myself as a member unless someone pries the information from me, and then I squirm during my confession. Lapel pins, flags, bumper stickers and decals are not my style.

The origin of this visceral antipathy eludes me, though I can trace several possibilities. A baptized Catholic, I attended public schools until seventh grade and returned home daily to a neighborhood populated largely by students of St. Martin of Tours Catholic School. Until third or fourth grade, I could not shake the thought that I was a Public, they were real Catholics. I considered my required weekly attendance at Sunday School a partly remedial, partly punitive program to reshape me so that I would become worthy of a promotion to whatever level they had achieved. Also, as a boy—an only child at that—I was quickest on the block to organize secret clubs and societies and install myself as president and chief of them. Following that, I was a Cub Scout for a year, a Boy Scout for 10 minutes and, as a teen, a member of a junior division of the Knights of Columbus, called the Squires.

If I were thus obsessed by the notion of belonging, as opposed to not belonging, the obsession must have matured into its diametric opposite. Membership for me became a subtle, passive form of committing the ostracism I may have inferred as a child. I became aware that by declaring myself a member, I simultaneously declared my nonmember neighbor separate from me—outside my new circle, unentitled, less privileged, less different, perhaps intolerably different.

Where the word "exclusive" once had glistened with meanings like special, blessed and chosen, its definition had rolled over in my brain and displayed a bellyful of unflattering opposites, like elitist, arrogant, separatist and cruel. In my religion, I had learned that if I behaved nobly and lived an exemplary life, my immortal soul would go to Heaven. My nonmember neighbor could follow my steps precisely, and his soul would not make it much past Elmira. Why? Somehow, by signing the application, taking the oath or paying the annual dues, I was always making a statement I did not believe and did not wish to make.

My daughters seemed at one time infected with my outsider's contagion. I vaguely recall a high school sorority initiation, known to be a playfully humiliating exercise, wherein the initiating members demanded behavior of pledge T.C. Lowe that evidently crossed over the personal line T.C. had drawn between playfully and genuinely humiliating. She refused to comply, and was, of course, threatened with expulsion from the applicant roster. She responded to the threat with a defiant, if melodramatic, resignation, and stormed off. In support, her younger sister, Colleen, who had completed her rites earlier that evening, followed suit instantly, abdicating forever whatever benefits membership offered. I viewed both gestures with titanic pride and said so, and they have not been good members of anything since. So, I wonder.

I also grew up—summers, anyway—within earshot of the joyous howls of a bayfront yacht club, with a huge, freshwater pool, a restaurant facility on the bay, a docking facility across the bay, and therefore a nearly private, oceanfront beach on the barrier island; plus a swim team, an elaborate program for swimming lessons, sailing lessons and safe-boating instructions. Many friends and acquaintances of mine from public school enjoyed their family memberships in the yacht club, but not my friends from the neighborhood, nor anybody I knew who was a parishioner of St. Martin's. That changed over the next 35 years, and eventually, after my sons were born; and I could afford it, I could articulate no convincing reason to deprive my family of the facilities, let alone the company of a host of fine people and great kids. So, despite my uncontrollable uneasiness, I applied to and joined the yacht club.

The value of this membership to my boys has been incalculable, especially considering the geography surrounding them. They are happy, active and confident; they have great friends, a sense of community, a special place where they feel welcome, and they have my club credit at the snack bar. I hope, however, that as they grow, they realize that their privilege makes them only luckier than nonmembers, not better.

Get It All Out

Parenthood inspires the oddest meditations. I am presently thinking about throwing up. I'm not planning on it, just wondering how those of us who have developed a confident expertise in the enterprise learned our technique, and whether we can articulate a method to our children.

I also wonder why such soul-gripping panic seizes certain people, and not others, when a mildly feverish, suddenly pallid child announces to his or her household that he or she, too, is thinking about throwing up. I have heard tales of adults leaping from unconsciousness, catapulting themselves into aimless fits, sprinting around a house like a horsefly caught between storm windows, knocking over lanterns and stumbling into closets, all because a 5-year-old meekly heralded his coming explosions. Presumably, the fits are inspired by fears of the uncontrollable soiling of the furnishings, which is exactly what happens while the parent is distracted in seizure.

On the other hand, I know a mother who does not panic at all at such announcements, but instead tries to reason with the stricken child, saying, "You ran down the hallway past two bathrooms to stand in my wall-to-wall carpeting and tell me you're going to throw up?"

One of my own four—I don't remember which—once launched into projectile vomiting as an infant. I had not witnessed that phenomenon before and could conjure no rational idea about what I should do to help the baby, except to sweep it up from behind and aim it, like a mortar, away from the piano, the rugs and furniture, and at tilework instead. I did the child absolutely no benefit, but I saved the couch. I later met a mother whose instincts drove her in an opposite direction from mine. In the same, startling crisis, she approached her baby face-to-face. She thus rendered herself just as unable to help her baby as I was mine, but much more likely to share the unfortunate consequences of his attack, which she did.

The initial experience of regurgitating must be absolutely terrifying to a young apprentice, especially one who has evaded stomach viruses long enough to be deceived about such control as he has over his body.

I for some reason can recall shaking in fear after an early childhood eruption, totally perplexed about how whatever had just happened had happened, and whether I had lost important parts; if I were about to blow up, or die, and, finally, if God or his counterpart had chosen to punish me with horror.

I recall that my mother exhibited a presence of mind about the experience that, over time and subsequent viruses, seemed to calm me immeasurably. She merely rubbed my back and reassured me while my insides proceeded with their violent business, as if to suggest that my body knew what it was doing and would finish the effort in due course. Eventually—and I think because of her approach—I became attentive to my system's subtle warnings and able, in most instances, to travel in a timely fashion to an appropriate receptacle and endure my spasms more philosophically.

In the last few days, my older son evidently has played host to a squadron of microscopic, parasitic invaders that raised his body temperature, lowered his eyelids, sapped his strength, erased his enthusiasm and twice threatened (once, successfully) to render his involuntary stomach musculature volcanic.

I thought at first pallor that he had fallen victim to his insistence on remaining active during the recent, homicidal heat wave. By Tuesday, the ambient air outside had gorged itself with water and exhaust fumes, and the sun seemed to be trying to cook the resultant concoction into an atmospheric soup stock. Jed spent the day on active duty at play. The evening before, following a similarly active day in what his air-conditioned, cowering father considered a prelude to hell, Danny had slumped into feverish dullness and seemed incapable of raising a limb. He displayed no other symptoms at all, and after a day of resting and sipping cold water, he re-emerged as the impossibly happy and active maniac he had been previously.

Jed, however, complained that a headache accompanied his feverish listlessness, then quite suddenly arose from the couch, mumbled his intentions and scampered to the bathroom.

I happened to make my appearance at the height of his eruptions and marveled at such natural calm as he brought to the work. After all, he is fairly inexperienced at post-infancy regurgitation. My wife and I could recall only one other intestinal explosion since diapers. As I remember it, he burst into tears when his expulsions were completed. This time, in my helpless sympathy, I managed to recall my mother's ministrations. I rubbed his back and mumbled that everything would be all right, momentarily. Danny watched us in awe, then joined me in my reassurances, saying, "You'll be all right, Jed." In a perverse way, it became a moment I will cherish.

I Can't Wait

My father had a perspective on such agony as waiting inspires, and I try to keep it in at least intellectual focus during periods between anxious anticipation and the relief of arrival. Generally speaking, his viewpoint would fit snugly into the category, Patience, but with a bit more determinism than the virtue's name implies. I would say, "I can't wait," and he would say, "Yes you can." I would ask, "How do you know?" He would answer, "You have to."

I have been waiting for the arrival of a grandchild, who is due . . . well, now—today, in fact—and as the inevitability of arrival draws nearer, and my nerve endings further distance themselves from such authority as my brain holds over them, I try different approaches to this most passive, non-activity of waiting. None of them have worked.

In the qualified euphoria following T.C.'s announcement of pregnancy, I managed most of the time to ignore the fact. Still reeling from the death of her first infant, and absolutely unable to influence the relative health of the pending person, it seemed most comforting at the time to simply not think about the range of possibilities between joy and heartbreak, so I didn't. I also didn't talk to her very much, as if to evade any reminders, and I accelerated that cruelty as her condition became more obvious. I ducked her, visited as infrequently as possible, received her telephone calls, but never made them, even excused myself early from a visit.

Alone, in the car or on the boat, I contemplated my felonies and determined that it is as painful and difficult as it is stupid to strain so not to think about somebody you love. Moreover, the resultant remorse lingers like the taste of gasoline. Cowardice must require more effort than courage, because I finally got so tired of myself, I began calling her every other day, always apologizing, first, for being a bother. She said I wasn't. I apologized, anyway.

Four weeks ago, I tried to adopt a reminiscent view of The Wait, recalling pregnancies and births from my past. It was a counterproductive exercise, because T.C., herself, my first child, chose to linger in the comfort of the womb for two extra weeks. Danny was 12 days late; Jed arrived on time and Colleen required chemical inspiration. I already knew of babies who were so eager to get out onto the planet and boogie, they gasped their first atmospheric lungful two weeks earlier than predicted. That left me with an over-under possibility for intense, moment-to-moment anxiety that encompassed a whole month.

My traditional remedy for such denture-grinding periods of my history is to escape to the bay, steer the boat between the emerald wetland islands and then stop and surround myself with solitude. In order to be comfortable with that sort of escapist pleasure, now, I would have to buy a portable telephone. Yet the very foundation of my restorative ecstasy is the absence of a telephone, the pure luxury of being unreachable. So, my comfort is no comfort.

Worse, as the anxiety intensifies individually, so does the

cumulative tension in the concentric circles of people in the family, even machinery. On Sunday, for instance, I thought my neurological system was going to blow a circuit. First, the air conditioner stopped conditioning the air. Once possessed of such righteousness that I considered air-conditioning an obscenely wasteful luxury, I have now lived in conditioned air long enough to require it in order to keep my sarcasm at bay.

My friend and air-conditioning wizard, Jim Connell, arrived just after my mother, who pulled into the driveway with her muffler bouncing from the underbelly of her car. Connell was at the front door, my mother at the back, shaking and nervous because she had promised to take a friend to a concert and now feared arrest or explosion, or something. Just then, Jed, Danny and their similarly animal-mad friend, Eammon, ran into the house screaming with excitement and delight that they had found and captured a beast of some species, which Danny was holding in the palm of his 5-year-old, right hand.

It was a toad. I did not want a toad in the house, let alone one whose captivity rested literally in the hand of Daniel Lowe, and I made my wish known too emphatically, judging by Danny's forlorn expression. Jed followed with another toad, and with Connell waiting patiently at the door, I repeated my admonitions, somehow managing not to scream them. I grew up in the same backyards as they and never once saw a toad nor entertained any desire to see or touch one, let alone room with him. I kept no rodents nor amphibians as a boy, yet they have, on Jed's dresser, in a menagerie of boxes, tanks and cages, four snails, three toads, one fire newt, two African frogs and a rabbit, to which Danny added a baby shrimp that he caught and housed in a plastic sandwich bag filled with salt water.

I escorted Connell to the basement and hid there while he discovered that the air conditioner's lines were frozen. I volunteered to stay down there and watch them melt.

A New Life

Shannon Marie, welcome to the world.
World, meet Shannon Marie, my granddaughter.
T.C. called at about 6:15 A.M. Tuesday, three days after her

due date. Nobody calls our house at 6:15 A.M. with good news. Because of my wife's job as a newspaper editor, the caller usually is announcing the death of a world-renowned movie star or a president or a pope. Otherwise, it's my mother, announcing the death of a relative.

The telephone is not on my side of the bed, so I could only eavesdrop, and then on only half of a conversation. Somehow, despite the cobwebs of early consciousness, I knew or thought I knew this caller was either my daughter or my ex-wife, who is T.C.'s mother and was to be her Lamaze coach. T.C. had made it quite clear she wanted as much family as possible near her for this birth.

I learned an hour later that T.C. also had telephoned her husband Bill's parents, his sister and brother-in-law and my mother, all of whom gathered that morning at the hospital. She had been awake and in labor since about 12:30 A.M., and her contractions were now in the neighborhood of three to four minutes apart.

I heard my wife say, "Oh, no!" into the telephone and thought my heart might stop, but the rest of her half of the conversation bore no further alarming intonations. I still don't know what the "Oh, no!" was all about, and I don't care. When I heard her repeat that T.C. and Bill were to meet their doctor at 7 A.M. at Good Samaritan Hospital, I simply rose and headed for the bathroom to shave and shower, thinking with each step of the four previous times I had repeated this same ritual this same way—without comment, almost as if I were mute.

Anxiety had pretty much taken over my system, and I must have decided I would ride out the period by taking care of details and keeping my mouth shut. Some part of my brain noticed the fundamental difference between the way my wife and I handled the same feelings—she talked nonstop—and I resolved to let myself laugh at the scene as soon as I felt relaxed enough to let go. Stupid thoughts bubbled up in my brain. For instance, I noticed the date on my watch—8:13—and recalled that eight-thirteen was T.C.'s birth weight, 23 years ago.

When I hear myself telling the story of that morning, I am aware also of the difference between enduring an event locked in time and recalling it in retrospect. We sat around a table in the hospital coffee shop for what then felt like days, and now seems so momentary. Incidents that felt disastrous at the time now float about my memory as comedic. We arrived at the hospital at 7:10. Bill waited in an upstairs waiting room, and at 10:01 we heard his name over the public-address system, evidently being paged by somebody who didn't know he was up there. We scurried to the receptionist, who didn't know if the call for Bill came from inside the hospital or out, but, the receptionist said, "They wanted him to see the baby." We said, "Is there a baby?" and the receptionist answered that she could not give us any information. We all spent the next 10 minutes poised somewhere between intense anxiety and certain madness, until the elevator door opened and Bill emerged with a shy grin and his arms opened for his mother. "It's a girl," he said. "She's fine. T.C.'s fine; everything is fine." Within minutes, the five or six public telephones in the lobby sounded like Las Vegas slot machines. The relief was colossal. I could feel nerves and muscles rattling in my forearms.

Hospitals have changed wonderfully since T.C. was born, when a doctor who had directed me to go home and wait finally telephoned four hours later and told me I was the father of a girl. I would be allowed to see my wife and my daughter in another three hours, he said. Three days passed before I touched T.C.

Shannon was born at 10 A.M. and placed in her mother's arms immediately. We all were looking at her at 10:20, the whole posse. By that time, we knew she weighed 7 pounds, 15 ounces, was 20½ inches long, had a headful of dark hair and no bruises, no blemishes and no heart problems. Twenty-four hours later, during a generous grandparents' visiting time, I held Shannon in my arms and talked her into swallowing an ounce of formula. Later that day, at a siblings' visiting period, my boys saw Shannon, introducing themselves as Uncle Danny and Uncle Jed. Twenty-four hours after that, she and her family were home.

Not wanting to be a bother, I waited until Saturday evening to visit the house. My wife and I intended to stay just a short while and then go out to dinner. I fed Shannon some of the tiny bottle, placed her belly down on the left side of my chest, reclined on the couch and remained there for three solid, blissful hours, in some vaguely familiar yet still new kind of trance; listening to her breathe, feeling her heartbeat, touching her fingers, stroking her hair, inhaling her sweet aroma and just allowing myself to fall hopelessly and eternally in love.

Forced into Roughing It

Anticipating the last gasp of summer, my son, Jed, for weeks had been pleading with his mother to convince me to spend a night across the bay at the barrier beach, camping out on the boat. I didn't know about his pleas, of course, until the eve of the last gasp of summer. My ignorance represented a tactical genius mutual to Jed and his mother. They know I don't camp out; they plotted secretly.

I used to enjoy sleeping overnight at the barrier beach on a boat. During the decade ending in 1987, we always owned one kind of cabin boat or another; first, an old wooden boat whose roof leaked; then, a 35-foot, fiberglass houseboat with a disappearing reverse gear and finally a classic, Egg Harbor sedan, which I later converted into tuition payments. My girls were 8 and 9 when we launched ourselves into boating vacations, and when they didn't feel trapped by the limitations, they seemed to delight in both the endless, night-and-day beach life and the ironically tenement-like society along the dock at West Gilgo Beach.

There exists a pattern among families of Long Island's South Shore, who already have revealed their weakness for the romantic allure of the saltwater by living there in the first place, to start out boating modestly, with a small boat. Realizing after a season or two the options that smallness does not offer, they then buy up, procuring a larger boat, perhaps with a V-bunk and maybe a head, or toilet. Ever discovering new inconveniences, they buy up, again, eventually approaching the fine line between convenience and luxury, and, finally, crossing it. They buy up to a level that costs too much, takes too long to get started and requires extensive care, study, prudence and a sort of renaissance mechanical knowledge, not to mention dexterity, patience and perseverance. I fell headlong into the pattern, up to but excluding knowledge, patience, prudence and perseverance.

The last and inevitable stage of the pattern requires selling the expensive albatross at a hefty loss and settling into a small and simple outboard motorboat that offers no comforts save speed of travel—no bunks, no toilet facilities, no cushions. I did that, too.

My boat has a canvas dodger at the bow, a collapsible, reinforced, cloth structure that, when raised, resembles in shape the canopy that might have sheltered the occupants of a turn-of-the-century horse and buggy. Viewing the dodger as a potential tent, Jed figured that he and I could sleep comfortably within its protection and spend the night under whatever weather the atmosphere offered. If I were 10 years old, I might have viewed the dodger similarly, but I am older and have slept many more nights in comfort than he. So I meditated, first, about the floor of the boat. Fiberglass over wood, it is unmercifully hard. Moreover, the floor space provided beneath the dodger would require a forced fetalization of my frame. Even then, my feet would likely sleep outside the canvas.

I had started to say I didn't think it was such a good idea, when mother and son looked at me as if it, The Plan, already were a fact, which it was. My wife had arranged to drive with Danny to South Jersey to see her new grandniece, leaving me and Jed, I had thought, to our own imaginative devices. Then she and Jed had conspired to preempt any contributions from my imagination. I was booked to take Jed to West Gilgo Beach to camp out on the boat. She had rolled a sleeping bag for Jed and an old comforter for me. She had packed pillows, sandwiches, snacks, towels, warm clothing and Jed's Boogie Board. We were scheduled to head out in our respective directions later that afternoon, the Saturday before Labor Day, to return home Sunday evening.

Feeling strangely surrounded by destiny, and seeing no ripe opportunity to articulate my misgivings, I nodded in passive agreement and packed a small travel bag. After the first contingent departed for Jersey, however, I slyly suggested to Jed that we begin our night of roughing it by smoothing it, first. We would slip away by boat and dine at a waterfront restaurant. He was unhesitant in his approval of the idea. My boy.

We encountered three men during our journey who asked and learned what were our intentions. The first asked, "Did you know that the temperature was going down to 55 tonight?" (I did not.) The second said, "You're gonna sleep in that? Hope you got plenty of extra insect repellent." (I had none.) And the third, after I had tied the boat so that it faced into the brisk breeze from the north, said, "The wind is supposed to pump up to 30 knots tonight. You'll have rollers headed straight at you all night long." (Oh, good.)

While Jed frolicked with his friends, sympathetic boat-owners took note of my forlorn expression and offered bunk space, but I was too cowardly to confess my cowardice to my son. So when the time came, and in a menacingly howling wind, I summoned a mock cheerfulness from deep within my vanity, and we crept together into the refuge of the dodger. Rocked all night as if by Grandmother Nature, we bundled up and slept like babes.

Boys, Pets, Love, Death

I once worried about how I would summon the tenderness and empathy required to seriously escort my children through such cosmic conversations as those that would attempt to explain death and sex. I suspected (accurately, so far) that I would fare better with the former; you could not avoid death, and it required no mysterious technique, nor the embarrassment of disrobing in front of anybody.

But I am learning that a natural distribution of responsibility exists regarding such indescribable complexities, and it should spare me any further anxiety, either in anticipation or regret. Daughters, for instance, begin learning about sex shortly after conception. They keep most of the acquired information to themselves or members of their gender, until they die, and they require no further edification from a father who probably is and will ever remain more ignorant than they.

Sons, in general, never learn very much about sex, but they studiously explore death in the slaughterhouse laboratory of boyhood. They squish, starve, drown or otherwise murder a succession of species samplings, ascending the food chain victim by victim until, as senior adolescents or junior men, they are conscripted by bandits or congressmen and ordered to commit homicide.

As different as I initially thought, and would have wished, my sons to be, I am loathe to admit that they are developing a callously high coefficient of remorse regarding abbreviated life spans, especially of their pets.

I began to notice it this past spring, with Jed's gerbil, Fuzzy, whose purchase, captivity and subsequent in-house liberties I vehemently opposed. Jed had pleaded to own a gerbil, and I had railed against the notion, until Jed escalated the negotiations by inserting the word dog into one of the discussions. He got a gerbil, quick. I admonished him regularly to both take care of the animal (which I cruelly called a rat) and to somehow prevent its periodic prison breaks. A parent more experienced with boys and gerbils had warned us that a liberated rodent was likely to seek the comforting warmth of the backside of the clothes dryer, where it was even more likely to get stuck and die, rendering the laundry room aromatic.

Fuzzy brought Jed and Danny great joy, but for some nasty reason, I ridiculed the little creature at every opportunity. One Thursday night, late, I returned home from a speaking engagement. While preparing myself for bed, I visited the bathroom, where I came upon the late escapee, Fuzzy, drowned in the toilet, its stiffened head bowed, its little front paws pressed together as if in supplication. As a father and a recovering boy, I had mixed feelings about the scene: I was terribly saddened for my son, who, though he didn't know all of it yet, was having a whopper of a bad day; I was, frankly, glad to know exactly where the rodent met his Rodent Maker, so I would not have to search for its cadaver; and, finally, I felt as queasy as guilty about my plans for extracting the carcass and presiding over its hasty funeral, Thursday being garbage night in our neighborhood.

Jed was saddened at the news of Fuzzy's death, but not so saddened as I might have predicted. He now wanted a rabbit. Again, I argued against the adoption. I said, "Divine Providence has liberated us from Jed's little rodent. Must we adopt a large one in response?" My wife heard my protestations, weighed their logic, nodded in agreement and then bought Jumper, a gray-and-white rabbit who lives in a cage in our kitchen, grows fat and less useful, manufactures pungent pellets and survives and survives and survives.

Jumper is singular, however, in his longevity. Most animals who have since entered our house have seen the last of their natural habitat, not to mention their old pals. Danny and our neighbor, Eamonn, recently scoured the entire house for change and re-emerged with enough money in coins to buy three tropical fish and a small heater for a fish tank. They don't own a fish tank, so they employed a more domestic and significantly smaller vessel to accommodate the three fish and the heater, which promptly poached the fish. Danny, Jed and Eamonn also have taken to collecting frogs, which they evidently find under rocks carefully placed in other people's landscaped lawns. Wednesday, I overheard Danny telling his mother what happened to his favorite frog pets. "Dinky and Pinky died," he said blithely. "And Slinky. Now I have Sprinky."

Jed interrupted, admonishing his younger brother: "Ma, Dinky died because Eamonn and Danny kept throwing him from the top bunk."

"Did not!"

"Jed," I interrupted, "how many of your guys have bit the dust?" He thought about it: "Well, Fuzzy. Two frogs. Two fire newts."

"Dan," I interrupted again. "About the fish in the container on the kitchen counter. His face was in the rocks last night, his tail straight up in the air. I thought he had become a plant. What happened?"

"Dead," said Danny, following the proclamation with a warning to me: "And it's not funny!"

Don't Knock the Rocker

My maternal grandmother, Mary (Mamie) Burns Dimond, rocked me to sleep and complained at the same time that my mother was spoiling me.

She complained that her daughter indulged me too generously with bottles of milk, for instance, and she pointed to my early girth as a consequence of that indulgence, even making snide comparisons to the beach-ball silhouette of New York City mayor Fiorello La Guardia.

In later years, she complained that my mother allowed me too much freedom in climbing the wild cherry saplings that congregated in our backyard, one day looking to me like the masts of a score of pirate ships, one day like the boughs of Tarzan's jungle or the trees of Sherwood Forest. Mamie scolded my mother for letting me swing from sapling to sapling, a rubber dagger in my clenched teeth, because I surely would fall and break my spine one day and humiliate the two of them in the emergency ward or the funeral home with my dirty undershorts and holes in the toes of my socks and the knees of my dungarees. She also scolded my mother for letting me read too much, swim too soon and ride my bike too far. But it was Mamie who rocked me to sleep at every opportunity, humming lullabies all the while, eliminating any chance that I might fall asleep on my own.

My earliest memory of falling asleep without somebody rocking whichever piece of furniture accommodated me involves a vivid sensation of my laying on my back with my left leg extended and my right leg apart from the left and folded at the knee. In my frustration at being unable to relax or otherwise abdicate consciousness, I began to allow the knee to sway from left to right, slowly at first and not very perceptibly but then with increasing enthusiasm, until my hips were rising alternately from the surface of the bed and even my head was beginning to sway back and forth. If I maintained this automotive posture at a consistently gentle rate, sort of an idling speed, and for a sufficient period of time, it somehow would become involuntary for a moment and deceive me into feeling that I was being rocked by an outside agitator. I thus would fall asleep.

If, however, I grew impatient, my system would accelerate the motion until the rocking became quite violent in appearance, as if I were struggling to awaken from a horrible nightmare.

Sometimes, the phenomenon merely happened while I slept. I remember my college roommate, Charlie Dunn, early in our roommateship, waking in the middle of the night and flipping on the light switch. He was staring at me in stupefied terror, as if I were about to erupt or grow fangs. I slowly realized that he must have heard and then witnessed my spasmodic, nocturnal rocking. He said that both my knee and my head were slamming against the wall. He worried what the guys next door thought.

My daughters always slept with stuffed animals, period. It worked; it caused nobody else a disturbance, and I think they still employ the method, from time to time, during fits of anxiety.

My youngest, Danny, however, turns out to be spoiled, or conditioned, actually, in much the same way I was, unintentionally but, I fear, permanently.

When Danny was new, his brother, Jed, was 5 years old and opposed to slumber. Jed stayed awake and made sporadic, obnoxious noises, sometimes using his voice, sometimes using projectiles, sometimes using battery-powered toys. In order to calm the infant Danny without insulting the ego of brother Jed, we parents conspired to introduce a distracting noise for Danny, the consistent and gentle hum of an electric fan placed near his head. No conspiracy ever worked better. No matter what the weather, we placed Danny in his bed, read him a story, cooed, kissed and eventually left him in the company of a 22-inch fan that caressed his hair and whirred him off to unconsciousness. In summer or winter, Danny dozed to the steady hum of an electric fan.

The resumption of the school schedule inspired more discipline in our normally relaxed household, and we parents have lately been insisting that the boys go to sleep in their own beds, in their own rooms and at a certain time, almost the same time every night. Danny insisted on the fan, of course, and we complied.

Danny tends to rise in the middle of the night, wander a bit and take up residence next to me, a nocturnal habit I have failed to discourage both because my powers are dimmed at 3 A.M. and because I like his company. But now he has added a new dimension. Thursday, at around 3 A.M., I half-awakened to the vague form of a small boy carrying a large fan in the dark. He placed it atop a stool next to my head, plugged it in and turned its dial to the high setting. He then snuggled next to me, so that we both faced a loud gale. By daybreak, my eyebrows were flattened against my forehead and my neck and shoulders ached. Danny seemed perfectly rested.

I know he's only 5, but someday a spouse is going to curse me for this.

The Dog Ate My Son's Homework

At our first parent-teacher conference of the year, we learned that Danny had experienced some difficulty meeting his homework obligations. Eyes turned directly to me.

I hated homework.

Around the time I first became old enough to be sentenced to homework, many of the fathers of kids I knew worked part-time. After they finished work, they would start work. I considered part-time work unfair. I considered homework part-time work, and unfair. I did not avoid homework at all costs. I avoided it, but

I often weighed the costs before determining what course of inaction I might take.

In junior high school, pages of science and math homework assignments began to slide out from my notebooks in the mornings, on the way to school. Wouldn't you know it: My careless and hurried colleagues inadvertently trampled many of them, in some cases beyond recognition; in some cases, enough to disguise the results entirely, though not the effort, nor the noble intent.

How confusing life must be for the child of a man who remembers not only that he hated homework, but how much he hated it, how he got out of doing it when he could, and what delightful distractions he found preferable to homework.

Poor Danny, my first grader. His place as youngest in the family forces him to conjure new tricks to put off his homework, new approaches, new tactics, new lies, all in the face of nearly insurmountable odds.

The boy does try.

We began the academic year with a new babysitter, Peggy. We asked Peggy to persuade the boys to come in from play at a certain hour so they could begin their homework. Jed complied without argument, at least to the extent that he left the field of play and entered the house. Jed's Zen-like preparation ritual for homework requires slinking down and slouching in a chair, hoping his body eventually blends with the furnishings, so his self disappears. He hasn't gone all the way, yet, but he escaped my conscious memory twice before I realized that he was not working.

Danny took an approach uncommonly direct, at least for my children. To Peggy's careful instructions to go home and begin the work, he answered, "No," and resumed play. In response to her subsequent, gentle prodding, Danny said, "No," again. Unsure of her authority (it was her first day), Peggy returned with Jed to the house and told me of the incident when I arrived 15 minutes later.

I roared authoritatively down the street in my truck, confronted the boy and intoned in my deepest, most serious voice, "You. Go home, now." His face contorted immediately. "Why?" he squeaked, as if insulted by the surprise. "Because you were supposed to go home to do homework, and when Peggy told you what time it was and asked you to go home, you said, 'No.' Now, go home."

Face turning to mud, he cried, "But I didn't hear her!" with a high, plaintive, dripping-with-sincerity emphasis on "hear." I did not buy it.

Within a day, he had a new tactic. His mother entered the house, greeted the occupants and asked, "Danny, how was your day? Did you finish your homework?" Danny answered, "Fine," for the day's evaluation and "Yes," for the homework, a truth and a lie.

The following week, he employed yet a new ruse. In a heavy rain, he came home a half hour before the appointed homework-inauguration hour, picked up the telephone receiver and began calling his neighborhood friends, acquaintances, associates and accomplices. He managed to successfully invite two of them over for a leisurely evening, some card games, perhaps, and an after-dinner juice box. When I arrived home, Jed was working on his homework and Danny and two pals were roller blading from the kitchen through the living room and back into the kitchen, again. In order to enforce the homework rule, I would have to eject the guests, banishing them to a rainy walk home, or drive them, myself. Wearing a knowing grin, Danny played happily until a parent called and picked up our guests.

Recently, stuck at home with his unforgiving Dad, again, Danny complained that he couldn't do the spelling homework. It looked simple enough: Write the vocabulary words in the spaces. They all contained *a*'s, he whined. He hadn't gotten to *a*'s in handwriting, yet. After examining his handwriting workbook, I almost yielded, but I told him to print the words, instead. He cried. I felt bad, for a while.

Last week, at his parent-teacher conference, we learned that Danny had been remanded to Room 4 that very day, for failing to turn in three days' worth of homework. He had tried every excuse, but his teacher simply insisted that he complete his homework, and in another room. She chose Room 4, Jed's classroom. Danny wailed, she said. He was mortified; tried, convicted and sentenced. Humiliated. He was banished, exiled.

"I don't think we'll have this problem, again," his teacher said.

I do.

Ball Return

Last week, with soccer season in full swing and Halloween scant days away, it seemed only natural for one of my boys to mention that, should anyone of our acquaintance be confronted with a seasonal dilemma in the not-too-distant future, a soccer ball probably would make a particularly appreciated Christmas gift. It seemed equally natural for the second son to second the first son's suggestion, and with doubled enthusiasm. That meant two soccer balls.

Miraculously, I managed to run my emotional reaction through my brain before letting it escape, a trick I wish I could perform all the time, or even frequently, or even at will. First, I strained to ignore the preposterous timing of the suggestion. It appeared to have advanced Halloween, which I secretly had considered to be the last day of summer, to a new, temporal benchmark status: Christmas Season Eve.

I also swallowed the temptation to inquire as to the disposition and/or fate of past soccer balls. I knew that I had provided Danny with, maybe, three soccer balls in his not-yet-6 years; and I knew that I probably didn't buy him any soccer balls until after he was 2 years old. I knew that I had bought Jed at least three soccer balls—maybe five—in his lifetime, three of them in the last three years. So, would it have been persnickety of me to require a full biography of just one, including cause-of-death and place-of-interment, before I trudged off to buy yet another, let alone, yet another?

Normally, I would have asked. Instead, I calculated the possible cost of two soccer balls—even designer soccer balls, if they existed—and I compared that to the cost of Christmas gifts of years past. The inflatable boat bobbed to mind, followed by the loan I floated the following year to finance the outboard motor. A skateboard whizzed past my recent memory, its price exceeding by $40 my first week's take-home pay as a junior high school English teacher.

I ate my consternation on the spot. I even cackled a bit, while I gleefully told the boys that, this year, soccer balls sounded like a great request for Christmas presents, and a timely one, too, considering their stellar performances on the fields of play. In high melodrama, I promised to consider honoring their request.

I thanked them for their forthrightness. I called them brilliant. They beamed with pride. I beamed, with smug, miserly, self-satisfaction.

Two days later, wracked with anticipatory shame, I spent $28 on two soccer balls and gave them away as I entered the kitchen door, during homework time, which I disrupted.

I knew right away that I was making an indulgent mistake, but I also knew that I was to be home alone with them this night until late. Aware that the consequences of my foolishness would be mostly mine, I forgave myself on the spot. I do that well, and often. I have to.

For the hour and a half the boys would have to themselves between a slightly late dinner and a slightly early bedtime, I repaired to my basement lair and left the boys to watch television above me, in the den. They, of course, played soccer in the den. I had to bound up the stairs three times with mock consternation before I was convinced that they could commit outdoor play indoors without harming much of value. After I heard the fireplace equipment topple with a handsome clamor, I could not think of any similarly endangered apparatus and so concentrated on my private leisure while they played, until I heard Danny's anguished screams.

I always am truly angry the fourth time I bound up a staircase, no matter what the reason, and so I fail to filter my emotions through my brain before I act. Danny was holding his soccer ball and wailing some awful dirge about Jed having thrown the ball and hit him in his back. Without thinking (of course) I took the ball, rounded the hallway, spied the alleged culprit and flipped the soccer ball into his chest. He fell down, grimacing and near tears, this fleet, consistently scoring, 10-year-old athlete, who limps back into tight games after being slammed to the ground and stomped on.

I retrieved the ball and ordered them both upstairs. I was angry with myself, but I didn't know it, yet. I should not have let them play indoors. I should have not have stayed downstairs. I shouldn't have given them the soccer balls. "Why do you two turn everything into a weapon?" I howled. "Why are you always trying to hurt each other?"

Becoming increasingly aware that I was out of control, I nonetheless yelled at Jed directly: "Do you know what it feels like to be hit . . ." Feeling stupid, I stopped. ". . . of course you know, dammit, I just hit you with it." Frustrated, I threw the soccer ball at the stairs in front of me. It bounced back, fast, hitting me in the face. Feeling more stupid, even ridiculous, I said, "Now I know how it feels, too." Now, feeling as if my pants had fallen down during a speech, I added, "I also know how it feels to make an idiot out of myself. What do you think of that?"

They were not amused, yet.

Party Line

A simple evening faced me one night this week; a quiet, throw-pillow of an evening. I and my sons would occupy the house from homework to bedtime, no additional personnel. My responsibilities were minimal and rote: Check homework; boil spaghetti; dice some leftover meat and toss it into the Ragu for texture; empty, refill and start the dishwasher, play Chinese checkers, preside over the boys' nocturnal ablutions, luxuriate for two hours in quiet solitude and, finally, watch the news and retire.

I thought Jed, especially, would like finding in his spaghetti chunks of Danish ham left over from my granddaughter's christening party Sunday, but he did not. He said he didn't like ham, period. Was I supposed to have known that? Why didn't I?

I told both boys then to sit at the kitchen table and not even think about taking their plates into the den and sitting on the floor, watching Nickelodeon. I then sat at the kitchen table alone and read the mail and the newsweeklies in peace, while the boys dined on the floor in the den, watching Nickelodeon. I thought about insisting that they comply with my directives, but they seemed content, and I felt content. As long as nobody spilled food on the rug in the den, what was the harm in their noncompliance?

After dinner, Jed and Danny both forgot to bring their plates to the kitchen sink, and I forgot to remind them. Next, Jed forgot that the plates were still on the den floor at the exact same time he also forgot he was not allowed to dribble a basketball in the den. He remembered after he had flipped a plate. I hated that.

With 45 minutes to go before bedtime, Danny perched himself in an oddly businesslike attitude at the kitchen counter and began writing letters on a piece of paper and mumbling names as he worked. I peeked over his shoulder after 10 minutes or so and made out, "frum danny," followed by "km1, em2, rm3, kk4," and a succession of similarly paired initials followed by numerals up to 8 or 9. I asked what he was doing. He answered with high-pitched, smiling innocence, as if I were teasing him, as if I were trying to pretend to be a blockhead who did not know that he was making a list of friends to invite to his sixth birthday party the next day. "K-M: Kevin McCarthy," he said. "E-M, Eamonn McLoughlin; R-M: Ryan McDonough; K-M: Katy Kretz . . ."

I nodded. "So, that's what you're writing!" I cheered, smiling warmly, frozen with secret terror. Could the next day be Danny's birthday? It was November. I scanned the kitchen for some sign of the date. "Your watch, idiot!" a voice in my brain said. I looked at my watch. My brain kept talking. "Weren't you supposed to stop and pick up a skateboard earlier this afternoon? How could you forget this boy's birthday?"

"I didn't forget it," I said aloud. "I just forgot what date today is. It can't be the middle of November!" Danny looked at me, as if I were talking to myself. "Tomorrow's not your birthday, Dan," I said, staring at my watch. "It's the next day. Friday." Nice recovery. Skateboard for breakfast tomorrow? And what party, anyway?

"Dan, about this party? Mommy didn't mention it. Is it different from the skating rink deal? Does Mommy know about this party?" I knew a debate had raged for months. We owed Jed a party since April, mainly because we couldn't agree in time on choice of weapons and battlefield and decided to have a double party around Danny's birthday. Jed wanted to host a sleep-over party with, say, 14 friends. We said we would rather drown, or pay for a skating rink party. He cut the sleep-over to a half dozen guests, and we said we would think about it. Months passed. November appeared out of nowhere, and here we were again.

Clever Danny. He declined an offer of a few berths for guests of his own at Jed's sleep-over; said he would endure Jed's friends alone. Of course, Danny's friends are not yet allowed to attend sleep-over parties. Plus, Jed's friends are the big guys, and Danny would have the run of them. Plus, by being so generous, Danny could insist on his own party.

"I'm having my own party. Eight friends. Maybe nine," he

said. I saw that Danny had gathered envelopes. He asked me to spell out each child's name and the words, "It's a birthday party." I helped prepare each of the nine envelopes for him, drawing lines next to From: and To: and printing messages for him to copy. He wrote, "It's a birthday," on the envelopes, but no date nor time, which satisfied me. Jed poked his face into the work, declared Danny's message stupid for its brevity and offered the infuriating suggestion that Danny extend the message to include both the undetermined, temporal details and "Happy Birthday," and "Wouldn't you like to come over?" All this to be painstakingly written on eight envelopes with 10 minutes left before bedtime. I whisked Jed out of the room, pronto.

After they were asleep, I checked Danny's little pile of envelopes. Instead of an invitation, each contained a tiny car, one of his cherished Micro Machines, a gift for his guests. Nice boy.

One on One with Teacher

Always in my past—and not for any reason I can recall or conjure—parent-teacher conferences remained wholly within the jurisdiction of the mother.

My own mother, who annually lapsed into rhapsodic reverie about her mother's performances at these autumnal summits, presided over mine whether accompanied by my father, as she often was, or unaccompanied. It was she who kept the schedule heralding parent-teacher night, and she who set aside all other recreations to attend, and she who, alone or with my father, introduced herself to the teacher, wearing the frozen smile of the politician awaiting the decision on his rumored indictment.

(Throughout my elementary school career, I must boast, my mother's inquiries always elicited polite pleasantries, at worst, and even some praise, on occasion. However, after I entered the catastrophic period of hormonal metamorphosis, during which I sprouted fangs, facial hair and An Attitude, parent-teacher conference night inspired in the poor woman the same anticipatory mood as would, say, a parole board hearing. When she introduced herself in those days, her smile jammed in first gear and limped along, straining and uncertain and probably somewhat jerky. Her head would fall plaintively toward her right shoulder, and her brow would ascend, so that the teacher could justifiably infer her nonverbal message as, "Hi. I'm Mrs. Lowe, Eddie's mother. So, I'm sorry, as you might well guess. You must be a very patient person. Are you the one he calls 'The Rodent?'").

I realized only recently—Tuesday evening, to be exact—how loyal I have been to the family tradition of passively relegating the parent-teacher-conference responsibility to the mother. Tuesday night was parent-teacher conference night, and the mother was not going to make it home from work in time, despite the fervor of my wishes. I was to meet the boys' teachers alone. By myself.

I was neither afraid nor intimidated; just new at soloing and, thus, a tad awkward. I likely would have little to say, I thought, and that made me fear the silences. On all previous occasions, with the daughters and with the sons, with the daughters' mother and with the sons' mother, I accompanied, mainly. I followed behind, opened doors, helped with chairs, held papers, produced a pen, if necessary, and offered weak, comic relief during errant lulls in the mother-teacher conversation. When the precise moment hit, I signaled our intent to depart by gently slapping my hands on my thighs, as if reluctant to leave but convinced that if I were to tarry another second, folded semi-fetally into the undersized, plastic chair, the delay would cripple me for life. Later, in the car, the mother (the mother of the girls, in those days, and later, the mother of the boys) would ask, "Well, what did you think?" or "How do you feel?" and I would answer, sometimes at insufferable length. But during the conference, I would remain mute.

Custom in the boys' Montessori school called for the conference to open with a parental perusal of a fairly elaborate, two-page, teacher-authored evaluation of the student's general academic achievement, work habits and social relationships. As I read Jed's evaluation, I felt the surrounding silence watching me and listening for signals, as if politeness required my audible acknowledgment of certain criticisms. I thus grunted approvingly when I encountered one, and snorted a sage chuckle at amusing observations familiar to me. I nodded affirmatively and allowed a knowing "Ah hah" to escape when I read, "More time should be allotted to math work . . ." and then, unintentionally, showed puzzlement at the line, "Jed has worked on the insets of equivalence for geometry . . . and has completed his work on the classified charts of vertebrates and invertebrates." I recovered as quickly as I could, so as to conceal my ignorance of the meaning of the insets of equivalence. I also registered genuine surprise at the line about Jed's passionate interest in Native Americans and the Bill of Rights. I didn't know that, and I felt pretty awful that I didn't.

I next spied the word "time" in the evaluation. I repeated it aloud and looked up at the teacher, Mrs. Cruz, who smiled with me. "Jed's time is different from our time," I said, as she nodded. "We have what time we have; he has all the time in the world." She nodded, again. If that was the down side of Jed, I was happy with it. I thanked her and escaped to Danny's first grade teacher, Mrs. Gisonda.

Danny's evaluation read that he had shown tremendous improvement in reading, which he had hated. Mrs. Gisonda explained that at one point Dan was convinced that he could not read. She asked him to read aloud to her privately. He did. She asked, "Who read that?" He answered that he had. She asked, "Can you read?" He said, "Yes," and that was the end of it. She also said that Danny would do anything to avoid work, which made me feel comfortable all over. "I'm familiar with that trait," I said.

Respect between the Sexes

My sons are not old enough to make love to anybody, let alone rape or be accused of it, so I tried not to think of them in the context of the William Kennedy Smith rape trial, which I also tried not to think of. I failed on both counts.

During the trial, and without all the pertinent information (because I felt sleazy whenever I caught myself listening for more details), I blithely though privately prejudged both the accused and the accuser. I still cling to such conclusions as I reached, however. The verdict would not have changed my feelings and did not.

Smith, like many men, has a cavalier opinion about sex and what I would consider a disrespectful if not downright low view of women. In this unseemly instance, he took advantage of a woman who shared both, though with fluctuating levels of conviction.

From Smith's perspective, he did not cross the ill-defined border between recreational sexual dalliance and rape. From the woman's viewpoint, he did. In the absence of clearer evidence of coercion or force, or of a committee of thoughtful and dispassionate eyewitnesses, only the two participants will ever know for sure, and their personal conclusions apparently will forever remain in diametric dispute (though I should hope that the world at least will forever evaluate his romantic proclivities as somewhere between oafish and sub-canine).

I don't care very much about Smith or his accuser. If he were my son, and I had just learned through his testimony that he equated making love with peeing behind the hedges, I would be embarrassed by my failure to have influenced him in any fundamental way. If she were my daughter and had her pants off within 90 minutes of an encounter with a man, I would ache for her confusion and wonder what I might have done to contribute to her self-disrespect—though, if she had known him for 90 hours, 90 days or 90 weeks, I cannot say how I would have responded. I don't know where my own boundaries fall.

Their sordid predicament hits home only when it reminds me of a responsibility I probably always had but did not feel so bound to or helpless about, until now. My wife and my ex-wife struggled with these issues during my daughters' adolescence, while I hid behind a comfortable curtain of self-proclaimed ignorance. But now I am the father of pre-pubescent sons, and I suspect I have fewer places to hide and ought to try to tell them at some point what little I have learned and whatever I believe about how they might best behave toward the other half of the race.

Cultural change has accelerated so that my responsibility differs from such responsibility as my father or his father had, or felt they had; and mine, now, is one for which I do not have sufficient knowledge or experience to address with any confidence. My father tipped his hat when he encountered a woman and employed "Ma'am" in his responses to her. I get the clear sense that I am considered somewhere between quaint and psychotic when I follow his example, as I do. (I should add, if only to head off the critic poised to pounce, that I also say, "Yes, sir," and "No, sir," and tip my hat to men when circumstances inspire the gesture.) But I would no more suggest those forms of communication to my boys than I would recommend that they bow from the waist and spread their Lands End parkas across a mud puddle to spare a female friend from soaking her Reeboks.

I would like to be able to tell my sons to treat everyone with similar respect, but that seems irresponsible, too, for its impossibility. Women generally don't rape. A man who would simultaneously communicate his respect for and his romantic interest in a woman will always have to follow more stringent rules than she does. The physiological relationship between the two sexes disallows equating invitation with invasion. Ultimately, only one is active; the other is passive. Only one, aggressive; only one, criminal.

Under circumstances that my sons will begin encountering relatively soon and continue to encounter for the next half dozen decades, the air between men and women always will be thick with invisible volumes of non-verbal communication, all open to interpretation—raised brows, lingering glances, double-takes, changes in tone, shifts in weight, accidental caresses, implied and inferred double entendres, wry jokes, bold suggestions and outright, nonverbal propositions. None of them would be admissible or effective in a man's defense, should someone accuse him of sexual aggression.

So, as modern and liberated a man as I would like to portray myself, I will have to tell them that we are different, us and them, and that we operate from different premises, different points of view. Thus, for reasons both noble and cynical, respectful as well as wary, I want my sons to behave toward women in a chivalrous manner. I want them to trust their instincts but make no assumptions about their rights to intrude.

Frankly, I wouldn't mind seeing them tip their hats one day, on encountering a woman.

Dads R Us

The 200 or so cold viruses said to be in a perpetual holding pattern over humanity must love Christmas night in America. Ready victims abound—overfed, exhausted, bankrupt, weakened to bacteriological ripeness, our immune systems sapped for our having summoned strength to vault absurdly artificial obstacles.

NOT AS I DO: A FATHER'S REPORT

I floated from dream to consciousness the morning after Christmas aware, first, of the new twinge in my throat and the new uselessness of my left nostril. Upon reflection, I realized how easily I could have predicted the onset of a cold the night before, as I languished stupidly in front of the television, stiff and wide-eyed, a wounded bait fish on an outgoing tide.

What exotic and uncharacteristic stimulus-response syndrome had driven me to attain so many superficial goals in such artificially compressed time? How, for example, in a world where people were losing jobs and struggling to eat, did I ever manage to whirl myself into a holy-quest frenzy over the relative unavailability of a Shinobi game cartridge for my son Jed's computerized, hand-held Game Gear game? He had not yet even received the operating equipment when I was scurrying from store to store, pleading for a specific cartridge and enduring corporate America's most demeaning insults for my efforts.

I recalled, for instance, the following exchange, herein including what I said and what I thought to say.

"Sorry we're all out of Shinobi. You should have been here two days ago. We had boxes of it."

"Oh, I see . . . I should have been here? Have I now flunked Christmas Shopping 101? I've arrived too late to give you inordinate sums of money for a game cartridge? Silly me . . . It's just that I was reading this advertisement in the newspaper this morning. Here, look: this very advertisement in my hand, here, instructing me to bring this very advertisement into the store and show it to . . . well, to you, I guess, so you could then give me $5 off the list price when I bought any of these Game Gear game games pictured here, like, say, Shinobi. See? In this picture here. Today's paper. Since the store so far has been open for only the half hour that I have been standing here at this heretofore unclerked, exclusively marked, Game Gear/Game Boy game counter—from which I finally telephoned the store's switchboard, reaching over the cash register to use the store's telephone extension to say that I would like to spend about $100 if only someone would take the money—I thought you, who now arrive so nonchalantly from whichever distant department has captured your heart, might actually have the Game Gear games that this newspaper advertisement from THIS MORNING'S NEWSPAPER says you have, and that you might want to sell one to me, THAT BEING YOUR DAMNED JOB and all."

"I know the ad is running in today's paper," said the clerk, whose obvious embarrassment made me feel relieved for not having said what I thought, and guilty for having thought it. "But the sale has been going on for three or four days, and that game was very hot. It sold out. Plus, we were robbed. They were after these games, specifically. Notice, all these games are here under lock and key. In fact, they're not even here. These are just the boxes. The actual games are in the back."

"Oh. You keep the empty boxes under lock and key? Guys steal the empty boxes, do they? Well, to tell you the truth . . . I hate it here, and I will do anything to get out and not come back, including buying my son all the other Game Gear game games that you do have . . ." I didn't even know what Shinobi was; still don't. I didn't know what Game Gear was, except that eventually it would render its predecessor, Game Boy, obsolete. My plan was to get a Game Gear game for my older boy, and one game cartridge he said he wanted, and to pass his Game Boy game down to my younger boy, but mask the insult by buying him several Game Boy game cartridges, plus this nifty, deluxe, Game Boy game carrying case. "So, if you could give me a couple of Game Boy game games and recommend just one, Game Gear game game, I will just buy all this gamey stuff and be on my merry way, and out of yours."

"How about this one? Joe Montana's Football Game."

"Well, I don't know. He likes football, but I think he likes the kind with the real foot and the real ball. But . . . yes. Give me that."

[Long search].

"Well, it appears we don't have that, either. In fact, we don't have any Game Gear games. I'm sorry. Toys R Us will honor our ad, if that helps."

Toys R Us had Joe Montana's Football Game, but not Shinobi. I decided to press on and hit department stores whenever I entered one's atmosphere. I finally got the last Shinobi cartridge locked away in Macy's in Manhattan.

Jed and Danny loved the gifts, but—and this is true—Jed said that their pal, Eamonn, had gotten an even better game than Shinobi: Joe Montana's Football Game.

YEAR FOUR

A Tree Whose Time Has Gone

My fatherly duty last Sunday was to remove the Christmas tree. I did not.

I am late to most duty, anyway, and for that alone would not live with me unless sentenced to it. But I never have discarded a Christmas tree on the first date requested, always putting it off until the next Saturday or Sunday; partly for no reason at all, partly for reasons that make only some sense and partly for reasons that don't make any, chief among them being a genetic predisposition for procrastination.

I know a dozen reasons for dismantling a Christmas tree and can enumerate them and their effects with little effort: First-through-tenth, the Christmas season has ended. All the good gifts that appeared under the tree on Christmas morning are in use, broken, lost or already have been laundered at least once; only the extra bottles of Old Spice remain, garnished with pine needles.

The tree by this time has taken on a painfully anachronistic air, even for the hopeless sentimentalist in the house, who carefully declines most opportunities to gaze at it in public for fear of attracting negative attention from the more fastidious occupants.

I have developed a private tradition of quietly basking in the glow of the Christmas tree at 1 o'clock in the morning, hours after the rest of the household has dozed and weeks after the holiday is over. I justify this behavior by maintaining that if you are going to decorate a room with as bizarre an object as a large, freshly killed evergreen tree, itself then decorated with impossibly delicate toys and tawdry lights, you ought to at least pay it some meditative attention when no other distractions are awake to interrupt.

By the second week of January, we have embarked on the season that bridges the New Year's hoopla and pre-spring hope, a season of gloomy weather and killer mood swings, wherein multicolored, sparkling symbols of giddy generosity and joy are believed to exacerbate the morose feelings of certain individ-

171

uals and inspire others to derision. In cynical minds, no artifact stands so lonely and out-of-place as a silver bell tinkling in a roomful of depressed adults and cranky children, unless it is a plastic misrepresentation of mistletoe above them or a brightly decorated Christmas tree, post Christmas.

I disagree. During the season, when everybody already is feeling pretty good, a Christmas tree is a still-life chorus of joyous song. Later, when we most need it, the tree becomes a free-standing, ever-available hug, a caress to be had on demand. For that reason, I would leave the Christmas tree dressed and standing through February, if I could.

I have spent some wintertimes in Vermont and envy the attitude of that state's residents toward Christmas trees, Christmas decorations, in general. Perhaps because of the tendency of snow to loiter there, Vermonters behave as if wreaths, roping, red ribbons and lighted evergreen trees were permanent accessories to their countryside's white, winter coat. They keep the Christmas spirit lingering until the March mud season. The result may amount to an extended, secularization of the sacred, but the twinkling thoughtfulness renders warm and welcoming what would otherwise be bleak, eventide panoramas.

Superciliousness aside, I also don't care to dismantle the tree because the work is strenuous, wet, filthy, disruptive and sweaty. It requires extensive follow-up tidying and results not in a feeling of personal satisfaction but one of emptiness and loss. When the work is completed, the decor reverts to late November. The house feels as if its must ebullient, entertaining resident got married and moved out.

The ritual of de-treeing includes a division of labor that I suspect is gender-driven and therefore sexist in some fashion, though it works pretty efficiently. Mother removes the ornaments, the most delicate and personally cherished first, the plain red and chromium-painted balls last. She places them in their flimsy, aging, cardboard containers and sets them aside for portage by Father to the Christmas closet, really a corner in the attic. Father then removes the strings of lights, which Mother then re-packages, because she is less likely then he to become impatient and entangle them forever.

Father then stares forlornly at the tree, wondering which jacket, hat and pair of gloves he will sacrifice to its itchy, sticky, sappy disposal.

My tree stands in an ingenious, commercial treestand recommended by my ingenious tree vendor, who correctly predicted that its simplicity would make raising the tree in the house easier than ever before. Removing the stand is another matter, however, requiring the deft application of the back end of a claw hammer and thus a warning to the children to protect their ears from flying shards of profanity.

This year, today in fact, once the tree is down, its water spilled, its carcass hauled out, its needles spread throughout the living room and imbedded deep into the hooked rug in the foyer, I will assault the place with the multi-gallon, wet-dry vac from Sears and, in the spirit of Christmas gone, suck up anybody who gets in my way.

A Fifth Grader Faces Bigotry

I have a letter from Sun Park, a fifth grader. I assume that Sun Park intends a compliment, calling me Editor. I will forgive him. Once.

On scan, I can see the letter summarizes Sun Park's fear and loathing of bigotry and those who participate in its violent liturgy. In a postscript, his teacher declares Sun Park's letter as representing the feelings of all of Class 5–1 at Public School No. 209 in Whitestone, Queens.

I don't know how to respond.

"My parents came to this country thinking it was the best country in the world," the letter begins. "At that time it was, but now it's horrible. The government might be all right but the streets are inhumane. It's sometimes dangerous to go shopping alone.

"When I hear about all these bias attacks it makes me sick. But recently the attacks are happening to kids around my age. That makes me just want to get up and leave this world. Sometimes I think that God made this world by mistake, that the human brain was made to destroy each other before the 21st century. It just turned to 1992 and there already have been more than four bias attacks.

"The world is already bad for my generation but think of the next generation, our children. We must try to wisen up these prejudice people so they won't teach their kids bigotry. If this world is at peace, think of what we can get rid of—like world hunger."

My older son, Jed, is in fifth grade, too, so the designation pops his face into my consciousness like a duck in a target game. In my mind, Sun Park and Jed become fifth graders together for the moment, asking me to answer the unanswerable, to offer an explanation for insanity. Jed's closest friend in school, Adrian, is black. Adrian cannot possibly have passed through his first decade without having encountered symptoms of the psychosis that so plagues this country particularly, even defines it, in many ways. I know Jed must have seen, heard or sensed its senselessness at one time or another, and I often have wondered whether my role as his father requires bringing up the subject or waiting until he does. He has confided to his mother that when the time comes, he does not want to attend a private high school whose population is characterized primarily by sameness. I don't know what inspired that thought, but I am encouraged by it.

I am not charmed by the notion of a fifth grader so worried as Sun Park about the world to which he will introduce his children.

Fifth grade: My teacher was Miss Lori, or Lory. We painted a mural on white paper that ran all along the right side of the classroom in what is now the administration building for the Amityville School District. I remember that the mural showed historical characters, buildings and battles, and that I drew a portrait of a famous character whom I believed to be noble and honorable. I later learned as an adult that this historical character also had bought people, had traded some, kept some, traded away the children of some and used some for breeding. Learning that so late and so dispassionately left me feeling betrayed.

I cannot remember exactly how conscious I was of the categorical differences among my fifth-grade classmates, though the significant categories were obvious: white and black, first; then within white, Catholic, Protestant or Jew.

I remember vividly individual differences. John Delves was blond and had a crewcut; Richard Mosley was tall, loose-limbed, deep-brown and had big teeth. Susan Stein sat quietly and wore soft, pretty sweaters. Louis Leftenant already had a deep voice. Bob Merrick had red hair and freckles. Richie Stewart, my best friend from kindergarten, was still short, might always be short, though his older brother, Junior, was tall. I envied tall, and old. I shared a secret closeness to a shy, skinny girl whose skin was darker even than Mosley's. I think her name was Ellen, and I have long hated that I don't remember for sure. We were born on the same day, same year. Everyone else was celebrating or looking forward to 11th birthdays; we kept quiet our embarrassing giddiness about turning 10.

I can recall no categorical animosity from those days, only individual, personal grudges. I'm sure bigotry existed, and in a big way. I don't know how I missed seeing it, unless I simply owe my parents my gratitude for their efforts either to conceal or to render it harmless. Whenever they discussed or joked about ethnicity, their arrows were rubber-tipped, their humor affectionate. I learned to notice first what was familiar about group differences. Blacks and Italians caressed and hugged their dead and wailed openly; the Irish stayed back, whispered condolences and then socialized. They all suffered.

I did not learn much about bigotry for a few more years; did not learn much about the forces behind it for at least another decade; did not clearly see its atmospheric pervasiveness until a victim taught me in a patient and elementary way, which I now owe my children.

Strong Feelings, Good Reasons

So far, I have kept relatively secret, from my sons especially, such political outrage as I feel whenever I have felt it, not so much because I want them to be uninfluenced by my prejudices—although I do, sometimes—as because I dread having to explain them.

I concluded long ago that my feelings were not within my intellectual control, that when I was performing at my best, I first felt, then thought, then acted. My neurological system responded involuntarily from its own memory and experiences to make me uncontrollably mirthful, weepy, suspicious, angry or wary, and my conscious mind followed after, hoping to rationalize, justify, encourage or suppress those hair-trigger feelings so that I could then behave reasonably.

Whenever I allowed my emotional self a greater voice in my

subsequent behavior, I operated at risk, sometimes achieving exhilarating and creative triumph, sometimes making a fool of myself. Whenever I gave the weighted vote to my intellectual side, I behaved in a publicly satisfying manner but eventually experienced pent-up, emotional consequences, alone and out of context.

I am not ashamed to be a compilation of my experiences, my ruminations and, to a lesser but undeniable degree, my conscious and subconscious memories of the experiences and ruminations of my parents, who, in turn, bore the influences of their parents. Smart people who know me well and know some of the components of my history often can predict how I will behave under certain circumstances and in response to certain stimuli. They therefore have trusted me, and we have been good friends or respectful enemies, and in one particularly satisfying case have remained good friends for decades.

I know other people who seem unimpeded by their histories, who suppress or evade almost all emotional reaction and manage to see all existence purely intellectually, and, therefore, in shadeless black and white, right and wrong, good and evil. For microseconds, I have envied the simplicity of their lives but then found myself overwhelmed by feelings, again, this time of pity for their emotional poverty and the futility of whatever hope they had of attaining wisdom.

Still, whenever I openly weep, laugh, mock or rail on hearing the news of an occurrence distant from me and my family and ostensibly unrelated to our comfort, safety and well-being, I do so knowing my children will always notice, if they are present, and always will remember, consciously or otherwise, that their father was moved to tears or rage by this or that kind of event. I know, too, that a fundamental part of each one of them, in their unwitting loyalty to me, thereafter will respond similarly to analogous events and/or stimuli for the rest of their lives, even when they think better of it. For instance, I am cursed and/or blessed with a ready instinct to imagine myself in the other person's shoes, and my children have picked up the identical, genetic disorder. I have watched my son cry to imagine that a frog captured by his brother must have left behind parents hysterical with anxiety over its whereabouts. I've heard my daughters storm out of the house after watching a television report of what each considered an injustice.

Everyone was out, Thursday morning, when I read the following headlines: "IRA Gunman Secretly Sent Back to Britain," and "U.S. Extradites an I.R.A. Killer to Belfast Jail." Nobody who lives with me saw or heard my reactions, which were demonstrative, if futile.

I have decided to keep the newspapers until a later date and to someday explain, formally, both my feelings and my thoughts on the matter to my children, especially, I suppose, to my sons.

I will say:

"You must know that everyone and every institution looks at the world from his, her or its own perspective, or point of view. They react, first by feeling, and then by speaking and then by doing. Usually, their language reveals their point of view ahead of time. To *Newsday* and the *New York Times*, for instance, and to the government of the United States, this Joe Doherty character was a 'gunman' and a 'killer,' because he used a gun and killed a man. The U.S. government also calls him a 'terrorist,' partly because, in general, men who carry guns and kill people terrorize the people who don't, but mainly because the word fits the point of view that suits their purposes. After all, the U.S. government ordered men with guns to kill 100,000 people only a year earlier and didn't refer to any one of them as a terrorist, gunman or killer.

"Anyway, Joe Doherty grew up in a town that I have been to, that one of your great-grandfathers came from, where from the time Doherty was 13 years old men with guns routinely jumped out of armored vehicles and, shouting very loudly, pointed the guns right in the faces of people who were shopping for groceries or mailing a letter or gathering to look at an automobile accident—old people, young people, little children, all people who were not carrying guns. They terrorized the people, sometimes beat them with bats, sometimes took them away for hours or even days at a time, sometimes shot them dead. In fact, they still do it.

"Sometimes, if you can imagine, they beat up fathers and mothers right in front of their children, sometimes children right in front of their fathers and mothers. The gunmen who terrorize the townspeople wear the uniforms of soldiers and fly the flag of a different country from the country the town is in. From the soldiers' point of view, they are under orders, keeping peace in a place they don't wish to be by constantly teaching

177

lessons to people they don't like, always warning them not to misbehave or be disrespectful, or else. The people, in many, many cases, especially the children, consider them an enemy army. Some hate the soldiers, and some grow up wanting to join an army—any army—that would fight them and drive them away, back to their own country. If you grew up there, you might be one. Me, too.

"This country, our country, always bragged that it cared about such people in such places, unarmed people being terrorized by occupying armies of other countries. But that's a lie, boys. Don't you ever believe it."

Holding the Fort on Privacy

In what must be one of the more glaring paradoxes of a life already replete with irony, I claim in these paragraphs to value my privacy and to have maintained a healthy respect for other people's, particularly my children's.

Of course, I make this unspeakably self-righteous boast before a million or so readers and then blithely proceed to chronicle the biographies of my children, detail for intrusive detail, month after month, year after year. As my mother would say, "Where does he get the gall?" pretending to such virtue.

But, as someone whose emotional nerve endings are particularly sensitive to embarrassment and humiliation, and whose combative passions arise quickest against threats to inalienable rights, I do try to keep a watch on my own curiosity as well as my occupational penchant for self-purging, lest I probe too deeply for such knowledge as a person considers his own and not mine, especially if that person falls within my parental jurisdiction.

I don't want to behave as if I have or feel any more privilege than mere paternity ought to provide. I believe that the contents of a daughter's purse ought to be her business, period, and no less sacred than the contents of anyone else's.

When my boy closes his door to change his pants, I don't presume to enter his room until I first knock, or, until after having already knocked four times, I realize that he is stalling, because he doesn't want to change his pants, he wants to wear the sweats that he wore the day before and slept in all night and would wear until they escaped from him of their own strength and energy. Only then do I barge through the door in memorable fashion, hoping he will not soon forget that both my patience and my respect for his privacy have limitations, and that he ought not to use one to test the other.

Mainly, though, I do knock. I trust. I respect. I also try to remember to say, "Excuse me," before I scream to one son about mashing the other son's head into the stairs, but I forget most every time.

My own quiet fervor for privacy first goes as far back as does my conscious memory, to messages and stories I recall from my parents, and then, further, to messages I received from them through their behavior, which I regarded as exemplary.

My mother told stories about her private attempts to escape the craziness of her family. Three of her older siblings were in show business, two as chorus girls, one, her brother, as a bandleader and later as a stage manager. The family lived in a railroad flat above a Brooklyn speakeasy, whose frequently ejected patrons now and then managed to climb the fire escape in the middle of the night. One even stumbled in a window, scaring my mother's sisters' chorus-girl colleagues into blood-curdling screaming fits. The poor sot vaulted himself back out, presumably to further meditate about privacy and the consequences of invading it.

My mother, meanwhile, became an inveterate reader. She spent a great deal of her energies in search of solitude, which in that family required elevating privacy to stealth and reclusiveness. She often told about hiding behind the sofa with a book while a posse of other family members searched for her, opening closet doors and calling out her name, wondering aloud where she had gone and whether she had survived the trip. She responded to their frantic summoning by turning her pages more carefully, to make less noise.

From my father, who was more declarative about proprietary rights—although, in his police emphasis, he leaned more on what you did not have the right to—I learned about the sanctity of such places as purses, wallets, top drawers and unopened mail. If my mother asked for an item she said was located in her pocketbook, he would bring her the pocketbook. He never asked his preadolescent son if I had cigarettes in my pocket (or in my sock); he asked, instead, "What kind of cigarettes do you smoke?"

placing the length and breadth of disclosure entirely in my hands. He also told how his father took him aside, privately, and recounted a remarkable dream he had remembered from the night before. In the dream, Patrick Lowe told my 13-year-old dad, "You were standing on the corner of North Sixth Street with two of your pals, and I walked up and saw that the three of you were smoking cigarettes. Ed, I was so surprised at that, I just kicked your ass all the way home, here. Wasn't that some crazy kind of dream?"

My boys and their friends built a fort in the woods last week. No place on earth is so deliciously and exquisitely private as a fort, whether made from blankets over straight-back chairs or discarded plywood supported by rusted supermarket carts. After days of hurried secrecy, as boys darted in and out with pieces of household inventory, I received a conditional invitation to view the structure.

First, I had to promise not to write about it.

Passing the Cue Torch

I realize that social ordinances against it exist in the collective mind of a whole caste of upstanding citizens; nonetheless, I am encouraging my sons to learn to play pool.

I would have so encouraged my daughters, as well, but my struggles throughout their childhood were insufficiently rewarding to afford me the luxury of either a pool table or the space indoors to accommodate one. In those days, I indulged my own yearnings for that specific, elegant form of recreation by paying for playing time at tables located elsewhere, sometimes in salons devoted exclusively to the rental of pool table usage, other times in saloons whose proprietors sacrificed valuable dance-floor space in hopes of attracting such occasional aspirants to momentary supremacy as my spasmodically competent self.

I am not advocating that my sons follow my example in frequenting saloons. Nor am I suggesting by the disclaimer that I intend to abstain from such visitations myself. In time, the boys will make their choices of social congregation and/or altar of worship. I have long preferred to clasp my hands together over a Chicago rail.

I merely want my boys to be acquainted with this one game in particular. Why? First-through-third, because I like it. I like sushi, and I introduced them to that. I like drifting in a small boat, scanning the bay bottom for blue-claw crabs, and I introduced them to that. I like Gilgo Beach, Mark Twain, the Jim Small Band, downhill skiing and getting my hair washed by somebody else, and I have introduced them to all of those. And I like pool.

Someday, I may sit with each boy and bore him to distraction with my rhapsodic dissertations on why I like what I like. Sushi, for instance, is sensuous, esthetically attractive and comes in small, diversified portions with a variety of sauces. It already is cold, so it can't get that way, which encourages conversation and permits periodic rest. Crabbing offers all the patient intensity of the hunt, but without blood, loud noises, exotic equipment or heavy lifting. It is fishing without cutting bait.

Pool has a rich history. Unlike Game Gear and Wheel of Fortune, it is three-dimensional, personal, subject to Newtonian dictates, intensely geometric and damned near as sensuous as loving, especially when approached similarly deftly and appreciatively. Also, it requires no heavy lifting, nor any head-butting, nor excessive stretching, extensive training or desperate panting for air. A Kelly-green felt beneath a bright, overhanging, pool table lamp is as striking and pleasing to my eyes as an opening-day infield, and the clicking of pool balls greeting each other sounds as exquisite to my ears as the clinking of crystal during intermission at a string quartet recital.

In my life grid I currently reside on the square: second marriage; fourth house. Miraculously, the house happened to be the first one in my life whose basement permitted the placement of a standard pool table in such an attitude that a player could walk all the way around it without once having to employ a pool cue he first sawed in half. With the encouragement and assistance of a sharper aficionado, I purchased a 50-year-old, Brooklyn-made, poolroom pool table from a New York City cop who was retiring and moving to Florida, where I bet he now regrets having left it behind.

I meditated for a long time over the thought of inviting my boys to join me. The table and its placid solitude were a lifelong dream realized, and I was loathe to share it, especially with people who were of the age where they equated rest with noise, conflict and exertion. Also, I was not so foolish as to overlook the potential perils of placing boys in a basement room equipped with long sticks and brightly colored, solid projectiles.

Gradually, I let the boys leak down the stairs and into the sanctum, first only to watch. Later, I let them roll the balls from one end of the table to the other, pointing out with ceremonial solemnity that when I thought they were ready, I would let them apply a pool cue to a cue ball; and if I saw that they could be trusted, brandishing sticks within striking distance of each other, I would indulge them some time to get the feel of the game, and then maybe show them some of its rudiments.

They behaved as predicted, initially, standing at opposite ends of the table, rolling balls back and forth to each other, first leisurely, then briskly, then aggressively. Finally, a speedy ball rolled back to the younger by the older, and in retaliation, as always, for a perceived slight, would arrive at the cushion one microsecond sooner than the departure of the younger son's escaping fingertip. Once the howling subsided, I would banish them both to the real world, upstairs.

It took many such incidents, and much feigned reverence, but they now respect the place and have got the hang of applying pool cue to cue ball with uncanny deftness. They now ask me to play, and I have heard each of them turn down an invitation to the ice-cream store, saying, "No, thanks. I'm going downstairs to play pool with my dad."

Clash of Titans in the Driveway

The last house I co-bought—the one from whose basement I record these musings—came equipped with a sturdy, basketball backboard, mounted on heavy-duty brackets bolted into the wall over the double garage door.

I recall smiling wryly when I first spied it, for it reminded me of the little depth charges of envy that exploded inside the boyhood me years before, whenever my father's car cruised past so luxuriously appointed a house.

In my childhood, paved driveways were not the neighborhood

norm, save for the occasional older home that boasted a pair of cracked, parallel concrete paths that flanked a bumpy mound of grass; good for learning to ride a bicycle, as long as you fell to the inside.

The driveway in front of my boyhood house, where my mother still lives, was made of pressed dirt, originally fashioned by repeatedly flattening the ground in front of the garage with a black applicator made in 1939 by the Ford Motor Co.

Years later, my father applied buckets of beach sand to the pressed dirt, presumably in an effort to blanch the dark, winter mud we tracked into the house during the months of February, March and April. Still later, he formed and poured cement curbs alongside the driveway, to keep it from spreading onto the crab-grass. As his police career advanced, he procured some yards of a pebbly gravel. He applied that to the pressed dirt by driving a 1952 Chevy back and forth over it for years, until he could afford bluestone, as if to match the street.

I owned my own driveway by the time he'd blacktopped his. Mine consisted of two parallel paths of cracked concrete, flanking a bumpy mound of grass.

In the time and place of my childhood, a basketball backboard mounted over a wide, blacktop driveway generally meant that the resident doctor had sons, or that the resident lawyer had sons, or the resident mobster, at least. My caste's prejudices required that such a manse be inhabited only by somebody whose hourly wage was pre-determined at a secret convocation of his larcenous colleagues. He had to be one of the three, or president of the Long Island Rail Road.

We bought our current house from a doctor and his wife, who had raised three sons. At the time, spring of 1984, my daughters were 15 and 16 years old, respectively; my sons, 3, and, well, minus 2. I was 38, myself, and had long abandoned any notion of improving such mediocre hoop skills as I had exhibited during my adolescence, associating with friends older, taller and stronger than I, and less dismayed by repeated collisions between their own teeth and other people's shoulders. Of course, their teeth, being higher up, rarely collided with anybody's shoulders, as mine did.

Anyway, I therefore intended to ignore the basketball backboard and its esthetic and spiritual relationship to the accompanying paved driveway, because I did not want my childhood fantasies fiddling about in my mental deliberations regarding the pros and cons of the purchase, in which I carried the responsibility of fully 49 percent of the vote.

After we had moved in, however, I visited Amity Harbor Sporting Goods and bought a top-of-the-line basketball. I bought it for my 3-year-old son, Jed, of course, and not for any subliminal, lost-boy, recapturing-youth folderol. I did test the ball with a shot or two, and, satisfied that it arced correctly and bounced back up when thrust down, I presented it to Jed and watched with anticipation as he wobbled under its weight and girth. He let go of it and then tried to follow it around the driveway for a while, until he was distracted by another 3-year-old boy, Kevin Kretz, who had skidded his Hot Wheels into the driveway with typically youthful abandon and offered Jed diversions more amusing than endlessly following a large, bouncing ball into the garbage cans.

Properly chagrined, but unwilling to waste such a worthy purchase, I shot baskets for the next hour or two, and for several more evenings that summer, and even the next spring. But no more. I had gone irretrievably from bad to worse. I was satisfied that my youth was where it belonged.

Last weekend, on a balmy afternoon, Jed invited me to play basketball in the driveway. I said, "Sure," though I was decidedly not. I figured we would merely shoot baskets. I felt capable.

My first shot missed the garage entirely. I laughed with a fake, cocky air, as if amused by so freak an occurrence. My second shot missed the garage, too, so I followed jauntily with a layup. It hit the backboard, rolled around the perimeter of the rim and departed without even peeking through the hoop's gaping hole. I missed a few more times, and Jed invited me to play a game. I twisted my ankle and tried to use it against myself, but he wasn't buying the act.

"A game?" I asked incredulously. "What kind of game? You mean, like, one-on-one?"

"Yeah," he said.

My heart sank. Somewhere between his last birthday and his looming 11th, a fortnight away, he had grown taller and more agile, and more accurate and energetic, and quicker and a little more deft.

Jed buzzed by me and hit a layup before I had a chance to tell him that I was going to take it easy guarding him. My chest was heaving by the time I had evened the score to 2–2 from an early shutout pattern.

I hate to revel in someone else's misery, but suddenly the entire Amityville Fire Department appeared two houses away at the home of a neighbor whose basement had erupted in what turned out to be a benign cloud of smoke.

The distraction saved my life and my pride, and I will make a contribution forthwith to the volunteer firemen's fund.

Kids Are Different from You and Me

My mother said she didn't know what to get an 11-year-old boy for his birthday. I thought of suggesting a basketball, because I also thought she ran over one in the driveway, but I said nothing.

"What does he want?" she asked.

"Ma, how do you expect me to answer that?" I said. "He's an upper-middle-class, 1992, American boy, and you're a fixed-income, widowed heart patient, raised during the Depression, no less. I can't tell you what he wants unless you put one of those little nitroglycerine bombs under your tongue, first."

After all, my mother's boy was in the last quarter of sixth grade when he arrived at 11. He was profoundly socially retarded by today's rules and a consumer of not much more than baseball cards, chocolate sundaes and plastic model-airplane kits.

His recreations were simple and primitive. With his pump-action, Daisy air rifle, he fired BB pellets into a target mounted on a cardboard box in the basement. He played baseball, read adventure novels from the library, built sinking rafts and faced but two brand-name choices in sneakers: PF Flyers and Keds. He had barely discovered Jocko's Rocket Ship on the Zenith radio bequeathed to him by his grandfather, and he was still a year and a half shy of purchasing his first two 45-rpm records ("Tom Dooley" by the Kingston Trio, and "A Lover's Question" by Clyde McPhatter), which he would play incessantly on his parents' Victrola. Also, he wore whatever clothing his mother pushed his semi-comatose arms into on school mornings.

Her grandson is from another planet. He is not greedy, not

spoiled, not presumptuous, and he does know the value of a dollar, but he simply cannot be compared to a chronological peer from history so different from 1992 as 1957.

He is in fifth grade, numerically, but eleventh socially. And as a potential consumer of goods, he is a postgraduate research assistant. He wears specific sweatclothes and footwear. He knows what sizes both he and his brother wear, and he knows prices. He shops for exotic computer games and the latest in stereo cassette-tape recordings. He reads advertisements.

After lunch weekdays, and throughout weekends and vacations, most of the incoming telephone calls are for him. "So, for starters," I told my dear, sainted mother, "he really would like his own telephone, presumably with call-waiting and call-forwarding. However," I added, to calm her, "I told him of the continuing cost of a telephone, after installation, and as dictated by usage, and he decided to put that suggestion on hold for a year or so."

He told me he would like a stereo, I told her. He knows exactly the stereo he wants, and he knows it is expensive, so he is perfectly prepared not to get it for his birthday. He just thought he would throw the idea on the table for consideration now or in the future. He described the thing to me as a portable, AM-FM radio with digital readout, dual cassette-tape decks, a compact disc player and detachable speakers. He specified Sony, by the way, as the preferred manufacturer.

"On the other hand, he also has expressed keen interest in a set of weights," I said.

"A sederwates?" she asked. "Whaddizzat?"

"No. A set. A set . . . of . . . weights. Weights. To lift."

"What for?"

"I love you, Mom. I've asked myself the same question a hundred times. In my life, I have no reference for understanding why anybody would want to buy heavy pieces of material that were difficult to lift, so they could lift them over and over again, so that they could become strong enough to lift them more frequently. But these kids' interests run from the futuristic to the primeval and back, in microseconds. One minute, their fingers are flying over a computer keyboard; the next, you turn around and they're grunting over hefting metal objects."

"But . . . why?"

"Muscles. They want to build up their bodies. I know, they're just different from you and me, Ma. I do remember high school kids wanting to build up their bodies, but only the biggest and the smallest boys. The biggest wanted to be even bigger and kill people on the football field. The smallest wanted to be bigger any way they could get bigger. The rest of us wanted pizza."

"He said something about a water gun."

"Oh, Ma, no! You have no idea. You're thinking water pistol. You're thinking squirt gun. That's not what he's talking about. Kids in this neighborhood have water guns with fuel tanks mounted on the sides and air compressors holding 200 pounds of pressure per square inch. You could clean elephant cuticles with these things. You could erode concrete, put out forest fires. You don't want to buy him that."

"What about a basketball?"

"Hey, now there's a thought."

"Would you pick it up for me?"

"Ma, basketballs haven't changed much. But, yeah, all the little bumps and the lines are worn off his. I'll get one for you."

Boys' Night Out, Dad's Night Up

Obviously, a colossal emotional thrill is readily available for youngsters who stay overnight, en masse, at the home of a friend; else why would my son and his pals behave so enthusiastically while plotting their next siege?

I suspect I could better understand the attraction if I put my whole mind to the effort. Most times, I prefer to shake my head in mock parental exasperation and pretend that I do not understand the phenomenon at all, that moreover, I am troubled by it, as if it were symptomatic of some deviance.

The truth—which I will keep mostly to myself and the loyal, trustworthy, nontreacherous confidantes with whom I share these paternal diaries—is that I have not yet reached the age when I no longer recall the scary but exhilarating thrill of spending the night away from the perceived clutches of my parents.

To this day, breakfast always tastes better to me when I am elsewhere. Of course, I do not take breakfast unless I awaken in a hotel, or on the rare occasions that I arise before dawn and attend morning services at a delicatessen near a fishing fleet or a golf course.

I do remember that in the last minutes before dozing on foreign bedding, I was delighted that other people's rooms and rugs and their sheets and bedspreads smelled so exquisitely alien to the boyhood me as to make each overnight an adventure for the nocturnal imagination. I do remember, too, that while I obeyed other people's parents quicker and more politely than I did my own, I luxuriated in the secret notion that I didn't have to.

I also remember certain liberties I associated with staying overnight at a friend's house, although I can't escape the suspicion that the passage of time has exaggerated those liberties beyond what I consider tolerable limits, but over which I seem to have little control. In our ancient day, for instance, we stayed awake late, whispering sinfully, muffling our laughter and sharing hidden treasures from the cookie jar before we fell off to sleep. Now, they stay awake, period, fueled by caches of artificially sweetened, chemical confections soaked in multicolored pastel dyes and vacuum-packed in nonbiodegradeable, synthetic wrap. Plus Doritos. Plus cola. And they try to keep MTV on all night as a counteracting sedative.

Through accidental eavesdroppance, I recently learned about a planned overnight gathering of 11-year-old boys. I overhear one half of many such conversations, because the conspirator over whom I claim tenuous authority talks louder into the telephone when I am nearby; louder still if I appear to be deep in thought or in a conversation of my own; loudest when he is not on the telephone, but I am.

At any rate, I overheard him talking to his friend, Dougie, about staying overnight at our house. In the very next instant, I heard him talking about Dougie, which meant that he had taken a call from another pack member. I might add that the second conversation was bizarre. I took notes on a telephone company bill:

"Did you know all Dougie's hamsters committed suicide? Yeah, really. One jumped off a washing machine and got drownded. The second one got drownded in the chemical thing for the dehumidifier, or the humidifier, or, whatever; and the third one got stuck under the refrigerator and couldn't get out to eat, so he starved to death."

The sleepover raid was set for a night that I would be presiding over the household by myself. I agreed to it on the condition that my boy's younger brother be included. Frankly, I didn't want to have to entertain him while we both could hear the older boys guffawing in another room, and I didn't want him falling asleep hours earlier than they and waking up hours earlier and waking them up and waking me up.

Soon, three boys bearing sleeping bags appeared at the back door and commandeered the den, which has the television, the VCR and the stereo. Smart boys. I tossed in the younger brother, some soda and the synthetic confections and kept watch outside until I could no longer stay awake.

In the morning, when they were gone, I found myself amazed at how contained to the den they had kept themselves and their aftermath. The den was carpeted in food remnants and wrappers, but the rest of the ground floor seemed undisturbed.

The portable phone was missing, and I have yet to discover its use to them in the middle of the night. I am happy nobody saw me trying to find the thing. I would hit the page button on the stationary cradle in the kitchen and then try to run into the den fast enough to hear the last bleating of the portable receiver. I always arrived too late to discern its location from the sound, so I got a broom and tried to tap the cradle from a distance, and then poke my ears into the den. Finally, I asked a friend to call me and let the telephone ring until I answered.

I found the instrument on the floor behind the couch. Maybe they were using it as a substitute football.

The Piano Man

Seventy-five percent of my children read music. I might be prouder if I could claim some credit for that, but I am satisfied, nonetheless. It means progress for the family.

My eldest and I appreciate music but remain ignorant of its written language. Now and then, she and I repeat aloud a lamentation common to our ancestors, basically saying that we wish we had studied music, or, as in our family's most repeated case, that we wish we had learned to play the piano, specifically.

My father passed on to me a genetic ability to approach a

piano, and, after a few minor clinkers, play any melody the brain might dispatch to the right hand's fingertips. He would finish each fleeting concert by repeating, "Every time I sit down at a piano, I could kick myself for not taking piano lessons." If he actually had kicked himself every time he sat down at a piano, he would have made headlines: "Frustrated Man Kicks Self to Death—Believed First Suicide of Its Kind."

My mother used to mutter the same lamentation and made a feeble attempt to spare me the same regret. I was in grammar school when she asked a music store proprietor about the possibility of my taking piano lessons. He tried to sell her an accordion. With messianic fervor, he maintained that the best way to learn piano was to learn to play the accordion, first. By amazing coincidence, he had a supply of accordions and an attractive payment plan.

Too innocent to understand his game, I knew only that I did not want to play an accordion or even try to hold one up. I didn't see the relationship between the buttons on the left side of the accordion and any similar devices on a piano. I didn't like the sound of an accordion. I didn't like the weight, and, more importantly, I didn't like anybody I knew who was taking accordion lessons. Not only did I decline the invitation, I forever considered it a betrayal that my mother would even think of asking me if I wanted to take accordion lessons. I know it's sinful, but I am delighted that none of my children care to take up the accordion.

My mother eventually did take piano lessons, herself, around the time I was in junior high school. She and my father also bought a piano that year, hoping, I always suspected, that its presence would inspire me eventually to take the piano lessons they always talked about kicking themselves over. I refused to fall for their ploy. I showed them. I never took piano lessons. To this day, the upright piano stands like a monument in my mother's living room, where I feel like kicking myself.

Meanwhile, as a sixth- or seventh-grader, I stood on line for a free flute during the formation of an American Legion marching band. The kid ahead of me got the last flute in the bag, so I got what was left: drumsticks. Throughout high school, I drummed my parents to hell and back, practicing in the attic and playing in a bad rock 'n' roll band. Finally, I taught myself to play the acoustic guitar, though not to read music.

All four of my children appear to be musically talented, at the very least to the degree that they can carry a tune around in their memories indefinitely and repeat its melody and cadence at will. They all started in elementary school, playing the recorder. Colleen, my second, then played the clarinet for years.

I would like the boys to learn to amuse themselves and maybe entertain their friends, or their own children, by playing a musical instrument, but I do not want them to feel that I am pushing them or, worse, that I am trying to erase my own regrets by tyrannizing them, living vicariously through their experiences. So, I remain mute, secretly hoping that they will ask me for music lessons, secretly willing to finance, if need be, the purchase or rental of instruments, and secretly wondering if somewhere in the cosmos it isn't written that I am paternally obligated to demand that they develop their talent by taking up a musical instrument.

Last week, days too late for his 11th birthday, Jed mentioned that he might like to learn to play the electric guitar, specifically the bass. Could I take him to a music store, so he could get the feel of the instrument? I launched myself into action. I borrowed an electric guitar from a musician friend and even bought a remarkable little battery-operated amplifier. I thought I would show Jed some easy, first-position chords, some sweet sounds.

He turned up the amplifier to maximum volume and turned the dial on the guitar all the way to treble. He squeezed an extended, sternum-piercing, howling sound out of the instrument and grinned from ear to ear.

"Sounds just like Metallica," he said proudly.

"Sounds like you set a cat on fire," I mumbled.

He said he liked it, said he was sure, now, that he wanted to take guitar lessons. I said that maybe he should give it more thought. Maybe he should try Grandma's piano.

The Fine Art of Living

My Colleen has come and gone again.

How adventuresome is having an itinerant, legally adult daughter blow into town once or twice a year, fan out displays of exotic artwork from her classes and photographs from her travels, whirl the younger children around with her imagination, view with generous interest their collections of baseball cards and rocks, make them sing and laugh hysterically and then disappear one day in a cloud of Ford-Tempo exhaust and the lingering strains of Van Morrison tunes.

She stayed for a week. Having most likely ended her undergraduate career in the Adirondacks, she aimed to touch base, reacquaint herself with her sister, enchant her brothers, absorb the textures of her baby niece, get some new tires, depart, visit friends in other states and alight, in early June, in the Grand Tetons, there to wait tables and explore the terrain until seasonal changes force new decisions on her.

It's easy for me to joke about how Colleen must have to scan the classifieds for a Help-Wanted ad in her field of major concentration—fine arts—and I yield to the temptation frequently, but not without envy. Although the pattern of my own life inspires me to wonder why she isn't already on one career track or another, the liberty of hers makes me wonder as well why I seem now to have been in such a hurry when I was her age. Of course, when I was her age, she was under construction, her sister was into destruction, and I was in the business of instruction.

I had majored in English and minored in secondary education, not because I wanted to be English—I did not—nor even because I wanted to be a high school English teacher. I wanted to write for a living, but the experiences of the generation before me, sons and daughters of the Great Depression, had so influenced my fears and those of my peers that only the children of extremes—privilege or desperation—could summon the gall to seek fulfillment in uncertain endeavors. The rest of us leaned more timidly toward what was assumed to be the security of civil service or unionized jobs. If you wanted to be a writer, or a dancer, or an artist, an actor, a comic or a musician, you were to first get a real job, then indulge your very nice ambitions on the side, at night and on weekends.

Colleen doesn't know what she wants to be, aside from being Colleen, or why she should make such a decision without first seeing the National Park System in its entirety. The argument against her procrastinating in the selection of a work life is compelling, but my heart so sympathizes with hers, I keep my mouth shut and marvel at the spontaneity of her life.

While disemboweling her overburdened little car last week,

for instance, she came across her mountain tent and set it up on the lawn for an airing, on the only day in the spring of 1992 that could have passed for a spring day. That night, Colleen camped out with her brothers in the backyard. Infected by her penchant for improvisation, I grilled cheeseburgers at 10:30 that night and told the boys they could take off the next day from school. I also gave them the portable phone for the night, prompting a friend to wisecrack: "What, and no fax?"

The boys finally nodded off after about midnight. Colleen never slept at all. She seemed surprised that boys of 6 and 11 years could create such a nocturnal symphony. Danny sleeps like an idling lawnmower with a spasmodic clutch.

Colleen departed on Sunday. She has offered her own heart to the mountain states, though she confessed once that whenever she settles there for a while, she lapses into reminiscing wistfully about strolling the sandy perimeter of the Atlantic. For my own solace, I keep a theory about the origins of her disenchantment with the coastal world her parents chose to introduce her to in 1969: that she awakened to a regional insult the very first time she encountered a self-serve service station whose proprietor asked for payment after she had pumped the gasoline into her tank, as if he did not assume she was a thief. I'm sure it did not happen until she was outside the New York metropolitan area, probably in Dutchess County, and that at first she was puzzled into stupefaction by the event. I have seen other Long Island kids stunned when first noticing the phenomenon, and I winced when they suggested teaching the attendant a valuable lesson, by leaving without paying.

Colleen considered the act a singular aberration, no doubt, until she found that most service-station proprietors north of Elmsford, New York, behaved similarly. Then, according to my theoretical scenario, she condemned the cynicism of the community that spawned her for its preoccupation with dishonesty and acquisitiveness. Thereafter, every cheerful, upstate stranger, every smiling department-store clerk in Boulder and every polite and personable Indiana cop added to her disdain for Long Island.

I'm glad she wasn't home Monday, when somebody stole the bike Jed got for Christmas.

Odd Kid's Out

I hate when a third kid enters the house. I like when a fourth kid enters; hate when a fifth arrives; I feel better when I see a sixth kid. I order them all outside upon the arrival of a seventh kid, but I still am slightly relieved if an eighth kid appears.

A third kid makes the worst mix. It doesn't matter who he is, or whose he is. He enters, and the atmosphere changes in the room. Magnetic poles realign. Gravity pulls harder. Time slows. The Cosmos squints in anticipatory pain. Dynamics change from creative to destructive.

No noticeable atrocities occur immediately upon the third child's arrival, and no system exists to accurately predict who will be the conspirators and who their targeted victim. One younger child might want to align himself with the oldest of the three and work toward that end with a sophisticated combination of flattery and treachery. The oldest, however, might be interested in one of the younger two, because of the value of his baseball-card collection. Siblings almost always conspire against each other. Two older kids often line up in opposition to a younger, although two youngsters might just as easily want to ostracize an elder who routinely abandons them when his peers are about.

Whole minutes have to pass before the general mood thickens. After, say, 10 or so, quietude arouses suspicion in the experienced parent. What sounded like peace now can mean stealth. Sweet, interrogative tones tend to take on the ragged edge of whinery. A child's normal curiosity flows into satanic envy with liquid ease. Ideas become schemes. Innocent children who were cooperating sweetly begin to hatch plots, each against the other. Possession—of anything—is tantamount to a Declaration of War.

Three is a nasty number.

It is Saturday—or Sunday, I don't remember which—and the Older Brother reveals to his Overnight Guest that his mother has promised to pay money in return for his cleaning out the garage. I overhear this, as does Younger Brother, who reads it (and correctly, I might add) as, (1) a public invitation to the Overnight Guest, a chronological peer, to join in the garage cleaning and share the profits; (2) a public disinvitation to the

Younger Brother to join in the same work and/or share in the remuneration.

I take a seat on the patio to read the newspaper . . . it probably is Sunday . . . and to meditate on Tom Sawyer and his fence. The Older Brother does not know that he has just managed to make cleaning out the garage attractive to his Younger Brother, nor that he could now effortlessly enlist his Younger Brother's servitude for the rest of the morning, and for a pittance. I don't think I ever believed a real boy could be as wily as Tom.

My first visit is from Younger Brother, who already is in near-whine. "Jed says I can't clean out the garage with him and Jonathan," he sings.

"You can clean out the garage," I pronounce. "Tell Jed I said you could."

Older Brother appears next. "Dad, Danny's bothering us. And, Dad, we can't find a broom."

"Did you look for a broom?"

"We looked all over. Everywhere. Searched the whole house."

"Look in the kitchen. Look, believe it or not, in the broom closet."

Older Brother leaves and then returns. "Dad, Danny's got the broom and he won't let us clean the garage, and Mommy said she would pay us if we cleaned the garage, and we want to make the money so we can go to Critterville."

"Why do you want to go to Critterville?"

"I want to buy two mice."

"You buy mice; I'll buy a cat."

"Dad! Tell Danny to give us the broom, please."

"Danny found the broom that you two looked all over the whole house for and could not find? Sorry, he gets to keep the broom. Besides, no broom is going to clean out that garage. Why don't you first take the extension cords from Christmas and coil them up, and then move the Ping-Pong table . . ." He leaves.

The Younger Brother appears, in full whine. "Dad! Jed says I have to give him the broom, and I found the broom, and it's not fair that he and Jonathan get to clean out the garage by their-selfs, and Jed always gets his way in everything!"

"Dan, calm down. You keep the broom. You sweep." He leaves. Older Brother returns, Jonathan behind him, prepared to corroborate.

"Dad, Danny has this pile of dirt that he's keepin' way in the back of the garage away from the garbage cans, and he won't let us even go near it or touch it, and we want to pick it up. Dad, it's so stupid. Danny's so stupid. He's such a . . ."

"Hold it!" I said, rising to visit the site and survey their progress. "Danny's stupid? He found the broom, right? Two of you older guys looked all over and couldn't find it? And he found it? Is that right?"

"Dad, do you know where the thing is, the pickup thing? The dustpan?"

"You should ask Danny."

"Dad! So stupid!"

Little People, Big Bucks

I'm going a little wacky trying to recall how entrepreneurial I was as a boy. Otherwise, I am at a loss for a pivotal reference for my latest puzzlements. I seem to be surrounded by little people who have dedicated whole segments of what I thought would be lives of carefree play to the pursuit of wealth, instead.

I can remember wanting to sell lemonade, or Kool-Aid, but I remember it as a diversion, as an activity designed for two or three boys to while away a hot and boring summer morning, not as the realization of a junior investment group's plans to reap a return on their respective investments, whose percentage values first were designated and agreed upon days earlier at an organizational meeting in a fancy, paved driveway.

In my memory, my playmates and I simply asked one of our mothers to find a card table, lend us a pitcher and some glasses, make the product, lend us some change, call her friends and neighbors and then buy two glasses herself to inaugurate our enterprise. We made the sign.

We kept her change. We drank much of the inventory but sold some product to the mailman, a deliveryman, one other mother and, usually, one patronizing older kid on a bike. Generally, we opened the business at around 9:30 A.M. and had filed for bankruptcy by 11, our dungarees sticky and our crew cuts sweaty with the heat, our enthusiasm for sitting by the road completely depleted. The skeletal remains of our industry—the card table, two folding chairs, a half-filled pitcher, some glasses and our painstakingly inscribed sign—remained by the roadside all the rest of the day, unprotected and undisturbed, like a vacated car dealership, until our landlord returned from his own business and erased the last traces of our venture.

If we made a quarter each, we were giddy with the economic independence and devoted our imaginations for the whole afternoon to envisioning the colorful menu sticker on the right rear corner of the Good Humor Ice Cream truck that jingled down our block just before dinnertime, cruelly mixing the emotions of the mothers who were torn between being annoyed at the pressure to spring for ice cream just before dinner, or grateful that they could use dinner as an excuse to not buy ice cream this time.

I don't know why we bothered to even look at the menu; we always selected toasted almond anyway.

My boys reaped a small fortune last week selling iced tea, made from what I called designer water—bottled Poland Spring water—ironically cooled and presumably polluted by ever-melting ice cubes made from the proletarian water of my youth, which came from our faucet. Every time I looked out to check on the kids, another car or truck had stopped in front of our house; home-improvement contractors, crews from the Suffolk County Water Authority, young adults in funky Jeeps and condominium dwellers in Mercedes and Lexuses (Lexi?).

I could scarcely believe the amount of business the boys did, the money they made or the substance of the arguments I overheard later about the relationships between dividends and investments, not to mention their prior agreements made about such compensation as each deserved for the use of real estate and equipment. I half-expected to hear them fighting about severance pay next, or unemployment insurance and extended health benefits.

Their fortunes made, they asked me to drive them to the baseball card store. I had heard about baseball card stores, but never had visited one. Having naively determined that so specific a merchandising limitation carried specialization to an absurdity comparable to, say, a toenail clipper store, I was certain the fad would not last more than the proprietor's first rental obligation.

The store was a revelation, as was their already familiar relationship with the proprietor, and the comfort and ease with which my older boy discussed the relative values of specific cards in his collection. Evidently, collector cards exist that commemorate every event that ever happened, from the Royal Wedding to Kermit the Frog's, from the history of baseball to the history of ALF. All have value. All the talk is about money.

I collected baseball cards, too, and I valued some cards more than others, because of a combination of the rarity of the card and the affection I heaped upon the player depicted on its face. So, because I held special places in my heart for Jackie Robinson, Duke Snider and Gil Hodges—places shared by the likes of St. Isaac Jogues, John Wayne and Fess Parker—I would trade away duplicates of Mickey Mantle and Ted Williams in a heartbeat for duplicates of my heroes. The values placed were purely emotional. I was a Brooklyn fan, specifically, and an underdoggist, philosophically.

Such emotion would amount to a severe handicap to today's 11-year-old collector, who is smart to buy a monthly periodical that will tell him in a typeface his father can no longer read without magnification that a 1990 Pro Set 1 378 series Bo Jackson card held fast at a value of 50 cents last month, while the values of most of the cards in that set, valued at $7.50, had decreased anywhere from 13 to 50 percent.

I do not yet know how I feel about all this economic reality. I was even beginning to take comfort in my son Jed's affection for his pets (which he calls bunnies and I call rodents), until my daughter revealed that she had driven her brother and his imprisoned, female mammals to the home of a friend who kept males of the same species. The implications boggle my every waking moment, and each night, before I turn out the lights on the rabbits, I stare at them.

Fitness and Firecrackers

In a spasm of health-consciousness, my body evidently starving for an aggressive, aerobic workout, I gave up the car for the summer mornings surrounding the celebration of America's independence and instead walked the entire block to the 7-Eleven store for my coffee and my glazed doughnut. My presidential physical fitness certificate probably is in the mail.

All along the strenuous route, I spied pyrotechnic carcasses strewn about the street: remnants of Roman candles, bottle rockets, firecrackers, smoke bombs and, occasionally, as my imagination exploded with anticipatory regret, some fingers from the hands of the Lowe boys, whose father was insufficiently stern about their independent celebrations of the Glorious Fourth.

The panicky image instantly produced what the walk did not —beads of sweat, and I nearly turned myself into a pedestrian fatality as I wandered across Montauk Highway ruminating distractedly about how I might have failed in my responsibility to forbid outright, in the name of safety, their involvement in personal fireworks.

Speaking in my own behalf, I did not buy any fireworks, nor distribute any, nor suggest that I approved of my boys procuring or using any. But I did not stand my sons aside, either, and tell them in the same kind of unforgettably ponderous, dirge-drummer detail my father employed for emphasis, that I would sentence each of them to a lifetime of protracted misery if I so much as suspected that they had stood within earshot of any explosion louder than that created by the average cap pistol, unless they had bought a ticket and attended an event staged by the world-famous Grucci fireworks family of Bellport.

Instead, I told them to be careful around fireworks and the kids who had them, and then I elaborated myself into a quagmire of equivocating. I said I knew that some kids they knew would have fireworks, and that some of the fireworks those kids had would not be all that dangerous, as long as the kids using them weren't stupid. I said I wanted them to remember to stay with not-dangerous and not-stupid, as a rule. Then, I dug deeper, saying that some kids would have fireworks that would be dangerous, and that some kids would be stupid, whether what they had was dangerous or not, which would make the non-dangerous fireworks dangerous, too. I paused to look at my audience.

They nodded, my sons, as if my admonitions were clear as crystal.

Danny took a smoke bomb out of his pocket and cheerily offered it to me as an example of a non-dangerous firework. He said that he wanted me to set it off for him in the driveway. He said it with a singsong innocence calculated to make me think that he never before had set off such a smoke bomb himself, which I took to be a crock. But I never had set off a smoke bomb, myself, and I was startled at the uncanny resemblance in shape, color, weight and texture between a smoke bomb, available just above the bubble gum rack in the average novelty store, and the cherry bombs of my own, vaguely criminal boyhood. Cherry bombs could remove the tightened lid of a galvanized garbage can or torpedo to bits the hull of a toy sailboat from beneath the murky surface of the Amityville River. I didn't like the idea that if Danny accidentally came across a cherry bomb, he probably would mistake it for a smoke bomb, so I revealed what I knew about cherry bombs, without elaborating on how I had learned these delicacies.

My paternal knowledge of and experience with smoke bombs thus challenged by a 6-year-old, however, I called for a book of matches. My 11-year-old handed me a butane lighter. Oh good, I thought. Perhaps now would be a good time to ask about the butane lighters and the two books of matches I spied in the drawer next to his bed when I was vacuuming his room and, I will have to confess, poking parentally around. I didn't have to say anything. Jed saw me look at the lighter and then look at his face. He immediately fingered somebody else—a good friend, no doubt—as having found the lighter and given it to him. That gave me the opening I needed, and I swear I heard my father's voice, tone and sentence structure fall from my lips, as I said, "Thanks. Where did he find it, in the drawer of your night table, next to the green butane lighter and the clear one and the purple one and the two packs of matches?"

Jed cleared his throat and proceeded to tell some fairly intriguing tales of how such items were being found with increasing frequency about town. I agreed that a hidden wealth of incendiary devices abounded for anyone willing to scan the ground around his person. I also used the opportunity to say that fire, however fascinating it most certainly was, could fast and easily get away from your ability to control it, and that I had only recently talked to a woman whose 15-year-old son had accidentally set fire to their house. So, I said, while approaching Danny's smoke bomb with the butane lighter, you had to be really careful with fire. I did not add, for some reason, that I had almost set fire to my friend's home while he and I were playing with matches in the crawl space underneath his house when I was about 8 years old. The smoke bomb rolled around the driveway spewing purple smoke, and the boys thanked me for my lecture and scampered down the street, where I periodically heard the report of a firecracker or two.

Choosing the Boy to Hurt

My boys had enjoyed a fairly exhausting, exhilarating Tuesday, though logistically complicated, even for a summer already replete with planned activities and a torrent of invitations. That steamy morning, their swim team had triumphed over their arch-rivals by a margin so narrow (313 points to 310) as to render each and every member's individual performance decisive to the collective outcome. Every contribution was crucial, and all day every kid brimmed with an explosive giddiness.

Danny lapsed occasionally into disappointment over his placing fourth in a freestyle race of kids 8 and under, until I explained to him over and over that since he was bested by three of his own teammates, all of them 8 years old, he stood a handsome chance to place first in that same race for the next two years. It took 10 minutes of artificially animated enthusiasm to bring up his mood, and I don't think the explanation had any effect on it so much as did the artificially animated enthusiasm. For Danny, the next two years bears the same conceptual weight as "after you die and go to Heaven."

The Lowe boys were scheduled to spend that evening and night with their dad, since their mother would be working late and staying in the city. But post-swim meet, Jed's swim team friends had plotted a mass, victory-sleep-over party at the home of a pal, Jonathan Kiely, whose parents had caught the dreaded, 24-hour, viral amnesia that temporarily erases the memory of the last time you hosted a sleep-over party for a horde of preteen boys (let alone on a humid, summer evening).

I did not mind. Group sleep-overs have been a hallmark of Jed's eleventh summer, and the group is happy and amazingly well-behaved, though their aftermath requires professional fumigation. Danny and I wouldn't have seen Jed at all Tuesday afternoon were it not for his requiring the delivery of clothes and sleeping paraphernalia to the Kielys'. He would bicycle there, himself, so that he could bicycle to the pool with his mates the next morning for swim team practice and more exultation.

Danny, Jed and I first had to deliver the bedding by car, then return home for Jed to get his bike and go back to the Kielys'. I knew as soon as we pulled up to the Kiely homestead that bringing Danny within sensate distance of the party was a mistake. Eleven-year-old boys swarmed over the lawn like enrapt religious fanatics speaking in tongues, while stragglers from other age groups shot baskets in the driveway. Danny's eyes bulged out of his head. I could hear his heart pounding. Jed jumped out of the car, flipped a baseball hat and a smart remark about it to pal Kevin Kretz (something like: "This is only the 29th time this week you've left your hat at my house") and forged his way through the crowd to deposit his sleeping equipment inside.

Meanwhile, an older Kiely boy, one for whom discourse with a 6-year-old had lost its social criminality, leaned into the car and with genuine exuberance invited Danny to stay. Danny turned to me as if he had seen the Face of God. Nodding in spastic anticipation, he chirped, "Can I, Dad? Please? Can I? Yes? Yes?" Dumbfounded, I stammered, "Well, if it's all right with Mr. Kiely," who at that moment was approaching with weary resignation.

Within seconds, while the beleaguered Joe Kiely talked to me, Jed returned to the car. Finding Danny gone, off playing basketball with the older-than-11-year-olds, he asked, and with obvious suspicion, "Where's Danny?"

I looked at Joe Kiely, the father of sons. He bowed his head. He knew.

I longed for, but did not have, an older brother who would love, teach, protect me and take me with him to places I might otherwise not be allowed to go without a grown-up, but probably also abandon me when he reached a certain age and call me a jerk for saying what when we were alone together made him laugh hysterically but when his friends were near made him snort. I also wished for—though less fervently—but did not have a younger brother, one I could help, teach, trust, wrestle, play catch and conspire with; though who also probably would follow me all over town precisely when I didn't want him around, and who with his smug little smile would weasel his way into every fun activity I ever invented or was invited to by my friends.

I have been watching with dread for the inevitably cruel separation of my older from my younger son, hoping with the insane optimism so predictably prevalent among sufferers of Parental Stupidity Syndrome that they might evade it, while at the same time certain as a New York cynic that they would not.

Midway through my answer about Danny, Jed pulled his hat down over his eyes and slumped into the back seat as if I had wangled an invitation for him to attend an antique show with his grandmother. In homicidal tones, he muttered a condemnation of Danny for ruining his life. I had to decide on the spot which of my son's hearts I would break in the next five minutes.

I chose Danny's, because his inclusion in the party was both accidental and late, chronologically. He wailed, of course, and tore me to shards. When we got home, he fell prostrate in the driveway, until I recommended the more comfortable front lawn, where I forced him to listen to me talk about how he would be 11 years old, someday. I knew it was stupid, futile and boring, but I couldn't stop myself. It seemed to be part of the job.

When a Boy Rides Shotgun

I bet some fathers of 6-year-old boys are fun to be with when they run errands. I bet I'm not.

My father might have been; I can't say for certain. I keep thinking that I really enjoyed accompanying him, recalling how much I relished even the invitation ("C'mon, Ed. Let's go for a ride."), let alone the exclusivity of his company, as we indulged such adventures as the Amityville Post Office, the bank, the Municipal Building, the drugstore and the barbershop.

However, I review those scenes through a 40-year-old filter, so I cannot trust their clarity. I know for instance that at every stop, every single one, he encountered somebody he knew, and that he and the other man—very often the father of somebody I knew—always talked and talked, probably until I could feel myself growing older.

I know, too, that on the hottest summer days, his car had to have been filled to suffocation with unconditioned air; no cars in that era possessed conditioned air. Worse, every car he owned was black, rooftop-to-tirewalls, so the summer errand rides must have been brutally hot. I don't remember that part vividly, though. Vividly, I remember the smell of his Old Spice after-shave, and the way his right hand rested atop the steering wheel—thumb extended, pressed against the inside of the wheel, in control. I vividly remember the sound of the steering wheel whizzing dryly against his palm, as he allowed it to spin back into place after a turn. I remember the snap-shut of his Zippo cigarette lighter and the way he exclaimed, "Eddie Lowe!" out of nowhere, as if he had just rounded a corner and spotted me for the first time in years. I would say, "What?" and he would just smile.

My Danny wanted to ride his bike to his friend's Wednesday morning. I said, "No. We have to run some errands." Right away, mine wasn't an invitation so much as a sentencing. I thought it might help to tell him what we had to do. The electricity had just disappeared, following a boom from around the corner. I had pulled myself away from my suddenly lifeless computer and said I might as well clear up some details. I had to procure cash and deposit it in an account for Colleen, who at the moment was en route between Wyoming and Arizona with no mailing ad-dress and a birthday approaching. She would have to discover her birthday gift by pressing the account inquiry button at an automatic teller machine. While I was at it, I said, I would straighten out some banking problems involving me and Grandma Doe, Doe being a childhood abbreviation of Dolores as well as doe-eyed, both of which she still is.

"What's the problem?" Danny asked, trying generously, I suspected, to seem interested, but placing me in an awful posi-tion. Good manners required that I now try to explain to him banking policies that I did not understand. I began my story. I told him that Grandma Doe had opened a savings account in the Roosevelt Savings Bank in Massapequa and that I wanted to put money in her account every month or so by sending a check to the bank. But the bank would not allow me, I explained. They said I could only deposit the money in person.

Meanwhile, Danny and I arrived at the bank where I had intended to withdraw cash from my account via the automatic teller machine and deposit it in Colleen's account via automatic teller machine, except that the automatic teller machine screen said, Temporarily Out of Service. We drove away in search of another machine-equipped bank, while I droned on.

I asked the information operator for the number of Roosevelt Bank in Massapequa, and I called them, I said, and someone told me I could deposit the check by mail if I wrote a letter asking their permission and had Grandma Doe sign the letter. So, I did that, but when Grandma offered my letter at Massapequa, the lady told her I still would have to appear in person, and that, by the way, nobody in Massapequa had ever told me to write such a note, as Grandma Doe said they had. I, of course, insisted that someone had, but I was wrong, because as it turns out, the people at the Massapequa branch don't answer any telephone calls. The information operator doesn't even give you a Massapequa number when you ask for the Roosevelt Bank in Massapequa. She gives you a number in Garden City. You go to Massapequa with wrong information from Garden City, thinking you got it from Massapequa, and Massapequa tells you they don't give out wrong information; you must have gotten it from Garden City, and they're right, but you don't know it.

Danny was laughing, so maybe he was having a good time running errands. We stopped at a second bank where the ATM was out of service, and I kept talking, while I looked around for a third bank.

So, Grandma Doe gave the Roosevelt lady my check, but the next day, I said that their policy was ridiculous, because I wasn't trying to take money out, I was trying to put it in; and so I called the Home Savings Bank next door and asked them if I could deposit checks in her account by mail. Turns out, when you call the Home Savings Bank in Massapequa, you get their offices in Farmingdale. It must be a virus they all have. Anyway, they said, "No problem," so we tried to close out the Roosevelt account, but we couldn't because my check hadn't cleared, and I have to meet Grandma Doe today and do that.

"Dad, it's probably because the electricity went out," Danny said.

"What is?"

"That the computers don't work, the bank machines."

I looked at him, for a long moment.

"Danny Lowe!" I exclaimed, changing the subject.

"What?" he asked. I smiled. I shook my head. "You're right," I said.

Alone—Like a Switchboard

I am alone.

The separation we have talked about for years is effected; we are partners in parenthood only, new members of the majority statistic of our generation. How surprising a relief is not worrying about it, any more.

The boys are away with their mother for a few weeks. The girls—the women—are busy in their adult lives. I am reclined on a sofa, by myself, in my own place, the television turned off; and the stereo, and the radio and the radar oven, all turned off. Listening to the monsoon summer of 1992, I am surrounded by pleasantries: a cold can of O'Doul's, a bag of M&M's peanut candy, a telephone, a book, *Newsweek* and *Time* magazines, some mail and a list of times and places where I am scheduled to talk about myself, which I claim to hate bitterly, but which I then do so frequently that I must be lying. A man could be far worse than merely insufferable, yet, for some reason, I seem to fear that most.

With no distractions, I am more distracted than ever. Every time I try to donate some of my attention to the book or to a magazine, I feel as if I should be contemplating an important issue instead, ruminating about the worth of my life, how it contributes to or damages somebody else's. As soon as I conjure an acceptably profound subject for meditation, however, the question arises as to whether this is garbage night. Or is it recycling night? Or is it one of the two remaining nights when the question ought not arise? And, if it is garbage night, do I have a respectable amount of garbage? I haven't yet created a volume of solid waste as would fill a garbage can. Do the collectors prefer to heft a full load twice a month, or a flimsy donation twice a week?

Wait a minute, I think. This is a peaceful night. Enjoy this. All your responsibilities are in the hands of other people, capable people. You can do nothing, worry about nothing, think about nothing. You've always said you prefer doing nothing to doing anything. Just do it.

The phone warbles. (They don't ring, any more).

"Hi."

"Hi, how are the boys?"

"Great; tired. They had a good day. We did a lot of bike riding. Is it raining at home?"

"It's different from rain, less relenting. It's more like atmospheric conquest. I just stuck my arm out the door to see if a drop of air would hit me. How's Nantucket?"

"Gray, but clearing up. The boys want to say hi."

"Hi Dad . . . Hi Dad. Dad, this house is awesome! It has decks all around the outside, and you can see the ocean. It's bigger than your house, but I wanna sleep at your house when we get back. We saw a rabbit . . ."

[Boooop] "Hold on, I have another call all of a sudden . . ."

[Click] "Hi, Dad. Are you doing anything tonight? Can I bring the baby over just for two hours. Great. Thanks. Be right there."

[Click] "That was T.C. She's bringing Shannon over. Is Danny near the phone? Wait . . . somebody's at the door. It can't possibly be T.C. She just . . . oh, it's Grandma. Come in, I'm talking to Jed and Danny. T.C. and Shannon are on their way over."

"Hi Dad, I love you."

"Hi, Dan. I love you, too. Are you having [Boooop] a good time . . . Hold on, I have another call. Is this amazing? No calls all day. Now I get three calls in the same minute . . ."

"This is the AT&T operator with a collect call from Colleen. Will you accept the charges?"

"Yes . . . well, no. I don't know. I mean, the problem is, see, I'm talking to her brother in yet another state. Can I call her back?"

"Excuse me, sir?"

"Dad, you don't know the number."

"I'm sorry, operator. Okay, I'll accept the call. I'll get the number. I'll call her back. Mom, open the door. Somebody just pulled into the driveway. It has to be T.C."

"Hi, Dad."

"Hi, Coll. I'm home alone. No, I'm not. Your sister just arrived with your niece. Your grandmother just arrived and is greeting them at the door. Your brothers are on hold from Nantucket. Where are you? And give me your number, so I can call you back."

"I'm in Phoenix, at Aunt Peggy's. I'm living for a month in Sedona, but you can't call me there, because my landlady screens all her calls on her answering machine, which she keeps in her bedroom, and since she doesn't get home until 7 o'clock every night, that's when I find out who called me. Then I have to call back from her bedroom, so it's easier to drive to Phoenix."

"How clear. Look, let me say goodnight to Danny and Jed and hello to Grandma Doe and T.C. and Shannon, and I'll call you back."

[Click] "Hello, Dan."

"No, it's me; they're going to bed. They're pretty tired."

"It's just as well. My mother is here, and T.C. just arrived with the baby, and Colleen is waiting for me to call her back. I'm in an avalanche. I'll talk to the boys tomorrow."

T.C. leaves. Grandma stays for a while, then she leaves. Shannon falls asleep on my chest, and I call Colleen, who quit a waitressing job in the Grand Tetons and traveled first to Boulder, Colorado, then to Utah, then to Arizona. She had taken the Wyoming job because when she waited tables at a busy resort in Yellowstone National Park last year, she was put off by the commercial hustle of the business. She wanted more tranquillity. The Grand Tetons job gave her plenty of tranquillity, but no income. "You won't believe what I'm doing," she says, bursting into hysterical laughter. "I start tomorrow at a Burger King. The manager is this cool lady, a little hard, a little tough, but good. She looked at my references and said, 'Just tell me why you would want to work at a Burger King.' I said, 'I've been waitressing and, well, no offense intended, but I wanted to do something mindless.' And she said [Boooop] 'I understand. I waitressed, too. You can start tomorrow.'"

"That's great. Hold on a second, I got call-waiting. [Click] Hello."

"Hello. This is Jim Small. I just wanted to see how you were doin'."

"Uh, good. I'm having a hard time adjusting to the solitude, though."

Havoc

I have not lived in a toddler-proof environment in some time; some, meaning a mere six years in actual time but much, much longer than that in emotional memory and mental preparedness.

The difference in real time and emotionally apparent time is significant. My son Dan's first year on Earth drew nigh in the fall of 1986. Other changes and events occurred in the fall of 1986 and seem very recent to me now; I can recall clearly the smell of the interior of my 1979 Chevy Blazer, the sound of small boys scampering up and down the stairs, the anticipation of Jed's first day of first grade.

Not so, however, Danny's toddlerhood and the precautionary measures and paraphernalia required to survive it. I recall vividly his bubbly laugh, but I have to strain to remember the sounds and sights of his creative chaos. I have to stare hard at photographs, ignore his long eyelashes and puffy cheeks to focus more intently on the stains on his bibs and the invisible coagulants pressed into his hair. By some mechanism as protective as the lush spring growth that follows an autumn fire in the pine barrens, I have lost the freneticism of that time; the period itself seems more distant, ancient even, as if it happened 10 years back, maybe further.

So, last week, when my oldest planted her 1-year-old daughter, Shannon, in my sole keeping for the afternoon and evening, I was shockingly unprepared, both emotionally and logistically. I had to hastily reprogram my brain for conditions my memory had long since blanketed with tricks of revisionist history.

Also, T.C. had neglected to tell me how her daughter had become so independently ambulatory in the days since last we nuzzled. No longer did Shannon simply stand awaiting the admiration of her audience and then waddle forward a half-dozen aimless steps as for a stunning encore; she now aimed herself forward and waddled with full intent and purpose, as if the audience might just as well go about their business or get lost. She seemed unconcerned about such impressions as she might make upon her admirers and determined, instead, to dislodge every movable item within her grasp and then eat the rest.

Just inside my doorway is a standing lamp with a round, glass table-top affixed at armchair height to its stem. In an attempt to create a new habit that would minimize loss and misplacement, I have been depositing keys and prescription eyeglasses on that glass top upon my own entry into the house. Shannon made for the keys, first.

Smiling, for I was amused, I reached for and grasped the keys before she got to them, but then realized that my eyeglasses were imperiled, too, and took them as well. So, she grabbed a pile of coins whose presence I could not explain and was tasting them by the time I had set down the keys and eyeglasses on a higher plane. I took the coins from her and put them in the pocket of my jeans. The act and such concentration as it required offered her enough time and freedom to snatch at the plastic cup containing the fat, black, felt-tipped marker whose origin or purpose escaped me and whose very existence, in fact, I had somehow managed to ignore entirely until the instant she appeared to be aiming the felt tip at her tongue. I grabbed the whole apparatus and wrenched it away, as gently as I could while still being timely. Surprised and thrown slightly off balance, Shannon then clamped her little hands onto the round, glass top of the table lamp, leaning backward with continuing imbalance as she seized it more securely, so that the table lamp in its entirety began to topple toward her in such a way as to threaten decapitation, or worse. I blocked the stem of the falling lamp with my right forearm, the lampshade skimming past my chin and resting on my chest, blocking my view of my granddaughter, who, by the sound of it, had meanwhile relinquished her grip on the glass, plopped down on her diaper, rolled to her left, stood again, reorganized her thoughts and priorities and was making for the den and another goal: my desk.

I hurried to protect the work, notes, letters, files, empty cups, computer disks, photographs, dishes, books, packages, checks, bills, telephones, calendars, wires and—ohmygodno—the keyboard of the computer, with which she could dispatch a week's work into outer space with the touch of her pudgy little, untrained fingertips.

Since it was dinnertime, anyway, I decided to distract her by airlifting her bodily out of the den and into the kitchen, where I previously had decided I would make myself a simple meal requiring only that I boil some frozen ravioli and heat some sauce to pour over it. While I turned on the stove-top flame, she knocked over a box of Cheerios. I moved her away a few feet, and she found the Black & Decker Dustbuster, grasped at its trigger handle and scared herself nearly into the next dimension with its resultant whine. While I filled a pot with water, she found a blue bag of hickory blend charcoal briquets and would have blackened her hands with their dust had I not whisked it away in time and tossed it into a cabinet under the sink, which drew her attention to the tantalizing array of door and drawer handles on either side of my legs.

I ate standing, pressing my backside against two kitchen drawers, the sole of my right sneaker crossways the juncture of the two cabinet doors directly beneath the sink, and stretching my left leg to press its calf against the cabinet doors adjacent on the other side.

I ate fast, too.

Homework, What a Kick

The boys pored over homework without break from immediately after dinner until it was past prudent time for bed. I felt like an ogre, a spinach monster, guilty and angry that their summer seemed to have ended without sufficient warning, and ugly for having carped steadily from the moment I greeted them until the moment I held up toothbrushes.

We had rendezvoused at 6:30 P.M., the apex of the last 90 minutes of hot September daylight. I did say I would let them have a kick with the soccer ball while I prepared dinner, but then I nuked dinner in the microwave, giving them upward of 2½ minutes of carefree recreation before I bellowed that their eventide schedule was about to commence. After that, I subjected them to my cooking, commanded them to start their homework, foiled every attempt by one brother to torment the other and now, after two hours of presiding ruefully over what I suspected was unremitting drudgery, I was forcing them to brush. What a guy, Dad; more fun than a barrel of Ceclor.

The adult in me, the recessive part, knows the value of homework—that homework is to academic pursuit what having a kick is to sharpening the deftness required for soccer—but the more logical child in me asks the same questions I can't help imagining a child would ask. After my children have retired for the night, I am left alone with my imagination and a curious compulsion to review some of their frequently baffling homework: magic squares, writing a script q, understanding the difference between rotation and revolution and homonyms and synonyms, using the dictionary. My imaginings of their questions are much kinder than my imaginings of what my own would be if I were back in their position. All of my questions would begin with, "Oh yeah?"

Oh yeah? If it's so good for you, this homework business, why does it feel so much better to kick a soccer ball than it does to look up the meaning of the word rachitic? and then not find it, by the way, and then have to ask your Dad to look it up; and then watch him not find it under rachitic but under rachitis instead (and how fair is that, by the way); and then hear your Dad mumble something like, "Rachitic must mean, looking like somebody who has rickets, whatever that means?"

I know somewhere in my mind it is worth the exercise to look up rachitic and find it at the bottom of rachitis, but I don't feel that it is.

And, oh yeah, why does it feel so much better to score a goal in a soccer game, when the opportunity arises, than it does to announce at some warp in your lifetime that you happen to know from your September 16, 1992, sixth-grade homework that if ever you should wish to describe somebody as looking like he is suffering from rickets, whatever rickets are, you can just as easily say that he is rachitic-looking and still be on target, linguistically speaking?

Re-imagining myself as a father again, I really cannot summon a convincing answer to the first question. Never having used the word rachitic, even in the word business, I imagined no good answer to the rachitic question. I did not dare conjure anymore questions I could not answer, because I already was feeling more ignorant than I had planned. Most knowledge doesn't make sense. I vividly recalled a friend of mine going through the junior high school years with a son who could think with terrifying precision but not spell at all, a deadly combination in a language wherein the rules follow the spelling, instead of the other way around.

"Ma," he would bark, "they spell Yugoslavia with a Y? Why?"

Or: "Wait a minute! A Filipino is somebody who comes from the Philippines? Are you kidding me? Who invented this? I'm not doin' this."

I was relieved, though, that when asked in real life about rachitic, I had consulted the dictionary first and refrained from prematurely blurting out my initial speculation (Uh . . . pertaining to ratchets?).

One of the other words was vagary. I had not used the word

much in my life, because I never could get a specific handle on what it meant. If anybody had asked me what a vagary was, I would have answered, "Ask a politician. Whatever he says, that's what it is. "With the boys asleep, I looked it up, imagining myself to be 11 years old, wishing I were outside having a kick and wondering whether life with my father was always going to mean dull work. I found it: "Vagary, n., pl—ries. An extravagant or erratic notion or action."

"Great. What's a notion?"

"What's erratic?"

"What's extravagant?"

As I read, I wonder at what point and in what grade I will become useless. Jed is now taking Spanish. Wonderful. I took Latin and French.

The earth rotates on its axis . . . yeah . . . revolves around the sun . . . Yeah, I remember all that . . . At what time of the year does the Northern Hemisphere lean neither toward the sun nor away from it . . . yeah, well, according to this picture, September and March . . . OK . . . and when the Northern Hemisphere is tilted toward the sun, what season is it in the Southern Hemisphere? OK, I can still do this. I can make it through another year, although I may look pretty rachitic by spring.

3 B's of Adjusting: Books, Bags, Bread

Every now and then life requires that I talk myself through a new schedule.

As a father under relatively new circumstances, I pick up the boys late on a Tuesday afternoon from their mother's house to bring them to my place, where they will eat dinner, do homework, watch television, sleep, awaken in the morning, wash, dress, get into my car and ride back to their other house to await the school bus.

Right now, I stand in my ex-driveway talking to myself the same way I talked to myself in front of my locker on the first day of my freshman year, reciting what classes I had in the morning, so that I could then recite what tasks I had to do and what items I needed to do them.

I have dinner covered, I think to myself. I have meat; I have a package of frozen, creamed spinach; I have leftover sweet potatoes I can nuke. After dinner, we'll do homework. That requires books. Books are in backpacks. I need their backpacks so they can do homework . . .

"Boys, where are your backpacks? Got your backpacks? Get your backpacks." If I say the word three times, I know they may hear it once.

"And gym bags." They have to have gym bags for the morning.

"And your gym bags. You have your gym bags? Put your gym bags in the car, too."

So far, very good.

"Sneakers." The sneakers should be in the gym bags. But, wait a minute. Don't be fooled, here. They're probably wearing the sneakers. Aha! They are. They need to put their shoes in the gym bags, so in the morning they have shoes.

"Where are your shoes? Get your shoes. Put your school shoes in your gym bags.

"School clothes?" I have school clothes for them at my house. I have pants, shirts and socks. Am I sure? I'm sure. OK. "We can go. Can we go? Food, books, clothes, gym bags, sneakers, shoes . . . Yes, we can go.

"All right, boys, let's go! Listen, I already started a fire in the grill. So, while I'm making dinner, you can play soccer in the back, but then right after dinner, you have to start your homework."

"Grill? Can't you make macaroni and cheese?"

"Macaroni and cheese?"

"Yeah," they chime in harmony. "That's what we want."

Should I object to this? Boil water, add stuff, serve. One pot, two dishes, two forks; case closed. A gift.

"Well . . . yeah, if that's what you want. I'll make macaroni and cheese. I hope you don't mind if I make real food for myself, but, hey, if you want macaroni and cheese, you got macaroni and cheese."

Two cereal-bowls-full they eat. I eat the meat and the leftover sweet potatoes; no point in cooking creamed spinach for one.

It is 7:35 P.M. While the sink is filling with hot water, and they are kicking a soccer ball in the living room, I begin chanting that homework time begins in five minutes. I hope to get them started by 8. Every five minutes, I subtract another minute from the countdown. At 7:40, I bellow that four minutes remain before homework time. "Open your backpacks and take out your books!" I yell five minutes later. "Only three minutes to go." Meanwhile, I talk to myself at the sink.

"I have to get up early to get them off. Obscenely early. I have to set the alarm. I have to make breakfasts and lunches. Do I have stuff? Yes, I have. I have cereal; two kinds. Do I have juice boxes? Yes, believe it or not. Good. What a guy. Peanut butter and jelly I have. Bread. I bet I don't have enough bread. Damn. Oh, good: six slices. But look at the milk; less than a quart. Not good. I can't leave them here alone while I get milk, not this early in the transition. And I don't want to put them in the car; I want them to start homework. Bag it. They'll have crisp cereal in the morning.

"One minute 'til homework time!" I sing. "Hey! What are you doing with the milk? That's all the milk I got. Aw, man! Now, what are we going to do for cereal in the morning? We'll have no milk for cereal!"

"So? You got eggs?"

"No, I don't have eggs."

"Oh. All right. You got cinnamon?"

"Cinnamon?"

"Yeah. We'll make cinnamon toast."

"I don't think I have enough bread, if I make sandwiches."

"You need six slices of bread; that's all you need."

"What are you, a calculator? Aren't you supposed to be torturing your little brother? Look at this, I got exactly six slices, plus two heels."

"So all you need is cinnamon, sugar and butter or margarine."

"Say, you from around here? Start your homework."

"Okay. Oh. Dad, do you have an encyclopedia?"

"No, I don't have an encyclopedia. Is that what you need to do homework? Because it's not in this house. The only encyclopedia we have is in Mommy's house."

"For Spanish, I have to pick a subject and research it and write a page about it. Like bullfighting . . ."

"Or jai alai, maybe."

"I don't know. Whatever. But I need the encyclopedia. Suppose I go back home tonight and do it and stay over here tomorrow night."

"Me, too," says the other macaroni-and-cheese hound.

"Why do you have to do everything I do?" says the elder.

"Don't start!" says I.

We have a family conference call. I drive them home. The next night, after they have eaten the meat and the creamed spinach, and while they are doing their homework, I ask the elder: "How did you make out with your Spanish assignment? Did you do it?"

"Yeah."

"Well, how'd you make out?"

"I didn't. It's not due until Friday."

Wrapping Up Days of Blunder

I watched with mounting anxiety as a backpack-burdened Danny Lowe trudged toward my house, dragging behind his 6-year-old-self two clear plastic bags filled with long tubes. The tubes, I feared, could only be gift-wrapping paper, which his customers no doubt ordered and paid for weeks ago—which might as well have been years ago—all of them relatives and neighbors who now had every right to expect delivery, and in amounts and patterns at least approximating the specifications on their orders.

I had been faring well, otherwise. The boys had been living with me for two school days and would be living with me for two more school days, while their mother attended a business conference in Arizona. The schedule she had left behind included basketball practices on Tuesday and Thursday nights for Jed and a registration appointment Wednesday night for both boys to join CYO swimming for the winter. No problem, I thought, with just a touch of arrogance.

The schedule did not mention that Jed also had soccer practice Thursday, overlapping basketball practice, and I did not read carefully enough the accompanying pamphlet from school officials suggesting that each student wear the color red on Wednesday in honor of one noble philosophical campaign or another. For reasons I assume are inextricably linked to gender-prejudice, it never before had fallen to me to peruse daily backpack correspondence, so I was not in the habit of heeding the medium. I will have to adjust. Tragically, I fear on my own account, my sons wore black-and-blue rugby shirts on Wednesday.

I hope it did not count against them as an intended sarcasm, because wearing the opposite of the recommended hue is the sort of gesture I habitually made in my youth as a student of the obnoxious.

Jed missed a gym class more or less on my account, too, for being unequipped. His gym bag, we learned with seconds to spare before the bus arrived, was in his mother's kitchen that morning, while he and the rest of his paraphernalia were in mine. I had the choice of panicking and then driving around town on a combined paraphernalia-procuring, bus-route run; or of allowing Jed to suffer the consequences of his inattentiveness to my gym-bag exhortations the day before. I chose to let him suffer instead of me. I still feel pretty dastardly about it.

Nor did I remember that Wednesday was pizza day, when I could have spared myself the trouble of making peanut butter and jelly sandwiches at 6:30 in the morning, when most of my biological bulbs are too dim for any culinary artistry, however primitive; nor did I bring Jed's CYO basketball raffle ticket stubs and monies to either of the two basketball practices, because I knew zero about any raffle.

Together, though, the boys and I unruffled all those minor complications with relative ease and success. It wasn't exactly seamless. We arrived an hour early for one of the basketball practices and were spared the embarrassment of waiting the whole time by a kindly security guard prudent enough to inquire about our presence and then inform us that we not only were early but at the wrong school as well. We arrived on time at the second location, so nobody but the security guard at the wrong building noticed our blunders.

The gift-wrapping paper played the high strings of my mind for days, though. I developed a private paranoia regarding it. She could not have predicted the arrival of gift wrap, I thought to myself that morning, as Danny swung the bag of wrapping paper against the trunk of the dying dogwood. She could not have conspired to attend this particular business conference in Arizona merely to evade the arrival of gift wrap.

Oh, yeah. You would, wouldn't you? By an earlier coincidence, Danny had happened to be in my custodial care weeks before, on the evening he had gathered together his gift-wrap orders and their corresponding monies. I recall that he asked me then to apply my scissoring skills to the order forms, so as to sever the names and addresses of his customers, and the numbers and dollar amounts of their orders, from the accompanying colorful photographs and advertising copy (showing how elegant and beautiful gifts would look if you were to wrap them in the gift wrap this bright-faced, innocent-looking boy was peddling, obviously as a way to entice unsuspecting citizens to help subsidize his education at a private Maria Montessori school. How I love the concept).

I recalled folding the severed order forms neatly into his backpack, hoping that he was correct in his dogged insistence that the advertising-photograph parts of the order forms no longer were useful and thus were supposed to be cut away, leaving behind long, wispy slivers of paper with graph-paper-style boxes bearing the names, choices, quantities and dollar figures pertinent to each customer's order. It had struck me that once separated from the bright, graphic, substantive part of the order forms, the long, thin business parts would be reduced in size to the likes of ribbons, or scrap paper, and might easily be mistaken for such and discarded.

I said so, but not often enough and not with sufficient passion in my voice. Frankly I know I thought that once I stuffed the slivers back into the backpack and zipped shut their compartment, my responsibility for them would disappear forever. I know that I was evading responsibility for the fund-raising sales program, as I had evaded it when we all lived under the same roof all the time, and as I evaded in my previous incarnations with my grown daughters.

"Dan, I got an idea," I said after a day or two of struggling to prevent them from conducting fraternal swordfights with the wrapping paper rolls. "Listen, it gets so dark so early, now, there's no way you're going to find out after school who ordered how much of what wrapping paper. Why don't you save it until Saturday," I suggested in the phony, singsong tone of a unconscionable cad. "First of all, Mommy will be home Saturday . . ."

A Double-Entry Family Account

Tomorrow, members of my family will commemorate the seventh anniversary of the birth of Danny Lowe, which, because of my mother's indomitable superstitious streak, will remind me of the death eight and a half months earlier that year of Ed Lowe, Sr., Danny's grandfather.

I am trapped in this morbidity by the power of repeated suggestion and no doubt have trapped my children in it, too. News of even a distant cousin's success at conceiving a new relative almost always inspires in me an uncharacteristic spasm of prudence—to make an advance payment of a monthly life insurance premium, for example—this, despite my insufferable, above-it-all insistence that I do not subscribe to the myths of the ancestors, including the one requiring one of us to drop dead upon the arrival of another.

Periodically, I declare myself opposed to the perpetuation of an ignorance but then blithely go about perpetuating it, myself, as if I somehow were mitigating my inclusion in the mythologizing process merely by declaring my awareness of it. If I were to examine myself more strictly than I have the courage to, I am sure I would find more preposterous examples of that insanity, but who needs to know so much about himself?

The fantasy is this: My mother believes, or at least strongly suspects, that a pattern exists regarding the exits and entrances of characters in our family cast; that every entrance upon our stage by a new member has been, and therefore will be, either heralded or followed immediately by the exit of another, in an uninterrupted, one-for-one pattern of birth-death, or death-birth, whichever order of succession applies at the moment of re-utterance of the belief.

According to my observations, the rules of succession and the qualifications for family membership loosen from time to time to accommodate the pattern's inconsistencies, which are, I must confess, infrequent. If someone dies, though, and no pregnancies erupt on the available horizon, the life-for-a-life theory basically goes unmentioned until distant cousins or their next-door neighbors conceive somebody new. On the other hand, if a child is born into the family, and no blood relative affords him the courtesy of choking to death in however unwitting a welcoming celebration, someone in the family will breathe new significance into the first available funeral procession sighted. Also, supporters of the superstition will quickly inflate whatever sliver of a relationship exists between the corpse and the innocent babe, despite the exaggerated wincing of such nay-sayers as my increasingly cantankerous self.

Danny's case set back the cause of reason by whole generations and could not be argued. We, his pending parents, knew at
my father's funeral in March 1985, that medical science had just
spotted traces of Danny in an amniotic puddle and then predicted his full-weight debut in mid-November. We had just
learned it. We even knew, microscopic though he was at the
time, that Danny would be Daniel Philip Lowe. Fundamentalist
proponents of the life-cycle superstition clucked and nodded
knowingly when the realization struck and became public that
Danny was conceived probably a week or so before the collapse
of his paternal grandfather's great heart, leaving absolutely no
doubt among them as to the Divine Plan to keep the clan numerically balanced.

I am certain that as soon as one person repeated the perceived coincidence aloud, the seed of superstition took root in
other young brains, requiring no further evidence, ever, for it to
be devoutly resurrected at subsequent funerals and baptisms for
another hundred years. I could tell Jed and Danny today that the
belief is merely a superstition and merits no remembrance, and
by the telling alone permanently inscribe it on their memories
and the memories of their descendants.

I suppose not much harm has been done to the family over
the centuries by this otherwise idealized method of population
control, except to such faith and skill as we have dismally failed
to show in evidentiary mathematics. The myth certainly has
comforted my mother at crucial moments in her life, and it
seems already to have served Danny well. He evidently feels as
connected as an understudy to his "Pop" because of the machinery of this superstition. Privately, he has boasted to me of vivid
memories of my father, and has regaled several of us with de-
tailed recountings of them, sights and sounds included, and with
a genuinely wistful fondness.

"Dad, 'member when Pop used to fall asleep in his chair with
Jed on his chest? I do." It is a remarkable feat to behold. I believe
that these manufactured memories will collide one day with
Danny's by then more analytical, adult mind as a subject of meditation and provide him with long fits of entertaining confusion,
but I wonder, also, what other myths and irreversible prejudices
have we already transmitted to the man inside this boy? How
formed is he by such messages as we passed to him inadvertently,
while we thought him inattentive or incapable of heeding us?

I recall the first time I addressed an auditorium filled with fourth graders. I had been hoodwinked by a school administrator into thinking I was appearing before another horde of high schoolers, whose skepticism I figured I understood and even sympathized with. When I learned that my fourth-period prisoners were only 9 or 10 years old, I feared I had no information to offer them nor any equipment to communicate it.

They then stunned me with their questions—more probing and challenging than those of any pack of adults. I remember feeling very strongly that these fourth graders already were formed, that their parents' opportunities for influencing them were all spent. The liars and cheats were visible before me, the saints, the strivers, the tough characters, the rebels and the sheep.

So, instead of torturing myself with the likely irrelevance of the unanswerable, obviously I should be fretting about the wisdom and value of a new, Nintendo acquisition. How infuriating is it that the old games won't play on the new machine?

If the Shoe Fits, Find It

Monday morning. I have roused the boys by squeezing their fingers and singing foolish songs. They still look imbecilic with sleep, but they are up.

Remembering the horrors of childhood bag lunches, I spread the peanut butter on both slices of bread. That way, the jelly won't soak into one slice during the bus ride to school, making the sandwich a peanut butter and wet-purple-bread sandwich, instead of a peanut butter and jelly sandwich. I place the boxes of Yoo-Hoo in the bottom of the bags, then the Drake's crumb cakes, then the sandwiches. Fresh from the dryer, the clothes are laid out on the living room floor in the shapes of a tall boy and a short boy. Even in their respective stupors, they will know who belongs to what.

Though it admittedly was limited, and probably deeply prejudiced, as well, my past experiences at fathering in a two-parent household cavalierly allowed for the mother to embrace the bulk of the responsibilities for whatever was supposed to happen to the children on school mornings. The apparent unfairness never seemed odd to me, or abnormal or even unfair.

It seems odd in retrospect, though, and I think about it while I plod through the morning rituals. "Danny, nice job getting dressed, but why are you walking around with one shoe? Where's your other shoe?" "I don't know." "Dan, you came here yesterday afternoon with two feet. Each foot was covered by a shoe. So, you must have two shoes. Did you have two shoes when you got out of the car?"

"Yes." "You've been in the living room, the kitchen, the bathroom and your bedroom. You have about 14 minutes to eat your Cinnamon Mini Buns and find the other shoe. You got that?"

"Yeah." "Jed, you don't have shoes on, either? Guess why your white socks are black on the bottom. Where are your shoes?" "Upstairs." "Good. At least you know. Go get 'em. What is it with you guys and shoes? Jed, did you brush your teeth?" "Yes." "I didn't." "You were supposed to brush your own teeth, not Jed's. Hello, Dan? I'm sorry, you're not getting this, are you? Too early. Just go upstairs with your brother and brush your teeth. And don't brush them the way you put on your shoe. Brush both the tops and the bottoms. Were you really thinking of getting on the school bus with one shoe?"

"No. Dad, I told you, I can't find my other shoe." "Have you looked? You have to look to find something. My guess is that it's probably right under the piece of air where your foot was when you took the shoe off."

"Dad!" "Dan! A shoe doesn't walk away empty. Where did you find the shoe you found?" "Right here. In the living room." "Any reason you would have taken the other one off in a different room? Don't they get along?" "Dad!" "Go brush your teeth and find your shoe." As a father cohabiting with a parental partner, I suffered no responsibilities for anybody's weekday morning ablutions but my own, nor was I expected to feed, clothe or equip anyone younger than I for either intellectual combat drills, lunch in the schoolyard or jumping jacks at gym class. These duties fell into the able hands of the resident mother, who I think suffered from an impossible dilemma: not wanting to share the ironic pleasure of the morning chores, while wishing at the same time that somebody competent would help her with them.

I, meanwhile, assumed quite comfortably that I was incompetent, despite such evidence as I presented myself whenever the mother was away and I presided over the alarm clock and the cereal bowls. Even then, however, I also assumed I owed my success to such preparations as someone else had made on my behalf, such as procuring the appropriate packaged lunch foods and folding the children's laundry in anticipation of my frantic, last-minute search. Finally, I never before noticed any pleasure in the work, ironic or otherwise; not until the whole of it became my responsibility, from junk food procurement, to laundry, to remembering to buy milk for breakfast cereal, even to setting the alarm clock the night before.

"Dad, I left my gym bag at Mommy's house. My shoes are in it." "I thought your shoes were upstairs." "No, my sneakers are." "Aha. Your sneakers are upstairs. Your shoes are in your gym bag. Your gym bag is at Mommy's, and you are not allowed to wear sneakers to school. Am I close? Do we have to get in the car and go to Mommy's to get the bus?"

[Silence. Obviously, the answer is yes]. "Dad, I still can't find my other shoe." "How is that possible? This is a little house. It has to be here." "But I looked!" "Do you have your other shoes at Mommy's? Do you know exactly where they are? Because we're gonna have to go to Mommy's for the gym bag. Do you know where you have two shoes, together, in the same place, one for each foot?"

"I think so." "Dan! Do you?" "Yes." "All right. Eat this, quick. I'll put your books in the car. When you're done, hop out to the car. I mean that. The grass is wet. Damn. I thought I had this covered. I thought I was getting good at this. I even liked it. I even made coffee. I can't believe this."

"Dad, take it easy. It's not your fault." "Hah?" "Yeah, Dad. It's Monday. Lighten up."

One Frozen Pop, to Go

I had expected to be alone for the first weekend in December, naively believing to be unalterable the information I had scrawled into the calendar boxes designating those days. I must remind myself that a kitchen calendar is merely a guide to a given month, in much the same way that the price of a boat is really only a down payment.

My sons were scheduled to accompany their mother to Boston, there to visit her second cousin (their second cousin once removed) and her second cousin's children (their third cousins).

The boys' mother and I don't have much to offer our sons in first cousins, having scant siblings between us. She has but one, the father of two grown children who live far away, and I haven't any. Almost all of Danny and Jed's cousin contemporaries are removed at least once from the family trunk, or they are located higher on the rungs of cousinhood, in seconddom or thirddom. It probably is important that my sons cling to what little currency they have in cousins, especially considering the cousin wealth to which they are exposed daily. Their neighborhood friends, the Kretzes, McLoughlins, McCarthys, McDermotts, O'Neills, Morans and McDonoughs, are all first cousins to each other, sometimes twice, Amityville being a smallish village. In one particularly exquisite case, a pair of my contemporaries, first cousins twice over who are the children of two mixed pairs of siblings, married sisters. Their children are more related to each other than they are to their own mothers.

Anyway, on the eve of the planned departure for Boston, Jed announced that he did not wish to go, but preferred instead to spend the weekend at his father's house, and for two specific reasons (lest the father suspect for a second that his scintillating wit and charming personality had any bearing on the son's preference): Jed wanted to attend the annual, outdoor Christmas-tree lighting ceremonies in the village Saturday night, and he wanted to try out for a soccer travel-team in neighboring Copiague on Sunday morning.

I would have felt more enthusiastic about the Christmas-tree lighting had winter not arrived abruptly at 3 Saturday afternoon. Later, in the cruel and howling dark, I hurriedly followed Jed around the gazebo in the middle of the village, not knowing exactly what he was looking for but knowing with certitude that I wanted to find the epicenter of the crowd, better to escape there the bitter wind. Suddenly, Jed spotted a platoon of pre-teen boys clad in billowing Starter jackets like his own and said, "Dad, I found my friends! See ya!" leaving me to frolic in the frozen street alone, absorbing the beauty and spirit of the inaugural evening of what the front office of the New York Islanders has dubbed the New Ice Age. I cannot be of good cheer after I have lost all feeling in my toes, and it's just as well that my son missed my involuntary, spasmodic evaluations of the ceremony.

Jed bunked that night with a fellow gang member whose mom returned him to my cleverly unlocked front door at 9 A.M. Sunday, in time to dress to try out with a dozen others for a travel team whose coach at an earlier tryout had already selected all but five members of his squad. I trudged out onto the field behind my son, surprised and dismayed that I was the only tryout parent in sight, though I had seen several familiar cars. If I were to freeze to death on a soccer field while staring into the jaws of the first unobstructed, gale of winter, I would have liked at least to have mumbled my final thoughts to a colleague father.

Eager for recognition as an all-pro father but keenly aware of the absence of any witnesses to my waning resolve, I steeled myself, leaned heroically into the killer gusts and withstood the frigid blast for two, maybe three minutes before beginning my stealthy retreat to the car. I passed along the way a squadron of dark-haired men publicly stripping off their coats and leggings to reveal brightly colored soccer shorts and jerseys. Each man kicked a soccer ball into the air repeatedly and in a pattern that would suggest the swirling shape of his personal signature. They were quick, deft and had thighs like the front fenders of a 1941 Lincoln, and they spoke a foreign language, which I took to be Eskimo. I raised my collar, ducked my head and started hustling my puny frame toward my car, when a man's deep, Sunday-morning voice interrupted my progress, crying, "Hey!" in a sort of friendly tone. Ahead of me was a full-sized station wagon whose owner-operator I recognized to be Steve Kretz, my lawyer, whom I first hired when I was 5, under the condition that I would still get to be captain, or chief, sheriff or president.

Four other men huddled in the car, one a McDonough so much a cousin of Steve's that they share all four grandparents between them. Each frozen dad had accompanied a son or daughter to the barren tundra and then fled its climate; all were happy to invite additional body heat into the car. There, in paternal imprisonment, we laughed with communal relief at the arrival of what appeared to be a semi-pro soccer team. They surely would drive the travel team coach off the field and end our ordeal sooner.

We also shared in that remaining half hour our knowledge, particularly of the nonverbal communications offered us during semi-conversations and non-conversations with apprentice adolescents and full-blown teenagers—what they actually would like to say while they are asking, say, for a ride to the high school. Translated accurately, none of the information can be repeated publicly without violating a bookload of ordinances on decorum, obscenity and blasphemy, or, frankly, without showing our hand.

But it was wickedly funny and, oddly, a great way to spend Sunday morning.

A Collect Call for Christmas

I had been gazing distractedly at my sons' creative tinsel distribution on my Christmas tree, when the computerized AT&T operator telephoned and asked me to press a button indicating that I would accept or not accept a collect call from my daughter, Colleen.

It has taken me some time to become cozy with computerized telephone operators, probably because I hate them. They lack a sense of humor, and they insist on plodding through the entire length of their deadly corporate recitations, despite my admonitions, despite my ready acceptance of the reversed charges and despite my eagerness to get them off the line so I can listen to my daughter, who was calling this week from an outdoor pay telephone in Gunnison, Colorado, where the temperature was 30 degrees below zero.

When computerized telephone solicitors first were introduced, and I was appalled and infuriated by the impersonal intrusion (as if I preferred personal intrusions), I would hang up on one as soon as it opened its smarmy speaker. Later, in a vain hope of discouraging whatever companies were trying to sales pitch products to me via automated sales pitcher, I would, upon discerning the telltale tone and cadence of a mechanical sales nonperson, place the telephone receiver on the coffee table and let the robotic smooth-talker drone on, spending message units on an unheeding mark who had literally turned his back on the monologue and seized the opportunity to go to the bathroom.

By the time long-distance operators metamorphosed into machines, I had lost patience even with my own petty vindictiveness and reverted to simply hanging up the instant I heard the telltale, introductory whirr of a computer. I thus hung up on computerized, collect calls from Colleen two or three times before I found out that the mechanical caller was heralding her and not selling a subscription to Toenail Clipper Collector Magazine.

So, this time, I waited eagerly for the temporal blank space the computerized operator would leave to permit Colleen to voice-identify herself, either as Dracula or Godzilla, and I then shouted my exuberant greetings. "Hi! Hello! How are ya?" I bellowed.

"Uh!" she answered. She'd had better days. I was surprised; Colleen had not called in four or five days, following a period during which she was calling almost daily. Generally, I read a diminution in filial call-frequency as an indication of financial solvency, social preoccupation, happiness and well-being. In establishing such prejudices, I referred to my own history as a college student. I called home more frequently when flat broke or facing a final exam in a course through which I had slept.

The wandering Colleen has been in Gunnison since she left Sedona, Arizona, where she spent some time examining her own head, which evidently is a preoccupation in Sedona. Having unearthed some unsettling secrets therein, Colleen made straightaway for the mountains. They have been her infatuation since she first met them. Ironically, they have let her down during this season of joy.

In breathless litany, to explain her mood, she began with a swift condemnation of the weather, whose intensity I could scarcely imagine, and reminded me that she was out standing in it because the telephone company there had insisted on her paying a temporarily unattainable deposit before they would install a line for her and her friend, Beth. She and Beth live in a tiny cabin they rent and already dislike, because the entry door leads directly into their bedroom (requiring, I imagined, a daybreak tidiness to which our genes are manifestly alien). I said I didn't like that they don't have a phone. I didn't like, either, the nagging feeling that I already ought to have done something about it, but I kept that private.

Waitressing at Crested Butte was not as remunerative as she had hoped, she said, and several too many of her colleagues seemed to have no more depth than they could replenish from a 12-ounce can. Moreover, her car now required an electric block heater, which would cost all the money she had earned during the weekend, and, in the absence of the block heater and therefore a car that started, she had bicycled that morning to the main road and then hitchhiked to work in a climate that made spit shatter.

I had planned to commiserate by suggesting that I was at a low point, myself, but most of my paltry forlornness was focused on the scarcity of ornaments for my tree, and a friend had just promised to deliver a surplus; so I kept my mouth shut about my sorry self.

Trying to find the key to unlock her mirth, I said I had heard about her having received a letter from her sister, T.C. It worked, temporarily, as she set aside her mood to whoop with joy about the letter. Earlier, T.C. had explained why Colleen would be so disproportionately jubilant about a mere letter. "Basically," T.C. said, "she left home at 17, when she went away to school. She's 23, now, and this was my first letter to her."

I stopped short of telling Colleen what Jed had said about her the day before, because, while I knew she would be charmed, I also realized why she might be feeling so saddened.

"This is going to be my first Christmas without Colleen," he had told his mother. "Colleen," I mumbled distractedly into the receiver, "Please. Call whenever you feel the urge."

YEAR FIVE

The Tracks of Christmas Past

Christmas of '92. A departure from the norm; whatever that is.

In responding to a weighty, metaphysical query once stage-whispered to me by a high school interviewer (something like: "What is the purpose of life?"), I blurted an elliptical pontification designed, however flippantly, to suggest that I hoped to positively influence the tenants of the lives whose paths I crossed while bumbling through my own lease. I said I wished to live so that I would leave tracks.

As a father, I am leaving tracks, all right, but they are muddy and lack direction, and I am beginning to hope that they do not influence anybody, not even a burglar (especially not a burglar, nor anyone who might profit from keeping his daily itinerary private: a lawyer, for example).

I thought I had pretty well covered the potentially awkward logistics of this most recent Christmas, considering the social knots I have tangled by my relatively new and unanticipated membership in yet another trendy demographic category. But, I omitted.

The plan, though it sounded complex, was truly simple: My sons would begin their Christmas day when they awakened with their mother at my ex-house. My just-recently-divorced older daughter would begin her Christmas day when she and her own daughter awakened at the home of her mother, my first wife. My mother, Dolores, would open her eyes in an apartment, which she moved into last spring so that she could: 1) satisfy the curiosity she has nurtured since widowhood about moving to an apartment, but without having to permanently relinquish her house; and, 2) offer me a reasonable rental opportunity not far from nor unfamiliar to my sons and possessed, conveniently, of charming familiarities, like plaques containing my father's police badges and clippings of mine tacked to the walls of the kitchen.

I thus began my Christmas day in the embrace of the walls of my most distant postnatal past, the rooms of my earliest memories. My Christmas tree, properly festooned, stood where its most ancient predecessor first stood during the last days of the Truman administration. Beneath it lay a modest array of brightly wrapped packages, some for my daughter and granddaughter, some for my sons, some for their mother, for my mother, and some even for myself.

The plan called for my mother to arrive at my house, which really is her house, at 10, and for us to drive to my ex-house-by-informal-agreement, where we would meet my older daughter and her daughter, and my sons and their mother, who had provided for the occasion a generous, even sumptuous, breakfast. The boys, their parents, their Grandma Doe and T.C. and Shannon would exchange gifts, insert batteries, include some assembly, listen to seasonal music (and some light rap), surround the dining room table and feast on scrambled eggs, ham, toast, bagels, orange juice, coffee and/or cinnamon mini-buns, should anyone so desire. Then, the boys would be remanded to the bathroom to serve a sentence in the shower; Grandma Doe and I would return to my house/her house; and T.C. would take Shannon to see her father until an hour or so later, when the boys would visit my house/Doe's house to exchange some more gifts and insert more batteries. At 4 P.M., the boys' mother would pick them up and take them to a Christmas party hosted by friends whose Christmas party they attended last year. For me, the day would then end.

But for one, unexpected wrinkle, all elements of the plan, which was designed to minimize on the boys the negative impact of their parents' life-rearrangement, worked as well as or better than planned; worked in sync; worked in harmony; worked to the convenience of all participants; worked in the spirit of the designated holiday and in the spirit of the best intentions of mankind on any designated holiday. The boys' mother presented their father with a beautiful silk tie. The father presented to the mother a lightweight, portable chair for attending soccer games. The boys now have Nintendo in two places. Shannon got more presents. Grandma Doe got presents.

At 3:30, Grandma Doe announced her intention to return to her apartment for a nap, tossing over her shoulder as she departed a vague comment about dinner, later. Jed and Danny's mother spirited them away at around 4 P.M., leaving the ancestral Cape exquisitely quiet. The daylight in the living room fell away, replaced by a tree-lit serenity that bordered on the hypnotic, and I fell peacefully asleep, staring at the blinking, multicolored lights.

At 6 P.M., when my mother called and asked where she and I were going for Christmas dinner, I discovered the hole in the plan.

"Ma, it's Christmas. No place is open. How could I have forgotten?"

"You have to eat. We have to have Christmas dinner."

"Ma, I could make ziti with Ragu. You could come over."

"The diner is open. I passed it on the way."

"The diner? Ma, me? A diner guy? I'm not into big food and epic menus. A man my age shouldn't be having dinner with his plate of butter."

Mothers prevail, always. We ate Christmas dinner at the diner. First time, ever, for me. Big food. I mistook one of my scallops for a saucer.

Eating Out Eats Me Up

I took four generations out to dinner for Grandma Doe's birthday. She had a nice time. I had gas.

My normally limber neurological network fossilizes whenever my children accompany me for a formal restaurant meal. My sense of humor seizes up. My jaw locks. My voice tightens. My eyes dart involuntarily, making my head twitch and jerk to catch up, and, invariably, I notice during the meal that I am sitting uncharacteristically stiffly, my fingers folded betwixt each other after the fashion of a prayerful, old, captured missionary awaiting his call to the guillotine. All this before we have disarmed the napkin rings.

I fear for the staff, mainly; no question about it. I nurture a deep affection for restaurant people, always have, and boast a high regard for the honor and dignity of their mission. I have long admired the people who tend bars, cook meals, take reservations, wait tables, host, bus and clean up after, people whose work lives are earnestly devoted to making their fellows feel welcome, including those patrons who are welcome, anyway, but especially those who are not, never will be and should not be, not anywhere by anybody, ever, not to a fight, not to a funeral and certainly not to a meal, let alone in a public place, where other people must witness the act. The degree of patience and humility and the colossal self-esteem required to politely serve the chronically unwelcome of our species stretches the limits of my comprehension and then even tests my capacity for admiration.

My empathy for service personnel is exaggerated and a tad pathological, true, but knowing that never diminished my anxiety over sentencing a waitress to 90 minutes with my young children, even when she indicated clearly that she might enjoy the task.

I do not suffer for my children's behavior, but from my own, unfounded, anticipatory fear. The children always have behaved well, at least for the three minutes the young ones could endure remaining seated at a table unequipped with an electronic mouse. But I worry long before they begin to fidget. I worry about what has not yet happened and then fail to appreciate until later that it did not. My anxiety is of the no-win variety. I worry about how the children are going to behave in the next minute, then the following one, then the one to follow that. I am relieved only after I hear the last slam of the car door.

A friend nearly collapsed with laughter on overhearing me telephone my reservations for Grandma Doe's birthday celebration, obviously at a restaurant familiar with me and my family. "I'll have five-and-a-half people," I said almost apologetically: "my mother, my sons, my daughter and her infant daughter. So, I'll need a table where we can't hurt anybody, something in a corner, or off in the distance. The new room in the back or something in the adjacent paint store, if that's possible."

I took a seat next to the high chair, hoping to intercept any ground-to-air activity from my granddaughter's right launching apparatus. I failed at that. Shannon yielded to only one urge to fling, and then, when I was distracted, shot her milk bottle straightaway at the condiments mid-table, as if bowling. Otherwise, she was perfect, sucking on her bread until she had soaked it for what she must assume is my taste before offering the soggy pieces to me. I already had removed her silverware and other percussion instruments. My daughter T.C. fed pieces of her linguine to Shannon, who sucked them up like an actress in a television commercial and then screamed a two-syllable, Long Island version of the word, "more," which sounded something like *moe-wah*! Other patrons seemed pleasantly amused, though I fretted about their patience.

I seated Danny to my own right. He asked me what he wanted, and I said, "Probably a soup and an appetizer. Try baked clams." I don't allow Danny to order dinner any more, because he annihilates his appetite on the complimentary bread and raw broccoli. He asked for the soup with the cheese on top. I knew he would hate onion soup, but I knew, as well, that he would be sated before he broke through to the liquid. He seemed to like asking for my help in severing each foot-and-a-half-long strand of cheese that he proudly stretched high out of the crock, and I complied without complaint, because it kept his visits to the bathroom to a manageable minimum.

Jed and Grandma ordered fish and had a grand old time together on the opposite side of the table. I would say I envied them, except that the sight of them made the evening worth the effort.

To the Doctor We Shall Go

I am driving Danny to the pediatrician's office. I did not expect to, so I am at work calming myself, trying to concentrate on how neurotic I am about unexpected, parental chores.

For instance, I know I should not be thinking, "Dan, you picked today to get sick? You couldn't have checked my calendar first? You couldn't have picked a different day? I have ten tasks to do in two units of time. Yesterday, I had three. So, you picked yesterday to feel good and today to get sick? Thanks, pal."

I say none of these thoughts, but I think them over and over.

Next to me in the car, Danny coughs and then lists listlessly to the left, staring at the steering column. His eyes are watery, and when he sniffles, he sounds as if his straw has hit the bottom of a Big Gulp. I reach over for his warm little hand, the left, and begin squeezing his fingers, one by one, from the knuckles out to the tips, five squeezes per finger, until I have squeezed five fingers. It distracts me, and I suspect it makes him feel better, if slightly.

He asks in a weakened, plaintive voice if the doctor is going to swab the back of his throat with that stick. Since he has been able to formulate the sentence, he has asked the same question every time we have visited the doctor's office, and in a voice that makes me feel like his executioner. He must dread gagging more than I dreaded shots.

I pause before I answer him, trying to weigh my fears before I risk my selected answer, either betting on what I hope will happen and maybe betraying him with what turns out to be a lie or coming clean with what I really think will happen, and making him cry right here in the car.

I decide to go with the truth.

"Well, Dan, if he's going to give you a thorough examination . . ."

"What's that?"

"Thorough? It means complete. If he's going to do his job well and check you all over, to make sure you don't have an infection, then he'll have to look down your throat. If he sees an inflammation, which means if he sees that the tissue back there is all red and swollen, he'll want to take a tiny sample to test it, to see if you have strep throat. Maybe he won't have to, but my guess is that he will."

"Mommy said that he wouldn't do it."

Oh, good, an ambush.

"Well, then I change my guess. She probably knows something that you and I don't know."

"I know I don't have a sore throat."

"Okay, then the both of you know something I don't know," I say, thinking to myself, So, why did you ask?

I crumple all his fingers together, shake them fast in anticipation of my next hand-squeezing maneuver, and then I crush the whole pack of fingers, with disproportionately dramatic vocal accompaniment (an intense, squeezing-grunt, garnished with grimace). Finally, I release the victim fingers onto his lap with a cavalier toss.

Slowly (as always, even in his sleep), Danny places his other warm hand in mine, to be similarly tortured, presumably for the sake of fairness. We have played regularly at this game for about six-sevenths of his life, usually in the mornings, in the semicomatose moments before his daily eruption, or when he is sleepy and scared, or restlessly overtired. All four of my children have felt their Dad squeeze their fingers like toothpaste tubes, and I don't know how it started or where I got it, but it calms me, and I think it communicates my affection in some mysterious way.

However, I now resume my teeth-grinding ruminations.

I should have heeded the warning from the telephone call last night, when Danny's mother called to say that she might not let him go to school today, and that her workday today was jam-packed, and that she was getting dressed and going out at that (very late) moment to the 7-Eleven for children's Tylenol, just in case. The Tylenol and the jam-packed sections of her lamentation were clear signals that she might make an appointment for Danny to see the doctor and then not be able to take him there, herself; and that therefore she would summon me. I should have been ready.

In my experience as a practitioner of a craft whose periodic completion and delivery no longer requires specific location— meaning I can work at home—I find that people tend to assume that if you work at home and at your own pace, you will and can quicken the pace to assume extra chores if need be. It is a conditionally correct assumption, in my case. If the extra duty is pleasant, fun or exciting, wedging it into the workday is inspirational and increases my ability to work fast. If it is mundane, banal or unpleasant, and, worse, inarguably necessary, it feels like a trap and impedes my progress.

You cannot convincingly explain that to anybody.

I pull into the underground parking lot that is my destination, remembering suddenly that when I picked up Danny, I was to scan the kitchen counter for the new group health insurance card. I forgot, and now that we are at the doctor's office (and, uncharacteristically, on time), I realize I don't have the card. How stupid. Stupid, stupid, stupid. How do I manage, I mumble through clenched teeth, to always place my psychic speed bumps so close together, in bunches. Will doctors let my Danny cough to death at their merciless feet if he visits their precincts without sufficient documentation assuring them of our ability to pay?

I reach into my jacket pocket for my checkbook and am comforted by the feel of it. I take it out of my pocket. It is battleship gray. My checkbook is navy blue. I have grabbed an American Express pocket calendar. If the doctor asks, I can tell him the time in Zagreb and the number of air miles from San Francisco to Minneapolis.

Danny turns out to have a plain cold. No swabs.

The Commission of an Omission

One weekday evening following the national celebration of the births of two distinguished American presidents, my boys' mother telephoned to say that everyone was fine. Not only had they survived a blizzard-like Vermont snowstorm but had delighted in it to the point of distraction and then exhaustion.

It was potentially an awkward phone call, presumably for both parents, certainly for me, because it called to mind a rather strenuous disagreement, months before, over a similar phone call that she anticipated I would make, and that I did not make. (Fathers, and husbands, for that matter, tend to invite more disenchantment by inactivity than by actually perpetrating a transgression. However frustrating, an undeniable lesson I have gleaned from unsuccessful marital pairings is that a man is better to have transgressed than not to have gressed at all.)

The last time mother and sons traveled to Vermont, which was the first such sojourn since she and I rearranged our lives to begin as gingerly as possible the process of physical separation pursuant to marital dissolution, I received with admittedly subtle enthusiasm a telephone call attesting to the safety, health and general well-being of the party. I thanked her with legitimate sincerity and gratitude, truly gladdened to hear that all had arrived safely at their vacation destination, as I had assumed they would.

I exchanged pleasantries with my sons, then hung up. Next, in the boys' continued absence, I continued to go about the details of my daily life, as if my sons were merely at play in the neighborhood, or upstairs fiddling with Nintendo, or off somewhere enjoying a four-day weekend with their mother and their maternal grandparents, whom I trusted unconditionally as their immediate guardians and caretakers.

I did not call Vermont the next day, or the next day, or the next, to inquire after everyone's continued good health, or to suggest that I missed anybody's company, or to remind my boys that their handsome faces, soft voices and potentially fratricidal antics did in fact occupy my mind from time to time when they were not immediately about. Loyal to accusations about my gender and confident about the effectiveness of my prior communications with them, I instead took for granted the children's secure knowledge that I loved them just as much when they were away in Vermont as I had the day before, when they were at home in Amityville.

After all, they were with their mother, whom they loved dearly, who loved them dearly, and in whose company they took demonstrable delight, except when they were playing Nintendo and took all forms of nourishment, rest, parental attention or bladder pressure as a diabolical form of life-interruption.

Later, I was soundly criticized for it—it being the unmade telephone call—on the ground that it sent the message to the boys that their father did not care about their whereabouts or about such pleasures, discomforts or triumphs as they might have been experiencing outside of his presence or at least his relative proximity.

I argued (lamely, in part but not entirely) that I thought that it, my not calling, might also have sent the "message" (Yes, I repeated the phrase sarcastically, as the quotation marks are meant to imply) that I believed the adults would lovingly feed the boys and keep them warm and dry at night, even provide joyful entertainment for them during the daytime and, eventually, return them with all such limbs and organs intact as they owned and operated when they left.

I also postulated, much to the mounting angst of their mother, who confessed that she had fully expected me to say it next, that if the boys had felt any need or even the slightest urge for telephone contact with their father, they had attained such digital dexterity and memory skills as might be required for them to call and say so themselves.

The debate ended in mutual withdrawal, each side presumably convinced of its rightness and resigned to the other's genetic intransigence.

Retrospect (damnable retrospect) has heightened my awareness and allowed leakage into my brain of the possibility that the boys' mother was more than half-right in her position—retrospect and the statistical reality that mothers almost always are at least half right; because I since have noticed that when the boys are with me, and their mother calls, and I assume the boys to be all too occupied with play to want to be bothered with a seemingly patronizing interrogation about how life is going for them in their mother's immediate absence, I am almost always surprised at the eagerness with which they hit the pause button on their video game or their videotape to answer what obviously are the usual questions from their mother. The clear implication has been that, however brief and apparently uninforming the content of the call, the existence of the call provides a comforting reassurance that they evidently need.

I did grin, however, with momentary male satisfaction, over the knowledge that during the most recent phone call this week, the boys were upstairs at play with their grandmother at some sort of board game, as they usually were at eventide, and evidently not at all interested in interrupting the game to chat with their father. Presumably, they—colleague males—knew they would see me again in a few days and had little doubt that I cared for and thought about them as much and as frequently as they cared for and thought about me.

Epilogue

Ultimately, writing honestly about life with family is not possible, unless you first kill the family members who otherwise might read the work. The more civilized author therefore must dance around certain observations and evade others altogether.

Citing reasons that did not add up to a whole truth, I abruptly ended the preceding series of personal essays in February 1993, after writing regular installments every other week for four years. I offered no warning to my editors, who thus were offended, nor to readers, who were puzzled.

In the final piece, I pointed out that my son Jed, especially, was approaching a stage of life where he did not yet want to struggle through my prose to learn my view of him, but neither did he want to learn it via well-meaning but nonetheless intrusive comments from people who had read about him in their daily newspaper. Readers who had been following the series understood my dilemma as I presented it and forgave my departure.

I had lied, mainly. Though I was sure that he would, and did, Jed had not yet reached such a stage of development. Instead, the column was beginning to disrupt the calm and amicable dissolution of a marriage (whose aftermath, though sometimes complicated, since has convinced me absolutely that children of a good divorce are much healthier than those of a steadfastly deteriorating marriage).

A newspaper editor who had developed an entire Saturday feature section around personal life columns of which "Fathering" and its alternate, "Mothering," served as centerpiece attractions, my newly-estranged wife now was becoming increasingly uncomfortable with my keeping a public forum in which I could continue to air my triumphs, failures and dissatisfactions with little or no warning to her. She did not want to impose her hierarchical prerogative to edit or censure my thoughts, but she knew from moment to moment that any one of those thoughts might be critical of her, when she possessed no similar forum to balance or refute it. If, for instance, she were to read in the newspaper that I had prepared breakfast for the boys, packed their lunches and sent them off to school, she had no vehicle to point out to the same readers that she had done all of the same work the morning before.

Moreover, she embodied a modern cliché regarding working mothers. Even in the best of times, she had suffered conflicting loyalties. Dissolving the marriage merely exacerbated the conflict. A full-time, working executive and the mother of two children, she felt that she was under the scrutiny—real and/or imagined—of two damning societies: critics in the traditional workplace and critics in the traditional homeplace, each demanding that she devote her attentions wholly to the work they considered most crucial.

Raised on the comfortable side of society's prejudices, I did not feel such heat. Any diminution in my work output was deemed understandable. Any additional parenting task I embraced won me sympathetic approval, even if only my own. My advantage was sublimely unfair. The tension became palpable. When I suggested almost sarcastically that I end the "Fathering" series, she concurred so quickly, I knew I had to do it or contribute to an inexorably increasing antipathy that we so far had proved we actually could skirt.

I stopped writing the column. It worked, and it was worth it. We consulted a mediator instead of oppositional attorneys. We sold our house and divided our possessions without assistance or even argument. Our boys saw an absolute minimum of animosity, and though they no doubt always will wish that their parents loved each other and lived together, they reveal little to none of the anxiety common to children of combative or vindictive separated parents. We maintain separate residences in the same town, and we share both physical and legal custody of our sons.

In the meantime, living alone, I have become a much better father for the physical details I must address. The boys live with me three and sometimes four days a week. I cannot abdicate any chore or any category of chore. I buy and clean and fold and locate their clothes, so I am attentive to what they wear and where they throw it in ways that I never was before or dreamed of being. I know what they need. I know what they like (unfortunately, some of it is mine). And late at night, when I am folding laundry or ironing flannel shirts, I find myself enjoying a new tactile connection that I suspect traditional mothers always have known and traditional fathers have not. It makes me wistful for what I have missed and grateful for what I am learning.

EPILOGUE

With my older children, I am less effective, less satisfactory and less satisfied with myself, although Colleen and I are developing the kind of father-to-adult daughter relationship that I fantasized about when she and her sister were toddlers. Currently, she lives in Portland, Oregon, where she is studying for a master's degree while also training to be a Maria Montessori school teacher. We talk almost every night and have for three or four years.

T.C. is divorced and remarried. Shannon, her daughter, is a pure, shining delight.

We all live in a different book now.

Ed Lowe
Amityville, NY